THE CRIMINOLOGY OF BOXING, VIOLENCE AND DESISTANCE

Deborah Jump

BRISTOL
UNIVERSITY
PRESS

First published in Great Britain in 2020 by

Bristol University Press
University of Bristol
1-9 Old Park Hill
Bristol
BS2 8BB
UK
t: +44 (0)117 954 5940
www.bristoluniversitypress.co.uk

North America office:
Bristol University Press
c/o The University of Chicago Press
1427 East 60th Street
Chicago, IL 60637, USA
t: +1 773 702 7700
f: +1 773 702 9756
sales@press.uchicago.edu
www.press.uchicago.edu

British Library Cataloguing in Publication Data
A catalogue record for this book is available from the British Library.

Library of Congress Cataloging-in-Publication Data
A catalog record for this book has been requested.

ISBN 978-1-5292-0324-0 (hardback)
ISBN 978-1-5292-0328-8 (ePub)
ISBN 978-1-5292-0325-7 (ePDF)

Cover design by Blu Inc
Front cover: Megan Powell (photographer)/Image kindly supplied by Dane Bolton
Printed and bound in Great Britain by CPI Group (UK) Ltd, Croydon, CR0 4YY
Bristol University Press uses environmentally responsible print partners

FSC www.fsc.org MIX Paper from responsible sources FSC® C013604

For my father Peter Jump, for
encouraging me to educate my way out

Contents

Notes on the Author

Deborah Jump is a Senior Lecturer in Criminology at Manchester Metropolitan University, and the Head of Youth Justice in the Manchester Centre for Youth Studies. Her research interests include youth crime and desistance, ethnographic studies and psychosocial methodologies. She has contributed to *Mischief, Morality and Mobs, Essays in Memory of Geoffrey Pearson* by Dick Hobbs (ed) (2016), published articles 'Fighting for change: Narrative accounts on the appeal and desistance potential of boxing' (2015) and 'Why we should think some more. A response to "when you're boxing you don't think so much": pugilism, transitional masculinities and criminal desistance among young Danish gang members' (2017), and co-authored 'Starting to Stop? Desistance: An exploration of young offender's narratives (2017) and 'Dropping your guard: the use of boxing as a means of forming desistance narratives among young people in the criminal justice system' (2020).

Acknowledgements

This book would not have been possible without the men featured in it. I am sincerely grateful for sharing your lives and stories with me. Frank, I really hope you are winning all the titles you deserve. RIP.

Thank you also to my supervisors Dr Jon Shute and Professor David Gadd; without your patience and support, this book would not have materialised. Thank you to all my colleagues at Manchester Metropolitan University and Manchester Centre for Youth Studies; your support and encouragement has not gone unnoticed.

Foreword

There is nothing like hearing the words, 'protect yourself at all times' in a ring, knowing you are about to fight. Even writing them they still cause my adrenaline to surge a bit even now, well away from any real fight, sat at a PC. They cause a special, rare sort of excitement that is hard to recapture. Occasionally as an academic a book comes along that has the same sort of effect, not so much adrenaline as respect and admiration. The sort you feel when someone in a boxing ring has hit you with a great hook or cross and you do that little grimace of respectful acknowledgement while slightly resenting their luck, fortune and skill. This book evoked all those feelings.

As an ethnographer, and a long-term fan and practitioner of boxing, the so-termed 'Sweet Science' (as well as the social form that we researchers practice), it was an absolute honour and a rare pleasure to be asked to write a Foreword for Deb Jump's phenomenal book, *The Criminology of Boxing, Violence and Desistance.* It is a fantastic and engaging work, and proves its author a rare talent, the once-in-a-lifetime prospect every coach seeks, but few find.

I grew up in boxing gyms full of men like those in the pages of this book, and these spaces proved a good place to make connections and meet people, a skill that has served me well for years subsequently as an academic ethnographer and criminologist. In ethnographic and qualitative research ventures, boxing has given me commonality with an array of people. In New Zealand I have talked Joseph Parker vs. Anthony Joshua with a full-patched member of the Notorious Mongrel Mob, Horn vs. Pacquiao with Australian gangsters, and used boxing to build a rapport with all sorts of staff and subjects in policing, prison and crime contexts worldwide. Boxing and the unlicensed (including the now burgeoning white collar fight scene) gave me the chance to introduce colleagues to the crime world often written about in crime fiction. I have also fought myself, and boxing, fast feet and big hands for a big guy got me out of countless scrapes. Still now I regularly spar (my real fighting days behind me) and know the appeal of boxing and combat sports to its fans and practitioners alike. It is more than just the violence. Yet, at its core, boxing is about one person hurting another. Only some of those lured to the sport know the practicality, that pain and adversity, intelligence and strategy, are all as much a part of triumphing. It is not all about violence, it is about learning and the self. Yet, at a base level, the truth is boxing is a way of doing violence, and violence is, or can be, a powerful resource for bad or good. Boxing is something that appeals to survivors of intimate partner violence as it does to some police officers or prison staff and gangsters (both the real and the aspiring).

The core win in Jump's excellent book is not just in its brilliant ethnographic and narrative interview-based content, which gives deep insight into her participants' lives, but that it also aims to give the reader a powerful and nuanced insight of both boxing's legitimacy and its more dark and sinister version of illegitimate violence, which the men that perpetrate it sometimes understand all too well. Indeed, boxing may be the perfect place to discuss the complexities of violence and the taken-for-granted manner that we often have concerning its role and function. While recognising the sport's utility as a gear for change, Jump never falls into the trap of seeing boxing is a panacea for all social ills. She realises boxing's place in the social strata and expectations of how masculinity and violence should be practiced, but notes that it may be a way of transitioning some from acceptance of illegitimate violence to healthier and better lives. Some may be enticed by the violence and aggression; others may like the artistry of the Sweet Science. What intrigues me is the psychology of the fighter, the mindset you must have to compete in the ring, shelving fear, pain, embarrassment, failure, the competition never just against the man opposite but also against the self. In producing this work, she has produced a real heavyweight contender of a social science book that I hope will be widely read.

Professor James Treadwell
Staffordshire University

Introduction

Violence is a powerful resource, and boxing is a legitimised version. This book aims to give the reader a powerful tale of legitimacy, and also a darker, more sinister version of illegitimate violence and the men who perpetrate it. I question common tropes that suggest boxing is a panacea for all social ills, and unpick the criminal justice responses to youth crime and the well-intended misgivings that boxing is the cure. Boxing is seen as a 'male preserve' (Dunning 1986), and policy makers and parents, as well as criminal justice agencies, believe that the structured disciplining environment of the gym is enough to combat criminogenic attitudes and violent behaviour. I dispel this myth. I propose that boxing is a convincing 'hook for change' (Giordano 2002), and the appeal of the gym is undoubtedly a powerful one. However, I suggest that more needs to be done to challenge the masculine discourses present within the gym environment, and I do this by revealing the fragility of these. I suggest that boxing's appeal is its ability to generate a defence against male anxiety and vulnerability, and that the environment itself is tailored to the prevention of repeat victimisation. In other words, the attendees are not just there to become boxers, they are there to sequester any form of male vulnerability and victimisation behind physical capital and gloved fists.

I begin with an outline of boxing, and how gyms are seen as sociological sites of research. I then go on to discuss briefly the method used in this monograph, and introduce psychosocial theories of desistance from crime. I present arguments surrounding boxing's appeal, as well as exploring what the gym actually offers, thus questioning its contribution towards desistance from crime. Through the use of case studies in Chapters 4–6, I suggest that boxing is not necessarily conducive to a process of desistance, and that in fact, it can compound violent attitudes and male domination. Employing psuedonyms to the pen portraits of men such as Frank, Eric and Leroy, I make claims that boxing's appeal lies in its ability to create physical capital, and allows for men to overcome structural and psychic obstacles that have impinged on their versions of successful masculinity. Moreover, I discuss how boxing as a sport sits firmly at the intersection of class, violence and masculinity, and how these conflated concepts are stitched together in the minds and bodies of men who box.

I conclude by making suggestions to practitioners and policy makers in the field of sport and criminal justice, and therefore recommend a rethinking of 'what works' (Martinson 1974). It is easy to fill boxing gyms with recalcitrant youth and walk away, hoping for a more disciplined and respectful one to walk out, yet this is not always the case. As previous work attests (see Jump 2017), the masculine cultural values transmitted in the gym environment, especially in relation to homophobia, hyper-masculinity and the accomplishment of such through 'masculinized vocabulary' (Deuchar et al 2016) are not necessarily conducive to desistance from crime. I align with Maruna (2001), when I suggest that any semblance of desistance must portend from a redemption script, and a belief in a new self; one that is at odds with criminogenic attitudes and lifestyles. Contrary to popular belief (Wright 2006; Sampson and Vilella 2013; Meek 2018), boxing in its current form does not do this. Giordano et al (2002:1001), who coined the term 'hook for change', refer to secondary forms of desistance as 'cognitive transformations'. These transformations are positive developments, whereby the environment in tandem with the individual reframes their identity as incompatible with continued deviation. I argue that the enclave of the gym and the majority of its members are actually compatible with violent criminogenic attitudes, especially those that pertain to the defence of masculine ideals. Ideals that buttress the varying forms of the patriarchal gender order in late modern social worlds (Connell 2005) are actually counter-productive to shifts in identity associated with desistance.

More recently, work by sport scholars such as Anderson (2002; 2005; 2008), Channon (2014), Matthews (2014) and Woodward (2007) have gone a long way in unpicking and challenging the 'hegemonic man' (Anderson 2009), yet it still pervades, albeit under the surface in a negotiated and contingent form (Atkinson 2011). Accordingly, 'participation in this hyper-violent recreational culture' (Atkinson 2011:63) allows men to think of violence as powerful, productive and aggressive, particularly in late modern worlds, where overt displays are seen as archaic and contestable (Faludi 2000; McDowell 2003; Woodward 2007; Atkinson 2011). Therefore, the mimetic display of violence and masculinity found in boxing gyms is the antithesis to lamented versions of desistance suggested by scholars such as Meek (2018), Sampson (2015) and Wright (2006).

This is not the most populist view, and I fully appreciate the benefits that boxing can offer. The boxing community is well intentioned, and I truly believe that the majority of its inhabitants take seriously the impact of crime in their local communities. This book supports this view and respectfully acknowledges the hard work that gym attendees and coaches put in every week. It is not my intention to disparage any member, nor question the diligence of its coaches and allies. Yet, in challenging this 'Emperor's new clothes' approach to boxing and desistance from crime, this book lends some gravitas to the debate. It does this, by suggesting that we look more closely at the mechanisms by which we promote boxing to young people, especially those who are deemed as 'at risk' of criminality.

1

Boxing as Sports Criminology

Why boxing?

Boxing has been part of Western culture for millennia, but has always been a contentious sport, one that attracts and repels in equal measure. Like other sports, it emerged from ancient Greece as a formalised and permissible form of martial violence, adapted to peacetime, and expressed the male imperative to take up arms and fight to protect citizen and polity. Boys were taught to box just as every able-bodied man was trained to fight to protect the city from foreign aggression and to uphold the prevailing ethos. Boxing was thus seen from the beginning as being a *civilising* influence in society, by providing an outlet for male violence, while at the same time helping to promote the masculine 'virtues' – courage, strength, ingenuity and endurance. This ethos has remained fundamental to boxing throughout its long history. Today, it still forms part of the sport's appeal, motivating its institutionalisation not only in the armed services but also within civil society and professional sport. As this book will demonstrate, the issues of violence, masculinity, self-knowledge and even heroism are still relevant preoccupations of those who partake in, and reflect on, the sport at the start of the third millennium.

Boxing featured heavily in the London Olympic Games of 2012, and as these games were the first to feature women's boxing as a matter of course, boxing found itself thrust into a gendered spotlight as the contention surrounding women's role in sports spilt over into both political and public debates. Boxing has further formed the basis of political debates surrounding its transformative potential, with many professionals and policy makers arguing that it is a useful vehicle for engaging and reforming those involved in offending behaviour (Wright 2006; Sampson and Vilella 2013; Deuchar et al 2016; Meek 2018). It therefore seems that boxing is increasing its appeal and exposure for both men *and* women. In this book, I begin to unravel the complex relationship between the two: boxing's appealing nature, and its potential to encourage or impede desistance from crime.

It was during the London Games of 2012 that this research was conducted, and throughout them, I was speaking to and engaging with men who had boxed for most of their lives. During the course of my ethnographic fieldwork, I spent six months detailing the lives of men in a boxing gym in England. I participated in the social world of boxing, and situated myself as a boxer; an insider of sorts. Woodward (2008:547) writes that there are a 'myriad of ways of "being inside" boxing, although engaging in the sport physically is the most dramatic'. I felt that experiencing boxing at first hand would further allow me a glimpse into the lives of men who box, and it also gave me the opportunity to engage experientially in the daily routine of this pugilistic world. Conversing with the trainers and the professionals, listening to and collating their life-histories, helped me to understand what boxing meant to them, how they established their identities as sportsmen, and what this mantle signified on both a structural and personal level for the likes of Frank, Eric, Leroy and many more of the men I interviewed.

As a result of working in youth offending for many years as a reparation and rehabilitation officer, I became specifically interested in why practitioners (myself included) often thought that boxing would contribute towards a process of desistance from violence, and also why it was so appealing to young men in particular. The primary aim of this research was to explore whether the sport of boxing could *actually* contribute towards a process of desistance for these men, or whether it merely reinforced pre-existing violent behaviour and attitudes. More specifically, the research sought to explore the relationship between violence, discipline and desistance in the lives of those engaged in boxing, and therefore explored both the appeal and the layers of personal significance and meaning attributed by these men.

I set out to discover how the climate of, and participation in, the boxing gym affected men's understanding of violence, and whether or not this could lead to a process of change. Using qualitative methods, I sought to get behind men's stories –beyond the self-serving defensive responses we all tend to produce when questioned – to broach their understanding of, and their relationship with, violence. I felt it important to ascertain what violence meant subjectively to these men. Moreover, I felt it important to ask how and why they participated in boxing – as opposed to just measuring their behaviour – as I believed that this would assist with theory building and further help to reveal men's understandings of violence in the context of their own lives. To summarise, to what extent does boxing transform, undermine or reinforce investments in their violent behaviour outside the ring?

Boxing gyms as sites of research

The activity of boxing and the spatial geography of the gym itself have been the focus of many recent studies, the most notable being Wacquant's (2004) *Body and Soul: Notebooks of an Apprentice Boxer* and Woodward's (2007) *Boxing, Masculinity and Identity: The "I" of the Tiger*. Other works include van Ingen's (2011) *Spatialities of Anger: Emotional Geographies in a Boxing Program for Survivors of Violence*, and Trimbur's (2013) *Come out Swinging: The Changing World of Boxing in Gleason's Gym*. Each offers a differing glimpse into the social work of boxing – an often closed world, usually only seen in popular films and documentaries.

The number of people registered to box has increased by 15 per cent since 2012 (Sport England 2016), and since the 2012 Olympics, boxing gyms are finally opening their doors to a wider audience. Indeed, England Boxing now records 30 per cent of its 160,000 registered fighters as female (Sport England 2016). Once seen as a site that housed only men, and usually located in areas that could be viewed as working class, boxing gyms are branching out and producing more inclusive spaces that incorporate female professionals, LGBTQ members, and female/trans trauma survivors. Shape your Life in Toronto, Canada, and Love Fighting Hate Violence in the United Kingdom are among the most inclusive and progressive. *Amateur: A True Story About What Makes a Man* (2018), by Thomas Page McBee, also demonstrates the changing face of boxing, with his biographical account of being the first trans man to box competitively in Madison Square Garden.

Regardless of the intersectionality now seen in the sport, it is still an undoubtedly appealing sport for young men. This is evidenced by the longevity of male-centric boxing clubs in both urban and inner-city areas. For example, England Boxing (formerly Amateur Boxing Association until 2014) was founded in 1880, and Ardwick Lads Club in Manchester first opened its doors to young men in 1896. Repton Boxing club in the East End of London has been producing fighters since 1787, with Daniel Mendoza the prizefighting champion acknowledged by a blue heritage plaque at 3 Paradise Row in Bethnal Green. Boxing is also keen to demonstrate its social impact, by promoting a mental health campaign called #fightingback. This campaign, launched in 2019, demonstrates the positive impact that boxing has on members suffering with mental health problems. Knife crime is also a social issue that England Boxing is hoping to tackle, and in 2019 the Kiyan Prince Foundation founder Dr Mark Prince received an OBE for his services to sport and youth crime reduction, citing boxing as one of the sports that can achieve the latter: "Boxing, I cannot stress enough, how important it is" (Sky News, 9 January 2019). These figures and campaigns are important and topical, because for the past decade there has been an assumption by policy makers and politicians that sport can be employed as a tool for increasing social capital and reducing offending, particularly among young men.

Boxing clubs do have a long history of engaging young men in what is seen as a positive, healthy activity, and they are often perceived as conducive to a sense of routine and discipline, whereby they engage youths who would otherwise be left to their own devices. However, in theory, boxing may or may not be anything other than a place of incapacitation, a community centre/gym that simply occupies young people's time, as opposed to changing their personal outlooks or behaviours. This would suggest that the sport of boxing does not necessarily offer a change mechanism, and that any sport that detains young people when they may otherwise be involved in criminal activity would suffice. Where boxing excels above other sport, however, is in its appeal: young men flock to boxing gyms, as they do to football pitches, for the image it represents. This image of the male boxer – like the footballer – provides evidence of a transitional culture (Hannerz 1996) or turning point, whereby the local lad becomes the global brand. The world of competitive masculine sport and the exalted local hero is often viewed as a bridge between the world of working-class juvenile struggle and mass media superstar. Anthony Joshua's *From Drug Offences to Heavyweight Stardom: The Making of Anthony Joshua* is a prime example of this (*The Telegraph*, 6 April 2016).

Not only does boxing promote the local-hero-turned-superstar discourse, it further provides (for the mass majority of young men who do not end up worldchampion) an advantage in the associated struggles over 'who rules the streets' (Cohen 1976). There is a close fit between sport and masculinity: the prowess demonstrated in sport is seen as the completion of a young boy's masculinity (Davies 1992). Organised sport came to have a central place in the new world of urban male working-class industrial culture, in as much as boys learnt to drink and tell jokes; they also learnt the language of physical aggression. Sporting choice therefore mirrored class positioning, and if aggression is the universal currency and style of working-class male relationships (Tolson 1977), then boxing and football came to be symbolic representations of working-class masculinity, especially those forged in, and associated with, the industrial heartlands of Britain.

In this book, I examine the structural and psychological positionings of young men and how this translates into the appeal and desisting elements of boxing. I unpack the ways in which young men employ boxing as a vehicle in the prevention of repeat victimisation, and draw upon the resources and skills learnt to deny vulnerability and subsequently to command respect. Building on psychosocial criminological theories of desistance, I present arguments that elaborate on how the sport of boxing is appealing in its promotion of physical capital, masculinity and peer admiration, and also how the logic of the gym can sometimes reinforce the logic of the streets. In short, the lessons learnt and the masculine discourses inherent in the boxing gym arguably reinforce the Code of the Street (Anderson 1999), and the men who attend the gym are well versed in its translation.

Boxing and narrative interviewing: introducing the boxers' stories and psychosocial theories of desistance

Narrative interviewing

Narrative interviewing techniques were chosen, as they help to distinguish personal stories and assist in the unpicking of constructions and subjective investments made into identities of boxing and masculinity. Ricoeur (1991) and McAdams (1996) posit that it is through narratives that we make sense of our lives, as they enable us to see the links to wider social contexts, whereby biographical approaches are able to conceptualise both the individual and the social, as both of these elements need to be engaged with in order to understand how men make sense of their experiences of both masculinity and violence. Exploring these individuals' biographies in an in-depth way through this method offered me the opportunity to appreciate the heterogeneous nature of an individual's experience. It also ensured that the biographical originality of these men's lives was not lost, but was employed in understanding the differences and convergences in their experiences. As David Gadd (2000:430) writes: 'psychoanalytical interpretive readings of men's lives not only serves to highlight what many men have in common, but also opens up the possibility of change to theoretical engagement without denying the multitude of socio-structural and psychological factors that militate against it'.

Engaging with these narratives helped me to examine the embodied nature of boxers' experiences, as this approach assists with the unpicking of complex stories. As Plummer (1995:170) has suggested: 'Somewhere behind all this storytelling there are real, active, embodied, impassioned lives'. The interpretation of biographical narratives also gives consideration to the narrative as a co-constructed account, combined and united through the interaction of the researcher and the participant (Wengraf 2001). This allowed for me to be included in the analysis, as it offered a reflexive account of how I, the researcher, impacted upon the story being told (Presser 2005). Lastly, as other researchers from the narrative tradition have highlighted, narrative accounts offer the possibility of considering various levels of analysis when interpreting accounts, including the social, the individual and the intersubjective (Gadd 2000; Wengraf 2001; Gunaratnam 2004).

The narrative interview is mainly used in the context of biographical research (Bertaux 1981; Plummer 1983; Denzin 1988), as its main purpose is to elicit the participant's *story* in relation to the research topic. Therefore, the interactions, relationships and 'meanings' that boxing encapsulated for men were explored using these techniques. All techniques of narrative interviewing generally begin using a 'generative narrative question' (Riemann and Schutze 1987:353) that refers to the topic of the study and is, therefore, intended to stimulate the participant's main narrative. In this research, the narrative was framed by asking the participant to, 'Tell me the story of how you became a boxer'. Overall, the aim was to open up a dialogue that would elicit a story about their life – and their subjective understanding of boxing and desistance as a result.

I specifically chose this method, as it has proven to be the most prominent methodology for documenting or 'storying one's life' (Plummer 1983). Indeed, it is through biographical narrative interviewing that lived experiences can be understood. In common with other narrative techniques (see Plummer 1983; Hollway and Jefferson 2000), the biographical method encourages the participant to discuss events and experiences that they consider to be important features of their life story. Thus, I was interested in these men's experiences of violence, community, boxing and desistance, and also, how they saw themselves in relation to these concepts, having chosen to participate in such a transformative sport like boxing. As Connell (1995:89) has suggested, 'Life histories give rich documentation of personal experience, ideology and subjectivity ... but life histories also, paradoxically document social structures, social movements and institutions'. Therefore, with this in mind, I intended to also listen for men's constructions of masculinities and also their relationships to the social institution of sport.

Interviews took place over various points in time, usually when the men had finished training or were having a rest day. I interviewed most men at least twice, as this provided further opportunities to explore the men's narratives. It was usually on the second meeting that the men would relax and open up; allowing me to observe the *mise-en-scène* of their lives, and see behind the façade, what Hoch (1979) refers to as the 'Mask of Masculinity'. These repeated interviews allowed me the space to pay attention to any issues that the participant may be avoiding, particularly absences and noticeable changes in subject, especially when the topic being explored seemed sensitive. They gave me an opportunity to develop trust, and to work alongside these men in the facilitation of their narrative, helping me to gain a better picture of the lives of Frank, Eric and Leroy, to name but a few, by asking further narrative questions in a jointly constructed, considerate manner. According to McAdams (1993), the theory of the life story identity is one in which the author constructs and reconstructs their 'personal myth'; the process of identity development in adulthood. I intended to elicit the personal myths; the integration of these men's past, present and anticipated future selves in my search for the truth. The truth in this case was whether these men's narratives and, subsequently, their identities, were conducive to a process of desistance from crime and violence.

Psychosocial research of this kind, particularly in the field of criminology, seeks to understand the dialectic between inner experience and the social conditions of people's lives, paying particular attention to the conflictual and dynamic nature of both psychological and social processes (Gadd and Jefferson 2007). Accordingly, this method assists in the discovery of how each process mutually effects both social action and change, and through the theoretical conflation of both structure and agency, psychosocial criminologists (Hollway and Jefferson 1998; Jefferson 2002; Evans 2003; Gadd and Jefferson 2007) are able to go beyond recidivistic structuralist debates of power and poverty, and enter the realm of the psyche and a more holistic approach.

Research into boxing that has deployed an ethnographic approach has much to offer, as it is particularly productive in exploring the embodiment, routines and rituals of everyday life. The case studies also presented in this book form part of this ethnographic approach. Case studies have historically been viewed – both sociologically and psychoanalytically – as a method by which narrative accounts of individuals' life histories can be brought to life (Hobbs 1995;

Hollway and Jefferson 2000). I consider my work to be grounded in the psycho-social tradition, and psychosocial criminology often uses N=1 to explore how the psychological and social constitute each other, without collapsing one into the other (Gadd 2004; Maruna and Matravers 2007).

Using these life story approaches allowed for psyches to be unveiled, as well as engaging with issues of social structure, power and discourse, commonly associated with structural reasonings and more critical criminological theorists. Jefferson (2002) suggests it is naïve to presume that certain segments of the population, especially the disenfranchised, share a common outlook because of their structural positioning; that is, that people offend because they have experienced 'strain' (Merton 1938), or that they have inherited poor self-control due to problem families. Accordingly, I intended to be more creative and to look more closely at the inter-subjective – the interplay between the individual's psyche and unconscious motivations – to the social indices of power and discourse.

Based on historical fact, the self-narrative is seen to be an imaginative rendering through which the past is reconstructed, edited and embellished in order to create a coherent plot and theme of one's life. As McAdams (1999:496) writes: 'they hold psychological truths', and these representations of individual truths can and do shape future action, as one seeks to behave in ways that correspond to our self-myths. Therefore, these case studies, and the narrative analysis therein, informed my understanding of cultural influence *and* the underlying psychic responses to issues of socio-structural impediments, while empathically bearing witness to the storyteller and their personal struggles.

Introduction to classic theories of desistance

Psychosocial theories of desistance complement narrative interviewing styles, as they combine the structural elements with the psychoanalytical or psychological. As Connell (1995) suggested, they allow for an exploration of personal experience and subjectivity, and the intersection of these experiences and worldviews with social structures and institutions. Criminology has moved with this tradition in recent years, and scholars such as Barry (2010), Gadd and Farrall (2004), Healy (2010) and McNeil and Whyte (2013) recognise the interplay between structure and agency in the desistance process. As Maruna (1997) suggests, few phenomena in criminology are as widely acknowledged and equally poorly understood, as desistance from crime. For most individuals, participation in low-level street crime begins in adolescence and tails off by their mid to late twenties. In fact, Gottfredson and Hirschi (1990) argue that this fact has remained unchanged for the past 150 years. Commonly known as the 'age-crime curve', this correlation between age and crime has baffled criminologists for decades. Moffitt (1993:675) consolidates this thinking, by suggesting that the 'mysterious' age-crime curve is the 'most robust and least understood empirical observation in the field of criminology'. Indeed, even the most serious of offenders undergo what Wolfgang et al (1972) refer to as a 'spontaneous remission' between the ages of 18 and 30 years of age.

While not disputing this fact, this book is more concerned with the processes involved with desistance, and the factors that impede or contribute towards offending behaviour. As Mulvey and LaRosa (1986:213) attest: 'we know that many youth "grow out" out of delinquent activity, but we know very little about why'. Beyond what is often referred to as 'maturational reform' (Glueck and Glueck 1943), the next most influential explanation of desistance from crime is 'social bonds', or 'informal social control' theories (Farrington 1992). These theories suggest that rather than age being the sole factor in the desistance process, the informal ties that an individual accumulates over the life-course contribute to whether a person will desist or not. These ties are often referred to as 'turning points' (Sampson and Laub 1993), and take shape in the form of employment, education, positive relationships and, in some cases, the military. Put simply, these turning points redirect an individual's loose affiliations with crime, and provide a more structured existence that occupies their time.

Matza (1964) refers to this as 'drift', and describes the way in which an individual can literally drift in and out of offending. This is common for those who lack these bonds or miss sight of opportunities to turn away from crime. Therefore, the social bonds to conforming society become weakened, and lose their sanctioning power. For example, the risk of losing a job or a partner become lessened for those who are unemployed and/or single; therefore, those who lack these bonds are most likely to stay involved in criminal activity, as their lack of fear of ostracism and social sanction become weakened. Moreover, for those who have more to lose (loss of job and earnings), the more likely they will be tethered to normative definitions of law-abiding behaviours.

Common sense would have us believe that social bonds contribute towards the desistance process, yet these theories are not without their criticisms. Gottfredson and Hirschi (1990:188) famously criticised these assumptions, by stating that it is impossible for 'jobs to attach themselves to individuals', and that subjects do not 'randomly assign themselves to marital statuses'. In response, Farrington and West (1995:252) reply that to 'accept this argument would accept that most causal hypothesis in criminology could not be tested'. Arguably, desistance also needs to have a subjective element to it, to be truly understood. In other words, factors such as employment, education, marriage and family have to have a somewhat rational decision-making individual behind the structures. Indeed, like biological age, employment and marriage interact with psychosocial variables in a complex fashion. In this vein, criminologists should make every effort to understand the more subjective and cognitive correlations, as well as the more easily measured and quantifiable measures of social processes of desistance (Maruna 1997).

As documented by Meisenhelder (1997), factors such as age, marriage and employment have little impact on those who simply do not want to change. This being the case, we need to consider the internal processes involved in staying married and staying employed, and therefore evaluate the agentic and cognitive processes involved in the desistance trajectories of individuals involved in crime. For Matza (1964; 1999:28–29), agency means having a 'sense of command over one's destiny', therefore arguing that actions have internal rather than external motivations. Put simply, cognitive approaches to desistance focus on the inner workings of the mind. How do offenders' attitudes and thinking styles facilitate crime? This is a key question among cognitive desistance scholars (McGuire and McGuire1996 in Healy 2010). However, cognitive approaches are not without their critics, and for the purposes of this book, I consider not only more psychosocial approaches that include the agentic internal forces, but also how these intersect with the structural components of class, gender and ethnicity.

Boxing and its relationship to desistance

Drawing on the narrative approach discussed earlier, and considering the internal and external forces at play in the desistance process, it is my aim to unpick the boxers' stories and their personal relationship and understanding of desistance. Each interviewee presented me with different concepts, and different ways of looking at violence. Frank, for example, saw violence as a way to accrue respect and to command obedience, whereas Eric sequestered himself behind a 'carapace of muscle' (Fussell 1991), to defend against feelings of inadequacy and vulnerability. Leroy's story demonstrates what Sennett and Cobb (1973) refer to as 'the hidden injuries of class' – a lack of self-respect that diminishes the ability to achieve success, carrying with it the burden of shame. Each of these pen portraits demonstrates how narrative accounts decussate with specific emotions of hope, shame, self-esteem and reflective meaning – more specifically, the meaning of boxing and its utility in their lives; lives which are often scarred with violent histories and, in some cases, violent outlooks.

Boxing therefore offers not only a distraction from the atrocities that these men may have faced, but also a potential 'turning point' (Sampson and Laub 1993) that offers a more structured, meaningful experience. Additionally, within the monastic drudgery that can accompany boxing training, the physical space required to commit crime is somewhat diminished. Indeed, men will be often heard saying that after a hard day's training, they simply 'go home, eat and go to bed'. In this sense, boxing works. Gyms and their canonical appeal undoubtedly incapacitate men who otherwise may be involved in criminal activity, and this is often where the theorising stops.

In this book, I wish to extend the thinking, and go beyond the incapacitating measures of the boxing gym and all its facets, therefore exploring beyond the *ad hominem* statements of 'boxing saved me from a life of crime' to unearth the ambivalent appealing nature of boxing. In other words, what does boxing *really* offer men like the ones discussed in the pen portraits? And how do theories of desistance become applicable to men who choose boxing as a way of life?

Summary

In this chapter, I have discussed how boxing is a site of research in criminology, and more specifically, how boxing's appeal may or may not contribute towards a process of desistance from crime. I have very briefly outlined boxing's relationship to masculinity and the changing tide of boxing as a historical and contemporary sport. Through the use of narrative interviewing, I have foregrounded the pen portraits of the men in this study, and evidenced how they buttress the musings around criminal desistance theories.

In the following chapters, I will outline in more depth the appealing nature of boxing, and how sport is seen as a key definer in masculine accomplishment and performativity. Second, I will cover more broadly the desistance-promoting potential of sport and how boxing is automatically presumed to work in this regard. While not disputing the latter claim, it was always my intention to present a more nuanced account, and thus, evidence the theoretical underpinnings in a way that takes boxing as something that holds great potential as an activity that can assist in the drift away from crime. Having said that, boxing should not be seen as a panacea for all social ills, particularly for those already on the fringes of, or entrenched in, the criminal justice system.

2

The Appeal and Desistance-Promoting Potential of Boxing

Introduction

In this chapter, I discuss the enduring appeal of boxing and why it also continues to be a popular sport, particularly among young working-class men. I begin by briefly outlining the history of boxing and how it was viewed as cultural entertainment in the 19th century. I further demonstrate how, towards the end of that century, the middle classes distanced themselves from the ideology of contact sports, in particular boxing, and refocused their attention on more definable class-based sporting activities. In other words, sport became stratified, and different activities became appealing to different classes of men.

Considering the ways in which boxing forms part of class and masculine discourses, I discuss the appeal of boxing from a class-based masculine perspective. I therefore outline how contact sports form part of male working-class identities, particularly those that are informed by 'hardmen' discourses and motivated by violent working-class habitus ideals[1] (Hobbs 1995; Winlow 2001).

I present literature that suggests that these male discourses are perpetuated by a gender order inherent in sporting practice, whereby men are able to accomplish their masculinity by validating their domination towards women and other males (Connell 1990; Messner 1990; Messner and Sabo 1990). Thus, boxing's appeal is enduring, as it not only supports and perpetuates identity formation among men who use violence as a mechanism of control and domination, but further allows them to express this in their performance of masculinity and sport. I then go on to discuss how boxing clubs have a long history of engaging young men in what is seen as a positive healthy activity and are often perceived as conducive to a sense of routine and discipline, whereby they engage youths who otherwise would be left to their own devices.

In theory, boxing may or may not be anything other than a place of incapacitation, a community centre/gym that simply occupies young people's time as opposed to changing their outlooks or behaviours. This would suggest that the sport of boxing does not necessarily offer a change mechanism, and that any sport that detains young people when they otherwise may be involved in criminal activity would suffice. Where boxing excels above other sport, however, is in its appeal. Indeed, young men flock to boxing gyms, as they do to football pitches, for the image it represents. I will conclude with a discussion on the policy and practice debates, especially those with *ad hominem* statements such as 'boxing saved me from a life of crime'.

A brief history of boxing

It is thought that boxing's origins began in ancient Egypt, with archaeological and artistic evidence depicting bare-fisted fighters and spectators as early as the Minoan civilisation in 2700 BC (Swaddling 1999). It was introduced into the Olympic Games in 688 BC and has continued to flourish as a sport since that time (Swaddling 1999). However, during the Roman Gladiator period of 393 AD, boxing was abolished due to excessive brutality, as slaves were often used as contestants and pitted against one another in a fight to certain death (Swaddling 1999). It was not until the late 17th century in London that boxing resurfaced – now commonly known as 'prizefighting' – with the first documented fight appearing in the *London Protestant Mercury* newspaper in 1681 (McGhee 1988).

The first recorded boxing match took place on 6 January 1681 in Britain between the 2nd Duke of Albemarle's butcher and butler, with the victor winning a prize (McGhee 1988). Early prizefighting such as this had no rules; indeed, there was no referee, and there were no weight categories, head protection or gloves. The first boxing rules, which were merely about preventing deaths in the ring, were introduced in 1743 and referred to as the 'Broughton Rules' (McGhee 1988). Under these rules, if a man went down and could not continue after a 30 second count, then the fight was over, and the other man was deemed the winner. It was not until 1867, that boxing as we know it, came to fruition, with the Marquess of Queensberry Rules introducing chalked rings, boxing gloves and timed rounds and knockdowns. Despite the Queensberry Rules, boxing was, and still is, a regulated form of consensual violence. It stands apart from other sports in this fact, as it is the only one whose main objective is to inflict intentional pain on another human being.

All sports are inherently competitive and therefore conducive to the arousal of aggression; yet boxing differs, as it employs violence in the form of play fight or mock battle between individuals that is both the central and legitimate ingredient. Because of this, and the excitement that goes with it, boxing seems to both fascinate and repel in equal measure. In present-day society, sports such as boxing can be enclaves for the socially acceptable, ritualised expression of physical violence that is often touted as the main appeal. It is often cited as a very skilful sport, and as Joyce Carol Oates (1987:94) has attested, 'Even the spectator who dislikes violence in principle can come to admire highly skilful boxing; to admire it beyond all "sane" proportions'.

This idea of a fascination with violence is not a new phenomenon. The roots of modern combat sports such as football, boxing and rugby can be traced directly to a set of locally variable medieval and early modern folk games that went by a variety of names, such as hurling, knappan and camp ball (Dunning and Sheard 1979). They were played according to spoken rules through the streets of towns, and there were no external agents of control such as referees or linesmen. In spite of the differences between these sports and modern-day combat sports, one of the central characteristics of such games are the high level of open violence they involve. Participants of these sports engage in relatively free expression of emotion, while exercising minimal forms of self-control, thus generating – in a pleasurable form – excitement akin to that aroused in battle.

Historically, games and sports of this kind evidently corresponded to the structure of society where the levels of state-formation, and of social development more generally, were relatively low; where violence was a frequent feature of everyday life (Dunning 1986). Indeed, 18th- and 19th-century boxing matches competed with public executions to satisfy audiences' desire for violent spectacles, and quite often, boxing matches were held as part of a larger open-air festival in conjunction with other sports such as horseracing (Sugden 1996). As a consequence, prizefighting came to be more and more accessible for popular consumption, particularly among the lower classes, from whose ranks the vast majority of prizefighters were drawn (Sugden 1996). The rising popularity of pugilism occurred during a period of poverty, when life expectancy was short, and both Hobbes (1968) and Elias and Dunning (1986) wrote about how life for the urban poor was both brutal and nasty during these times. Accordingly, pugilism was able to flourish, as 'The bloodiness in the ring and the pit paralleled the bloodiness of society' during these times (Gorn 1986:27).

As the 19th century progressed, Stearns (1987) argues that the gymnasium and sport movement became informed by an ideology of social and moral development, therefore suggesting that the exercise of controlled aggression in sports was a good thing for the physical and moral development of young men. Indeed, Gorn (1986:202) claimed that boxing provided the perfect vehicle for this, as pugilism with its '[b]lood-letting, merciless competition, and stern self-testing in the ring addressed the newly perceived need of middle and upper-class men for a more active life'. In short, boxing was seen as counteractive to 'effeminizing tendencies' and prepared men for education and military training in Britain's expanding empire; and sport in general, was seen as 'a vehicle for the inculcation and expression of "manliness"' (Dunning 1986:82).

However, a rising tide of opposition that had previously formed in the United Kingdom began to take shape in the United States, and the middle classes started to distance themselves slowly from the sport of boxing (Dunning 1986). Towards the end of the 19th century, a change in class structure among sporting activities started to become apparent, with the middle classes slowly beginning to turn their attention to gymnastics and other college-based scholarship sports in a more discerning manner (Dunning and Sheard 1979). It was in this context that players became subject to written rules in sport, with many of these rules expressing a control or an elimination of more extreme forms of violence. As a result, boxing began to gain popularity among the working classes. This was due partly to: 'unskilled and casual workers being only able to afford sixpence regularly each week for entertainment' (Shipley 1989:91). It was also a way for working-class men to establish their identity and class positioning as separate to that of the newly formed middle-class gentlemen.

The Victorian public school was the main site for a new kind of masculinity that focused on the physical characteristics of the loyal, brave and active man – the natural counterpart to the spiritual, sensitive and vulnerable woman. According to Weeks (1981), it is the marriage of these ideologies that paved the way for the new standards of psychological and social normality based around the nuclear family, and with that, the emerging forms of sexual division and labour. Sport, therefore, was the fulcrum of this newly 'civilised' masculinity, promoting, as it did, the cohesiveness of team effort and the sanctity of fair play in a creative vacuum of competition (Holt 1989). Thus, organised sport, and the fair play ethic of the public schools, came to have a central place in the new urban male, working-class, industrial culture (Holt 1989).

Charitable and religious bodies, promoting the muscular Christianity of the public schools and the temperance of social reformers, played their part in the spread of team games – especially football – but the clubs, pubs and factory associations of working men were much more significant in their effects (Holt 1989). New professional sporting clubs – both boxing and football – developed vigorously in industrial towns and cities, and more or less replaced the chasm left by the passing of the often violent and disorderly festivals and traditions that were proving difficult to import into city life. Despite the violence, drinking and gambling that seemed to be a regular occurrence around the staging of professional sporting matches, especially those between local rivals (Dunning et al 1988), women did attend. In the main, however, organised sport provided a rite of passage for males – a bridge between the world of working-class juvenile street gangs and the masculine affirming adult world of work and leisure (Holt 1989).

This cohesion between boys and men, with its references to heavy localism, solidarity and defensive conformity, was born of hardness and maleness, and therefore as a direct contrast to the more formal and institutionalised notions of toughness and manliness. 'Aggression is the basis of style, of feeling physical, of showing feelings and protecting oneself ... a kind of performance' (Tolson 1977:43). If aggression is the universal currency of working-class male relationships, then local footballers or boxers accrued this currency through their demonstration of aggression both in sport and at a community level, usually being perceived as local legends.

In summary, particular sports such as football and boxing started to mirror wider working-class male solidarities – mainly those forged in, and associated with, the industrial heartlands of Britain. As a result, these sports began to reflect traditional working-class masculine ideals of self-sufficiency and straightforwardness. Working-class men, who formed the bulk of audiences at boxing and football matches, wanted from their sportsmen generally what they expected from their male peers at work, in the pub and on the street. This became known as 'grit', especially in the north of England, in which hardness, stamina, courage and loyalty became fundamental attributes, if one was to succeed.

Dunning (1986) realised this, when he argues that these working-class communities tended to generate norms that, relative to other social groups, tolerated a high level of violence in social relations. In his *Quest for Excitement: Sport and Leisure in the Civilizing Process*

(1986), Dunning attempts to explain how such communities exerted comparatively little pressure on their members to exercise self-control over their violent tendencies. Moreover, several aspects of this structure tended to work to this premise. Hence, the comparative freedom from adult control experienced by working-class children and adolescents meant that they tended to interact relatively violently and develop dominant hierarchies, of which age and physical strength became central determinants (Dunning 1986).

This pattern was also reinforced by the standards set by the dominant adults in communities of this sort. Sexual segregation and the dominance of men over women contributed to these ideas, and further reinforcement came from the frequency of feuds between families and street gangs at this time. In short, working-class communities of this type appeared to be characterised by a positive reinforcement cycle, whereby the employment of violence was rewarded and normalised in most areas of social relations, especially among males.

One of the effects of this cycle is the prestige placed upon males who could fight. Accordingly, there was a tendency for these males to develop a love of fighting and to see it as a central source of meaning and gratification in life (Dunning 1986). The central difference between those of working-class descent and those classified as middle class is that the latter generally viewed violence as something to be condemned and non-gentlemanly, whereas in the former communities it tended to be normatively condoned and rewarded. A further difference identified by Dunning (1986) is the fact that there was a tendency in the middle classes for violence to be 'pushed behind the scenes', and when it did occur, for it to take on a more instrumental form and to result in feelings of guilt. By contrast, in working-class communities, violence tended to be expressed to a greater extent in a public domain, and to take more of an expressive than instrumental form. As such, it tended to be associated with the arousal of pleasurable feelings (Dunning 1986).

With this in mind, it is reasonable to suggest that it is the working-class, violent masculine style that is generated, and principally expressed, in sports such as boxing. That is to say, the currently available evidence suggests that it is young men from this section of society who form the majority of boxing clientele (Sugden 1996; Wacquant 2004). This is partly due to class positioning, but also because boxing is a site where this masculine style can be so freely expressed. Furthermore, the boxing ring is viewed as a form of play fight that is centrally about the expression of masculinity, particularly in a form that is socially approved and controlled. The central difference between the masculine style expressed in boxing and combat sports, to that of male sport more generally, is that physical violence and toughness for middle-class men tends to be channelled into the socially approved medium of the game, whereas the violence of working-class men forms more of a central life commitment that shapes part of their habitus and guiding norms in this class culture (Hobbs 1995; Winlow 2001).

Finally, this historical trajectory of sport is what contributed to the main debates on men and sport in the 1980s (Connell 1987), as sport in industrialising societies developed as a 'male only preserve' (Dunning 1986) separate from women's spheres of life. However, correlatively, sport also served to differentiate between men themselves, between those classified as hegemonic and those classified as subordinate. It is this discussion that I turn to next.

Sport as a definer of hegemonic masculinity

Sport is a key terrain of contest for gender, as well as for race, class, sexual and global relations (Connell 1990; Messner 2005). It is a highly visible forum, in which male and female bodies are literally built, their limitations displayed, and their capacities debated. As such, it is a key site for ideological contest over the meanings of masculinity and femininity. In the 1970s, with the emergence of second wave feminism and inspiration from the 'men's liberation movement' (Connell 1990), a small amount of work on men, masculinity and sport started to appear (for further discussion, see Farrell 1974; Schafer 1975). However, it was not until 1980 with Donald Sabo's book *Jock: Sport and Male Identity* that scholars started to develop critiques of sexism, homophobia, violence and militarism at the heart of men's sports. Sabo (1985) developed these ideas and laid the foundation for specific questions to be asked surrounding boys' socialisation through sport, competition and success, bodies, emotions and pain, domination of women, and aggression and violence. Additionally, these questions paved the way for feminist writers such as Theberge (1991), Bordo (1989) and Hall (1991) to conduct research in pro-feminist directions and look at how women fit into an overall structure of power.

As discussed earlier, in the United States and increasingly in Britain, men's sport was formed during industrialisation and urbanisation, at a time of shifting work and family dynamics for both men and women (Kimmel 1990). This was at the tail end of the first wave of feminism and also amid racist fears of immigration. Thus, sport served to bolster faltering ideologies of white middle-class masculine superiority over women, and also over race and class subordinated men (Kimmel 1990). Based on these concepts of gender, feminism, masculinity and sport, Connell (1987) supplied sport studies scholars with a conceptual framework with which to examine the complexities of gender dynamics in men's sports that revolutionised the way we think about masculinity.

Traditional sociobiological theories of masculinity stated that a man's body and gender were purely anatomical (Wilson 1978), yet, in the social sciences, bodies and gender started to be viewed as neutral surfaces that could be imprinted upon, constructed and performed. This wave of thought was in response to notions of sex role theories of gender and the idea of a male sex role, as scholars could see that sport was an institutional realm in which men construct and affirm their separation from, and domination over, women. According to Bartky (1988), Lensky (1986) and Theberge (1991), this was particularly relevant, as women's exclusion from most aspects of sporting activity contributed to men's continued control and dominance over women's bodies. Sport did not just seamlessly reproduce men's power over women; sport was also a realm in which men of dominant groups affirmed their dominance and superiority over other men.

Connell's (1995) concepts of hegemonic, marginalised and subordinated masculinities gave conceptual form to the idea of gender as multiple. These concepts produced discourses with which to speak about seemingly paradoxical gender dynamics, with hegemonic being the currently dominant and ascendant form of masculinity (Connell 1995). Put simply, hegemonic masculinity is constructed as not feminine, but also simultaneously, not-gay, not-black, not-working class and not-immigrant. Thus, hegemonic masculinity recognised the connection between two important social patterns – hierarchy among men *and* women, and also hierarchies among men (Connell 1995).

Sport became a perfect starting point for investigating how individuals actively construct meaning around gender, power and masculinity. The idea that sport is, on the one hand, a modern bastion of patriarchal power and, on the other, a terrain that has been contested continually by women and by marginalised men, has been imperative to studies of sport and gender to the present day. Since the 1980s, concrete studies of gender and sport, such as those mentioned, have repeatedly demonstrated how the once unquestioned bastion of powerful, competitive, hierarchical and often violent heterosexual masculinity is not a seamless patriarchal institution (Messner 2005). Rather, the very crux of the gender order of men's sport is contested and wrought with contradiction and paradox (Messner 2005). These contradictions and paradoxes cover thematic areas such as bodies, relationships, violence and domination and, for the purposes of this book, I turn my attention to the latter.

Sport as a form of domination

As discussed, sport plays an important role in the 'masculine validating experience' especially in the formation of identity in adolescence (Connell 1983). Connell suggests that to learn to be a male is to learn to project a physical presence that speaks of latent power. He therefore argues that sport is empowering for many young men precisely because it teaches them how to use their bodies to produce effects, and also, because it teaches them how to achieve power through practised combinations of force and skill: 'What it means to be masculine is, quite literally, to embody force, to embody competence' (Connell 1987:27). This is especially important among adolescent males, for whom other sources of recognised masculine authority (based on earning power, sexual relations or fatherhood) are some way off.

Therefore, the male body, and its capacity to express force and skill becomes an urgent task. Sport serves as an important conduit for achieving this, as according to both Connell (1995) and Merleau-Ponty (1962) our sense of identity is firmly rooted in our experiences of embodiment. It therefore becomes integral to the reproduction of gender relations that men are encouraged to experience their bodies and themselves, in forceful, space-occupying, dominating ways (Connell 1987). This is precisely why sport matters in the total structure of gender relations, as it can be argued that masculinising and feminising practices associated with the body are at the heart of the social construction of masculinity and femininity.

In linking embodied constructions of masculinity identity in structural concepts of patriarchy, Connell (1983:27) suggests that it is through a combination of both strength and skill that this is possible. Hence: 'Men's greater sporting prowess has become a theme of backlash against feminism, as it serves as symbolic proof of men's superiority and right to rule' (Connell 1995:54). It is through this combination of strength and skill that the body can be symbolised as masculine, and arguably, nowhere else but in the discourse of sport can this be so readily harnessed. The masculine body moved from symbol of beauty to symbol of power (Dutton 1995). In sports such as boxing, the ability to demonstrate the embodiment of force and competence is second to none, as 'sport has come to be the leading definer of masculinity in mass culture' (Connell 1995:54).

In the main, however, this idea of force and competence is accomplished through competition, as this develops hierarchy and is thus deeply embedded in social structures of gender, race and class. Moreover, with the cultural meanings accorded to masculinity, men employ techniques that allow them not only to *be* masculine, but also to 'do' masculine (Messerschmidt 1993). This 'doing' not only preserves the exclusion of women from masculine validating practices such as sport, but further serves to create and carve further identities based on domination and aggression.

Messner (1990:100) argues that: 'Violent sport as spectacle provides linkages among men in the project of the domination of women, while at the same time helping to clarify and construct differences between various masculinities'. Boxing therefore offers a specific, traditional, physically aggressive site that invokes hegemonic masculinity, subordinates homosexuality, and by and large excludes women from the higher echelons of success (Hargreaves 1997; Woodward 2004). Boxing therefore forms part of a practice that depends heavily on binary oppositions – especially between women and men – and this is what supports claims to exclusivity and notions of a stronger sex. Indeed, Woodward (2004:8) writes: 'Boxing is ever more constructed around resistance to the rhetoric of transgression and interconnections and remains entrenched in a binary logic'.[2] Woodward's point is that, whilst theories of identity, especially gender identities, become more of a fluid dimension, the site of boxing becomes more entrenched in its resistance to anything not classed as 'manly', and with that, an intrinsic aversion to 'femininity'. Accordingly, this dualistic rigidity pervades the sport, with its inherent language of heavyweights/lightweights, strong/weak, pro/amateur, courageous/cowardly, and the constant negotiation of these semantics performed and practised by men who participate.

According to de Garis (2002), the disciplinary practices in boxing gyms form part of a social relation in which social identities are formed and expressed. This is particularly evident in fighting and sparring, as they are seen as being strongly associated with masculine identities and performance. This is because sparring practice involves a negotiation and representation of subordination and dominance, with de Garis (2002) further arguing that sparring practices create rituals of 'somatic intimacy' that are important and relevant for men in sporting arenas. He observed that sporting practices in boxing gyms offer a space in which men may share somatic intimacy that otherwise would not be socially sanctioned. The example he provides is that boxing is: 'one of the few times in which two scantily clad men may, in a socially acceptable manner, emotionally and intimately embrace each other is immediately after they beat each other up' (de Garis 2002:97). de Garis claims that the gym is a 'safe' place to express this intimacy, because the textual representations of boxing as masculine and violent deter any allegations of weakness and femininity.

Somatic relations among men outside of a sport are controversial. Culturally, it is seen as a subordinated version of masculinity and in opposition to that of hegemony. Gayness, weakness and other forms of intimacy between men can be classified in these negative subordinated terms, which in turn, allows for the patriarchal ideology to expel homosexuality from the hegemonic order. More recent work by Anderson (2002; 2005; 2008; 2009), however, suggests that this may be slowly changing. Yet, bodily weakness is still affiliated with subordinated masculinities, and the non-sporting male can often be taunted and symbolically linked to femininity, contributing to this idea of the insistently masculinised male. Emasculating words such as 'pussy' and 'gay' are often still banded around sporting arenas, as references to men who fall below the expected competitive standard set out by the dominant masculine order (Eder et al 1997; Kreager 2007).

The textual representations and the rhetoric used to describe sporting activity, particularly boxing, evoke masculinity, as aggressive boxers are often referred to as 'macho' or 'hard'. Messner (1990) argues that one of the main attractions of sport is the macho quest to assert dominance through competitive victories, suggesting that masculine domination in combat sports promotes an attitude in which the body is used both as a weapon and as a tool to achieve goals. According to Messner (1990), this form of masculinity is destructive to the body, as it denies emotional intimacy, with the body merely acting as a medium and target of destruction and domination. Messner therefore argues that any intimacy shared is covert, and only characterised by doing together rather than mutual talk about inner lives. Klein (1986) and Oates (1987) both see it as a further attempt to employ aggression in the domination of others – opponents, teammates, women, ethnic minorities and gay men. Therefore, rather than discussing forms of 'somatic intimacy' vis-à-vis de Garis, we should pay further attention to the ways in which sport is employed to invoke hegemonic masculinity.

According to Messner (1990), sports do provide some form of positive relationship. This is accomplished through having teammates, participation in group activities, and the emotional salience of men's earliest sporting experiences in terms of their relationships with other males. It is not so much the competition (although this is a dominant masculine value of organised sports) that seems important here, but something fun to do with fathers, older brothers or uncles. Indeed, Messner's (1990:100) respondents reported that the most important thing about sport was 'being out there with the guys – being friends', and this for them, led to 'some kind of closeness'.

Though sports participation may have initially promised this intimacy, Messner discovered that the less skilled, less competitive boys started to become alienated from the hierarchical system. Those who did experience some early experience of success in Messner's sample, started to receive recognition from adult males (especially fathers and brothers), and therefore received higher status among their peers. As a result, participants invested more and more of their energy and identity into athletic participation, developing a self-concept to that of an athlete, and internalising the rewards that came with it. These young men therefore learnt that athletic participation was a guaranteed way to obtain recognition, contingent on being a winner, and that performance and winning were extremely important. For some, this created pressures that served to lessen or eliminate the fun of athletic participation, whereas for others it was a way to achieve and obtain status among peers and male family members (Messner 1990).

The downside to domination: sport and male vulnerability

Connell (1995:45) argues that: 'True masculinity is almost always thought to proceed from men's bodies – to be inherent in a male body or to express something about a male body'. In his 1990 work *An Iron Man*, Connell demonstrates how the mental, emotional and physical training regimes in becoming a top athlete encourage men to deny fear, deny anxiety and pain, and avoid any other inconvenient emotions, while mentally controlling one's body to perform its prescribed tasks. 'The decisive triumph', Connell concludes, 'is over oneself, and specifically over one's own body'. The 'magnificent machine of the iron man's physique has meaning only when subordinated to the will to win' (Connell 1990:95).

However, Jefferson (1998:78) claims that the embodiment of masculinity is deeper than just the male body as a centrality to the sense of self, as he writes: 'It is thus about representations of the masculine body *and* their psychic underpinnings; for without the latter it is impossible to comprehend how masculine body imagery has sufficient affect to be reproduced across the generations' (emphasis in original). Jefferson posits that while masculinity is embodied, it is also carries with it an emotional investment – the suffusion of both desire and anxiety – thus providing a further backdrop for the construction of masculine identities. Jefferson argues from a psychosocial perspective, and eloquently frames the notion of anxiety in a pen portrait of Mike Tyson – Iron Mike – the heavyweight boxing champion of the world.

This is important, as Jefferson demonstrates that 'hardness' – the interiorised quality extracted from risking the body in performance (Jefferson, 2002:92) – is de rigueur for anyone serious about boxing. Moreover, Jefferson (2002) suggests that psychoanalytical reasonings have at least a small part to play in the way masculinities, and indeed hegemonic masculinity, is framed. Viewed from a Kleinian perspective,[3] vulnerability – and male anxiety – manifests itself as parts of one's personality, and this becomes too painful to confront or admit. In psychoanalytical terms, this 'persecutory anxiety', is a projection or splitting off that must be disavowed, and projected onto another, where it can be safely attacked. A classic example would be the extreme homophobe; unable to deal with the ambivalence and mixed feelings of homosexuality and the 'truth' that this may reveal about themselves, the homophobic male projects feelings into violent action, and employs words such as 'faggot', 'poof', and so on. Accordingly, this projection into violent words and actions acts as a purification process, whereby the homophobe can cleanse himself of unwanted desire and anxiety, and therefore attack the ambivalent feelings from afar. Using this projection/splitting thesis, Jefferson purports that any threat to masculinity, especially those that are invested in the discourses of the 'hardman' discussed earlier, will inevitably project any feelings of softness and weaknesses into the 'other', thus avoiding threats to self. In Jefferson's words:

> the extreme hardman would seem to also fit this pattern: unable to tolerate any hint of weaknesses or softness, because it is too threatening to his sense of selfhood, he must split off this unwanted part (and the reservoir of hate), and project it onto others, and mercifully attack it there. (Jefferson 1998:93)

Using Mike Tyson as a case study, Jefferson (1998) argues that Tyson, in his quest to embody the 'hardman', did so by the employment, or rather the disavowing, of psychic and structural anxieties that facilitated his transformation from '"little fairy boy to compleat destroyer"' (Jefferson 1998:18). To assist in this transformation, and to completely embody the hardman, Tyson had to imbue a set of social and psychic congruences that add up to a compelling satisfaction in inflicting – or desire to inflict – punishment, and therefore triumph over the threat of having it inflicted on oneself (Jefferson 1998). This is an important point, because men such as Frank, Eric and Leroy in this study demonstrated at times an inability to sit with any concept of softness, vulnerability and potential loss. Drawing on Jefferson's arguments, it became clear that to imbue this sense of hardness, the men had to literally inflict punishment on other's bodies and minds (as well as their own) to negate feelings of psychic loss, anxiety and vulnerability.

Indeed, Sam Fussell's (1991) book *Muscle* lends weight to Jefferson's argument, when he discusses how he took his body to an extreme physical limit to gain a sense of 'control', and was able to diametrically oppose concepts of feminization, by 'extolling the masculine virtues of sacrifice, distinction, discipline, dignity, self-restraint, and commitment to a cause' (Featherstone 1992:174). While Fussell's book is specifically focused on bodybuilding, the parallels to boxing are not lost here, and I would argue that both sports inhabit a social world that places onus on the body as a defence mechanism.

Dubbert's (1979) work on the significance of sport as a 'primary masculinity-validating experience' canonises ideas that feminist psychoanalysts such as Chodorow (1978) and Epstein (1991) have been writing about for years. They suggest that masculinity is an inherently fragile identity, because it is anchored in a positional – as opposed to a relational – sense of self. Put more simply, masculinity and its many manifestations are somewhat governed by the fear of attachment, and therefore in need of constant reaffirmation. Certainly, the concept of 'hardness' that Jefferson discusses in relation to Tyson, sits neatly with psychoanalytical object relation theories, whereby some men are endowed with fragile self-boundaries and a deep ambivalence towards intimacy, and will defend against this exposing vulnerability, by disguising it behind a carapace of muscle and bodily capital (Wacquant 1995b).

Similarly, Klein's (1990) ethnographic study of male bodybuilders illustrates not only the quite literal construction of hard male bodies but also the emotional insecurities, health costs, sexual anxieties, and contradictions that lie beneath the layers of muscle. Indeed, athletic careers construct masculine bodies as machines or tools, and often in this process alienate themselves from their health, feelings and relationships with others. Hall (1991) argues that accounts such as Fussell's or those seen in Klein's ethnography, are reflective of a personal 'hidden anxiety', with Glassner (1989) and Pleck (1982) arguing that these anxieties tap deep into the core of conventional masculinity, and that the majority of men's self-esteem correlates highly with having a muscular body. Conversely, those men with small or 'soft' physical attributes have lower levels of satisfaction than more athletic peers (Pleck 1982). This pursuit to obtain muscles highlights men's 'passionate battle against their own sense of vulnerability' (Glassner

1989:315), and therefore reinforces particular embodiments and hierarchies of masculinity in sport. Moreover, one of the ways in which these hierarchies can be established, and the vulnerability denied, is through the credible use of violence and domination in sport. Indeed, by honing the body and denying intimacy, male athletes not only protect themselves from inner anxieties, but also further allow for the perpetuation of a dominant gender order seen in sporting discourses, especially those of a combative, violent nature.

Combat sports, masculinity and intersectionality

Much of the literature views sport as a masculine validating experience. Violent sports, in particular, provide linkages among men in the project of the domination of women, while helping to construct and clarify differences among various masculinities in the gender order – or, as Matthews (2014) suggests, more localised pastiche forms. The employment of the male body in violent sports forms the basis of male identification and competition, and therefore becomes an important organising institution for the embodiment of masculinity. Additionally, men's power over women becomes naturalised and linked to the social distribution of violence, and then, largely through the media, weaves a structure of symbols and interpretation around these differences, which naturalises them (Hargreaves 1986).

Not only does the hegemonic pattern construct difference between men and women, but it also serves to construct difference between class, race and status. As a result, violence in combat sports such as boxing is often seen as primitive and uncivilised, and thus reduced to men from lower-status backgrounds, in which socioeconomic circumstances prevent status from being achieved in academic and financial ways. Sport therefore becomes an avenue to assert a sense of masculine 'style' – a masculine self – when other methods of accomplishing one's masculinity seem limited. As Messner (1990:103) argues, men who herald from higher-status backgrounds generally abandon sports after high school as they transition into other 'middle-class cultural endeavours that encourage the performance of masculinity in more rational directions such as education and non-sporting careers'.[4]

For men who are unable to express their masculinity in conventional middle-class ways, being successful in sports (particularly those associated with working-class masculinities such as football and boxing) was often their only hope of achieving public masculine status. Various research has suggested that men, particularly adolescent men who suffer socioeconomically, view sport as an extremely important avenue for constructing masculine identity and status (Messner and Sabo 1990; Connell 1995), as it is seen as an avenue to achieve respect in a masculine quest for recognition through public achievement, and unfolds in a system of structured constraints due to class and race inequities. The institutional context of sport, therefore, and the constricted structure of opportunity in the economy makes the pursuit of sporting careers the most rational choice for some young men. Research into this idea has suggested that these social contexts that are stratified by social class and race form part of a choice for young men in whether to pursue or not pursue a sporting career, and becoming explicable in an individual's assessment of the available means to achieve a respected masculine identity (Messner 1990).

For most men, particularly those from lower-status backgrounds, the status and respect that they can achieve through the medium of sport becomes important simply through being achievable. Nonetheless, this does not equate to overall social mobility, as Jefferson and Walker (1992:4) observed: 'That the next heavyweight champion will almost certainly be black has nothing to do with chromosomes and natural aptitude but everything to do with the racial and class disadvantages combined.'

Indeed, this hegemonic pattern evident in sport merely serves to perpetuate a gender order that is constructed and legitimised by the overall domination of women, and also the marginalisation of certain men. Yet, Anderson (2002) has suggested that this may not always be the case, and has put forward arguments for a more 'inclusive masculinity', stating that we need to rethink our categorisations of fraternal sporting institutions as merely monolithic. Or as Matthews (2014) suggests, masculinity that is only viewed through Connell's (1995) hegemonic lens is not enough to currently theorise masculinity and sport.

I agree with both Anderson (2002) and Matthews (2014), yet I am still convinced that combat sport provides an arena in which men can deny vulnerability, disavow anxiety, and thus distance themselves from the intimate feminine other and the subsequent marginalised male. Boxing, therefore, is appealing to men as an investment; an investment in physical capital and muscular armour that allows for the domination of both women and other men who do not meet the standards prescribed by the hegemonic gender order. This standard inherent in male sporting culture is what arguably contributes towards violent attitudes and behaviours among male athletes, as one of the most widely discussed research areas to develop from masculinity and sport is the relationship between male athletes' on/off the pitch violence.

In the next section, I will discuss how a combat sport such as boxing subscribes towards the arguments surrounding male athletes' understanding and practice of violence, and, more importantly, how this may or may not contribute to a process of desistance for those who box.

Contemporary ideas surrounding sport and desistance from crime

Although the health benefits of sport are well established, the evidence for sport's impact on education, crime and community cohesion is limited and largely anecdotal (Collins and Kay 2003; Wright 2006; Laureus Report 2011; Meek 2018). Coalter (2007) argues that vague and unexamined claims about sport's ability to address issues of antisocial behaviour and crime have always underpinned public investment in sport. Since the 19th century, concerns with social order and the moral condition of the new urban working classes via the 1975 White Paper's concern to reduce 'boredom' and 'urban frustration', the supposed role of sport in combating crime and antisocial behaviour has been key for public sector rationale and investment.

In the main, sport has traditionally always been regarded as having moral components; having the ability to instil values that are transposable to other areas of life. These values often range from character-building attributes to the development of self-efficacy, locus of control, self-discipline and fair play. Qualitative policy documents can often be littered with *ad hominem* statements of how sport 'saved me from a life of crime' (Coalter 2007). The main focus, however, is on the relationship between sports participation and crime reduction. Can participation actually reduce criminal activity, and if so, how? The answer to this question can be broadly broken down into theories: one being the rehabilitation of known offenders; and the second being theories concerning crime prevention – or 'diversion', as it is more commonly known.

On the one hand, the former approach of rehabilitation tends to involve smaller projects with a specific focus; usually the targeting of known offenders. They generally have a specific remit in terms of a counselling-based approach, in which participants are risk assessed and their needs identified as part of the project's mission. These types of programmes are usually adapted to meet needs, and aimed at developing personal and social skills, while building self-confidence and esteem. More importantly, these programmes are specifically focused on the development of a locus of control, whereby participants believe that they can control events that affect them, and are therefore less likely to blame external forces for their own behaviour. In short, locus of control can be said to be about personal responsibility and core evaluation of one's self; therefore, this locus, once developed, is presumed to be transposable to the wider social context, thus reducing offending (Coalter 1988; Nichols and Crow 2004; Wright 2006; Laureaus and Ecorys 2012).

Diversionary programmes, on the other hand, which are the predominant concern of social policy initiatives, tend to be relatively large-scale, open-access sports programmes, targeted at youth at risk in specific identified areas during times when antisocial behaviour is perceived as being at its peak. This approach was specifically sanctioned under the New Labour regime as part of its social inclusion agenda, and part of a cross-cutting scheme that saw all agencies under the banner of crime and disorder coming together in a holistic, targeted approach. Indeed, the significance of this approach was indicated by the establishment of a national sports-based programme called Positive Futures in 2001 (Crabbe 2006; Kelly 2011).

The absence of systematic evidence of the effectiveness of such programmes can be explained by a number of factors. According to Coalter (2007), at the level of practice there has been an absence of a culture of monitoring and evaluation, bolstered by a range of factors and a simple belief in the efficacy of such interventions. However, the fundamental issue is the fact that there has been a widespread lack of clarity about the nature of outcomes and their measurement. Furthermore, there have been substantial methodological difficulties in controlling for intervening variables and in assessing the cause and effect relationships of these programmes (Nichols and Crow 2004; Smith and Waddington 2004). These same problems are also said to be evident in the more focused, small-scale rehabilitation programmes (Smith and Waddington 2004). Similarly, Taylor and Godfrey (2003) argue that the major problem in identifying and measuring the effects of sport on criminal behaviour (if any) is that the influence on behaviour is indirect, working through a number of intermediate outcomes or processes, such as improved fitness, self-efficacy, self-esteem or locus of control, and the development of certain social and personal skills. It is therefore clearly not sufficient or wise, to measure changed behaviours or to simply assume that they are as a result of sport participation. In short, it is difficult analytically to separate the developmental changes related to sports participation from more general developmental changes in young people's lives, and also from the influence of social and structural factors unrelated to sports.

Finally, it has been consistently noted that many of these projects have a number of common weaknesses, such as vague rationales, overly ambitious objectives and a relatively unsophisticated understanding of the variety and complexity of the causes of criminality (Utting 1996; Coalter et al 2000). It is a complex relationship, one that can only ever be partially understood, and I discuss this later.

Sport and conformity: theoretical arguments for sport's potential to increase pro-social behaviour

Over the past thirty years, a number of studies have indicated that involvement in sport can be associated with reduced delinquency and violent behaviour. They argue that sustained involvement in sporting activity contributes towards an overall decrease in crime and antisocial behaviour (Landers and Landers 1978; Mahoney 2000; Langbein and Bess 2002; McMahon and Belur 2013; Meek 2018; Vazsonyi and Jiskrova 2018; Walpole et al 2018). It is arguments such as these that lend legitimacy to delinquency prevention programmes such as Fighting for Peace and The Boxing Academy in the UK, and the Midnight Basketball Leagues in the US. Schemes such as these promote sports as a means of keeping young urban males off the streets, while arguably, and simultaneously, increasing participants' bonds to schools and conventional peers, and also increasing self-esteem, social capital and upward mobility.

Authors writing about the relationship between sport and delinquency commonly invoke social control perspectives – particularly Hirschi's (1969) social bonding theory – to examine the linkages between sports participation and youth offending (Larson 1994; McNeal 1995; Crosnoe 2001; Cryer 2005; Groombridge 2016). These authors suggest that it is the constraining influence of conventional bonds that explain variations in individuals' delinquent behaviour, rather than merely focusing on individuals' motivations. Conventional sites such as schools, gyms and youth centres are seen as important places for adolescent integration into conventional societal norms, and adolescents who are tightly bonded to such sites and their peers are more likely to refrain from violent behaviour than other less bonded youths. Because school sports and extracurricular activities are institutionally sanctioned activities governed by schools, youth centres and conventional gyms, then social control perspectives predict that sports participation should increase the bonds that adolescents feel towards society. When considering the benefits that sport has to offer, Hirschi's (1969) social bonding theory comes to mind, as it incorporates elements of 'attachment', 'involvement', 'commitment' and 'belief', all of which can be applied to an individual's positive participation in sport.

To elaborate, sports participation should increase attachments to coaches, teammates and institutions (Coleman 1961; Purdy and Richard 1983; Cryer 2005), and the bonds to these influences should arguably reduce individual tendencies towards aggression and delinquency. Additionally, the time required to practise and be successful in the chosen sport should increase involvement, and with thissshould result in adecrease in time spent on other non-conventional/illegitimate activities (McNeal 1995; Walpole et al 2018). Also, because the rules and values of sports are assumed to lie in the value system shared by conventional society, participation in sports should increase an adolescent's belief in the moral order, and therefore promote pro-social behaviour (Larson 1994; Fitzpatrick et al 2015). Indeed, many youth sport initiatives have explicitly promoted pro-social behaviour through the learning of fair play, teamwork and conventional values (Fine 1987; Cryer 2005), and this element is considered extremely important in reducing and sustaining desistance from violence and delinquency.

Evidence for these theories generally comes in the shape of case studies, or qualitative interviews with bonded participants, and this can be seen in projects encompassing both rehabilitative and diversionary elements. For example, work by Nichols (2007) examined a host of projects – both rehabilitative and diversionary – to examine the processes by which participants were said to have reduced their criminal involvement. Nichols (2007:199) states that: 'In the long run, sports participation might provide a diversion from crime, in the same way that it is obvious that someone cannot be committing crime at the same time they are on a programme'. Indeed, the same long-term effect would be achieved by long-term sports participation, and in this respect, crime reduction and sports development objectives coincide. This mechanism of involvement is the rationale behind many sporting programmes, and it is often felt by policy makers that if participants developed a long-term commitment to sport, what Stebbins (1997) refers to as 'serious leisure' or 'major life interest', then this alone would prevent them from getting involved in anything else. This is because the commitment developed through the love of sport would maintain a long-term interest across the life-course.

Nichols (2007:199) discovered, however, that there was 'limited evidence for the latter effect in the case studies', as after 12 weeks of participation on a rehabilitative programme only three out of nine case studies were progressing to independent sports participation.

Furthermore, out of the 45 clients who began the rehabilitative programme, only 12 went full term. This does not necessarily mean that the mechanism of developing a commitment to sports participation that will then act as a long-term diversion from crime is invalid; it just means that this particular programme has not succeeded in overcoming all the barriers for that individual. Additionally, McMahon and Belur (2013:17), in their synthesis study of 11 sport-based programmes aimed at reducing violence, ascertained that 'programmes cannot be easily compared and generalised conclusions valid across cases cannot be drawn, without signalling a few caveats'.

This is important, as all too often, sport is seen as a panacea for all social ills, without a rigorous evidence base (Cox 2012). Long-term sporting programmes are important as hooks for change, and certain sports will be more attractive than others, as evidenced by McMahon and Belur (2013). Scraton and Flintoff (2002) identified that attitudes towards a specific sport are strongly linked to gender stereotypes, and consideration needs to be paid to how sport might reinforce a certain image of masculinity for some young men, especially when masculinity is incorporated into the programmes' 'hooking' potential. Generally referred to as 'male specific' (Scraton and Flintoff 2002), some sports, such as rugby and boxing, incorporate the gendered element of toughness into their appeal (Jump 2015). From McGuire and Priestley's (1995) conclusion, however, it would seem as if the main aim for policy makers, and indeed community leaders, is that the activity should attract the largest number of the target group, regardless of gender exclusion and potential reinforcement of gender stereotypes. Evidence suggests that diversionary activities that attract large numbers are sufficient enough in the short term to combat crime, yet more consideration is required, especially regarding the messages that are being transmitted in the longer term (McMahon and Belur 2013; Jump 2015).

It is arguable that the most significant factor associated with positive long-term behavioural change is its staff and trainers (Purdy and Richard 1983). Indeed, Wright's (2006:168) work into boxing as a form of social work to reduce violence, states: 'The likeliness of violent behaviour is lessened if an adolescent forms meaningful emotional attachments with others who do not condone violence'. Pawson (2006), Nichols (2007), Taylor et al (1999) and Hendry et al (1993) further suggest that the quality of the relationship between a sports leader and a mentee depends on the qualities of that leader.

Pawson (2006) suggests that functions of befriending, direction setting, coaching and advocacy are positive attributes, and that mentors who are seen to assist the mentee with wider relationships, especially those with other agencies, are beneficial and reciprocal. This implies that mentoring works better if it is embedded in sporting programmes that offer additional support (Witt and Crompton 1997). More specifically, and more importantly for this book, Nichols (2007:202) identified that the key characteristics of leaders on sporting projects were that they must create an atmosphere of mutual respect and must certainly not respond aggressively to aggressive outbursts. Nichols states: 'Staff had to be role models in the values required to live together harmoniously'.

Taylor et al (1999) report in their research that some managers of sporting programmes claim that high-quality staff are essential to the success of their projects, and when assessing and recruiting staff, these managers place more emphasis on the values that the recruits display than on the technical skills they possess. The managers felt this to be imperative in the recruitment of staff, as young people attending their sporting programmes were said to be in a transition in their own sense of self. Hendry et al (1993) also attest that the staff themselves must have a depth of maturity for the process to be in any way beneficial.

It is often assumed that participation in sporting activity will provide access to new peer networks. Indeed, there is some evidence that this is successful for participants on the rehabilitative programmes (Nichols 2007). This was as a result of participants gaining support from conforming peers, and the assistance in the development of new self-identities and lifestyles that are at odds with criminality. Moreover, this change in self-concept and self-identity has also been further identified as important in research by Graham and Bowling (1995) and Maruna (2001) into those who desist from offending.

Nevertheless, in the more primary diversionary sporting programmes, there was little evidence that participation in sport offered new peer networks, and if it did, there was little evidence that these peers were any less likely to be involved in offending (McMahon and Belur 2013). This contradicts ideas that involvement in 'diversionary activities' automatically bonds youths to socially valued themes, and is more reminiscent of theories surrounding differential association (Sutherland 1947) – the idea that criminal behaviour is learnt behaviour specifically in interaction with deviant others.

In summary, the concept of sport and its relationship to control theory (Hirschi 1969) is a highly intricate web of complementary and contrasting interactions that are difficult to untangle. In the context of programmes to reduce youth crime, sport is a tool to facilitate a process, much more than an end in its own right. Sport's value rests on its ability to hook young people in, followed by the ability of its programme staff to develop attachments and foster its participants through transitory periods of self-discovery. As Hodge and Danish (2001) suggest, 'self-esteem is not enhanced automatically through participation in sports, but rather through supportive interactions with adults and peers'.

These interactions, coupled with person-centred approaches, require an awareness of the process of 'mutual aid', whereby staff can provide a realistic base for young men to test ideas and be respectfully challenged if not meeting group norms and values (Malekoff 1997 in Wright 2006). Additionally, it may also require an awareness by members and coaches, of how perceptions of sport – masculine physical prowess and physical risk – may jeopardise what the programme originally set out to achieve.

Having said that, there is a lot of empirical evidence to support the fundamental claims of social control theory outlined earlier. Mahoney et al (2003) and McNeal (1995) argue that adolescents are less likely to drop out of school, more likely to attend colleges, less likely to behave delinquently, and more prone to upholding rules and elements of conventional society (Fine 1987; Walpole et al 2018). However, these theories do not specifically address violence, nor do they specifically address attitudes towards violent behaviour.

Control theorists assume that the motivation to commit delinquency is a constant across individuals, and that group norms supportive of crime are weak or non-existent (Hirschi 1969). This is because control theorists choose to focus on pro-social bonds and omit the idea that individuals may be tightly bonded to groups or subcultures that promote antisocial behaviours. Working to this premise, violence by male athletes would be interpreted as evidence that either sport is not a conventional activity, or that violent athletes are not as fully bonded as one would expect. Considering that there is a lot evidence to suggest that sport involvement is generally regarded as conventional behaviour, sport scholars are left assuming that those athletes who commit delinquent acts are somehow alienated from institutions such as schools, peers and families, as it is *this* lack of association that would free an athlete to behave violently.

The argument that an attachment to role models in the form of trainers or coaches immediately reduces delinquency is a common misconception. While it is acknowledged as important, it also becomes imperative that the coaches and trainers on sporting programmes have the skills to develop and align participants' behaviours with more conventional values inherent in wider society. Purdy and Richard (1983) identified that the length of contact between participant and coach is crucial to the development of a relationship, and therefore they are critical of the more 'open access' diversionary programmes that Positive Futures (Crabbe 2006; Kelly 2011) and Street Games (Walpole et al 2018) offer. The evidence for successful personal development in some young people in the more intensive rehabilitative programmes was 'more heavily influenced by the role model of the sports leader with whom they had developed a strong personal relationship' (Coalter 2012).

Additionally, there is some evidence that young people's attachments to role models can be negatively influenced by the coach's value system, as Collinson's (1996) analysis of young males' search for self-identities through drugs and crime attested. It may be possible that the bond that athletes develop with their coach could negatively impact upon their behaviour, and therefore *increase* their propensity for crime and delinquency. This is a contentious thought, and does not always chime positively with policy makers and practitioners. However, I feel it is an important point to make, and will discuss it further later.

Sport as criminogenic: a discussion on the learnt behaviours in sport and its relationship with violence and masculine-enhancing properties

As with the potential for negative bonds to be formed with coaches, there is also the risk with certain sports, particularly those with a combative nature, that the bonds created and the lessons learnt can also have adverse effects on an individual's behaviour and attitude. In contrast to control theories, social learning perspectives allow for subgroup variation in attitudes towards violence and delinquency. Some theorists argue that individuals learn antisocial values and violent behaviour as part of group interaction (Sutherland 1947; Akers 1998), whereas Sykes and Matza (1957) argue that some groups have positive attitudes towards criminal behaviour, or at least find ways to justify and neutralise behaviour.

Social learning theories posit that individuals may be tightly bonded to others, while simultaneously possessing attitudes that are favourable to violence and delinquency. Trimbur (2009:263) writes: 'One can be an accomplished drug salesmen and an accomplished Golden Gloves champion'. It is this very idea that separates learning theories from theories of control. Work by Akers (1998) has developed this idea of differential association reinforcement theory, by suggesting that individual violence and delinquency is as a result of continual and reciprocal processes of observation, attitude internalisation, and real and perceived reinforcements from demonstrations of violent behaviour.

Hughes and Coakley (1991) apply these theories to the debate around athletic deviance, suggesting that rather than athletes' deviant behaviours resulting from social alienation or rejection of specific cultural values, they emanate directly from the normative definitions learnt in the sporting environment. They refer to this as 'positive deviance', stating that the values associated with sports – obsession with status, sacrifice for the team, playing through pain, and refusing to accept limits – are generally associated with individual success and conventional behaviour. Moreover, these values and normative definitions can also create dilemmas, in which 'athletes do harmful things to themselves and perhaps others while motivated by a sense of duty and honour' (Hughes and Coakley 1991:311). This idea arguably contributes towards a participant's aggressive attitude and behaviour, as the aggression displayed is often an essential component of sporting success. As Kreager (2007:708) has attested: 'By applying lessons learned in sports, athletes may perceive violence and intimidation as acceptable means of achieving off-the-field goals and solving problems unrelated to sports'.

Peer relationships in the sporting context can also play a pivotal role in the learning process, particularly during the teenage years, when identity formation and status-conscious processes play an important part (Coleman 1961). As Eder and Kinney (1995) highlighted, sport provides males with clear trajectories for increasing peer status, and team sports in particular can provide consensus to group norms. Humiliation and hierarchy all apply to group loyalty – particularly among sporting males – and ridicule and status competition serve to reinforce it (Warr 2002).

The defence of masculine reputations both in and outside of a sporting context may see men resort to 'character contests', where violence becomes an acceptable solution to a problem (Goffman 1967; Luckenbill 1977). These character contests form part of a systematic hierarchy of masculinity commonly seen in masculine peer groups (Goffman 1967; Luckenbill 1977).

In his work on athletic off-the-pitch violence, Curry (1998) observed peers simultaneously encouraging retaliation through violence as a means to build cohesion and display courage. Violent reactions – both in and outside of the sporting context – bonded teammates to exclusive peer groups based on normative expectations of honour, masculine courage, risk-taking and ridicule, whereby individuals were forced to compete for status to secure their identity and avoid humiliation at any cost.

Research into masculinity and sport suggests that not all sports are equal in terms of their relationship to violence (Messner 1992; Connell 1995; Crosset 1999; Coakley 2001). The debate from these authors, is that 'hyper-masculine' combat sports, such as boxing, wrestling and rugby, create conditions where violence becomes acceptable as a means of 'doing' masculinity and maintaining valued identities.

Eder et al (1997:69) offer evidence to support these claims, as their research demonstrated how young men were able to successfully construct masculine identities in combat sports. In their research, Eder et al observed young men initiating patterns in which, 'higher status was associated with intimidation of others, and lower status was associated with submission', particularly when athletes were responding to insults and issues of disrespect both in and outside of a sporting context. According to the Eder et al, these intimidating responses established a system by which those who participated in violent sports had access to resources that enabled them to respond more violently. This behaviour guaranteed higher status among peers in the same sporting milieu, and additionally served to prevent future attacks. The aggression shown by athletes, and more importantly, the willingness to respond to challenges, identified leaders in the group, while further helping to promote disdain for those unwilling or unable to retaliate in defence of themselves (Eder et al 1997). Because of this, those unwilling to use violence were derided as being weak and effeminate, and were either expelled from the dominant group or subjected to violent victimisation.

Kinney (1993) identified that this lack of retaliation can also result in a stigmatised label, as those who cannot fight or prove their 'toughness' are placed at the bottom of the status hierarchy and assigned an identity as someone who is weak and ineffectual, thus promoting violence among athletes as a way to maintain status and dominance in group activities.

In addition, studies by Messner (1990), Begg et al (1996), Eder et al (1997), Curry (1998), Miller et al (2006) and Jump (2015) have all documented a positive relationship between sustained sport involvement and violent behaviour. They argue that participation in sporting activities can actually contribute to an increase in aggression and violence for participating individuals, particularly if the sport is classified as 'combative'. To support these claims, Edreson and Olweus (2005) conducted a cross-sectional design over a two-year period to specifically analyse the effects of 'power' sports (boxing, wrestling, martial arts and weightlifting) on aggressive and antisocial behaviour in male adolescents, as there is a strong argument that those who participate in combat sports such as boxing may have a higher probability of being involved in violence than other conforming peers and/or athletes who may choose and pursue less combative sports (Kreager 2007).

Edreson and Olweus's research produced results that distinguished between contact and non-contact sports as important in determining violent attitudes, with the contact sports category demonstrating an above-average risk of being involved in violent behaviour. Edreson and Olweus (2005:477) concluded that:

> From the practice of power sports itself and, very likely, from repeated contact with 'macho' attitudes, norms and ideals with a focus on muscles and physical strength and a belief in the value of toughness, and maybe violation of societal norms. We found no support whatsoever for the fairly common view that participation in power sports serves as cathartic function and actually leads to a reduction in violent and antisocial behaviour in everyday life outside of sport. It rather seems that boys with fighting skills and physical strength are particularly likely to use these 'assets' outside the sport situation as well. (Edreson and Olweus 2005:477)

However, as the latter research does not provide any concrete evidence to support claims for the use of violence 'outside the sport situation', Kreager (2007) has argued that the reliance on cross-sectional designs that are unable to distinguish selection from socialisation effects is a problem endemic to sport-violence research. Yet, despite these limitations, Kreager's (2007:721) results suggest that 'male dominated contact sports have important consequences for male adolescent violence', and as a result, could therefore have serious implications for social policy design.

To conclude, it would seem from these arguments that boxing would most certainly be classified as combative, therefore raising questions around its efficacy as a sport to reduce desistance from violence. Boxing is a successful hook in recruiting young men, as it is seen as a way to construct a dominant form of masculinity that some young men aspire to (Messner 1990). Work by Fletcher (1992) and Meek (2018) argues that boxing can actually develop self-control and self-discipline for young men, but, if the main ideology in boxing and combat sports is to win at all costs and maintain desired identities, then the messages transmitted and the rewards procured can arguably serve to reinforce violent behaviour. The work of Kreager (2007) would reinforce this argument, as the dominant forms of masculinity often seen in combat sports increased the likelihood of these forms becoming transposable to wider arenas unrelated to sports. It is this very argument that I intend to discuss and elaborate on throughout this book.

Summary

I began with a brief history of how sport came to be seen as welfare, and how sport was used as a vehicle to generate social capital, foster inclusion and contribute towards tackling poverty. I then proceeded to provide brief arguments for the desistance-promoting potential of sport, looking at theories surrounding sport's ability to incapacitate, bond, develop and involve young people in conventional activities, even though these may not always be methodologically sound.

I have discussed the criminological theories and policy implications in relation to sport, and provided arguments that suggest that not every type of sport provides the same outcomes in terms of pro-social development, and desistance from crime. I have also looked at theories of masculinity, arguing that sports – particularly violent, combative ones – reinforce a sense of hegemony and promote attitudes favourable to violence, especially when concepts of status or winning become threatened. This is because sports violence forms part of the dominating element of winning, and an imperative part of maintaining valued identities and status-forming attributes. These identities and attributes form part of a habitus of respect, honour and status, where violence forms part of a system to maintain these and ensure the continuation of dominance and respect. As a result, this habitus of sport and the 'win at all cost' mentality often fostered in combat sports becomes embedded in men's self-concepts, whereby violence becomes part of an everyday occurrence. Moreover, the status-promoting aspects of sport and violence become neutralised in certain men's frame of reference – they see it as normalised behaviour in the pursuit of winning or maintaining face, and part of their identity as successful sportsmen.

Combat sports, therefore, can be said to be symbiotic, whereby they involve and incapacitate young men at times when they otherwise may be involved in criminal activity, yet they contribute to a habitus where violence and hyper-masculinity dominates other values (Sabo 1986; Connell 1990; Messner 1990). By creating and sustaining identities that are favourable to violence, combat sports such as boxing can form part of an activity and a sporting culture that takes violence and masculinity as a central theme. Coaches and teammates play a huge role in the formation of identity and self-concepts, and arguments fall on both sides of the line. Work by Wright (2006:172) suggests that 'when youth feel honoured and valued, they are more able to build respectful relationships with the adult leader and fellow members; creating a safe space for growth and change'.

While I see the merit in these arguments, and can clearly see the value of positive role modelling, I am inclined to be slightly more critical than Wright, and to suggest that individual growth and change will only come about by the development of a 'redemption script' (Maruna 2001). This is a process where previous behaviour becomes acknowledged and worked through, and subsequently 'knifed off' as a part of oneself no longer valued. In boxing, this is a difficult process to undertake, as young men often draw upon the social capital that violence can offer, regardless of whether or not they take it 'out of the ring'. For true desistance to occur (if this actually exists), one must be able to resolve the meaning that violence has in their lives. Therefore, boxing and violence – and the relationship that men have with both these things – brings into question the very precarious nature of desistance.

A further question we have to ask ourselves is: how can the culture and coaches in the boxing gym impede and assist in the desistance process, especially considering the current political climate, and potential benefits of mentoring programmes designed to reduce serious youth violence?

To answer these questions, I turn to three case studies of members in the boxing gym, and outline the differing struggles each man has with his own concepts of violence. Frank, Eric and Leroy are not symptomatic of all males, but they present a snapshot of men's lives in an inner-city boxing gym. By using case studies and stories, I hope to provide a glimpse of the struggles that men like this face, and how boxing may – or may not – lead to a process of desistance. These stories are personal journeys of condemnation and redemption; stories of real lives and real men in the homosocial world of boxing and inner-city life.

Notes

1. This being a set of socially learnt dispositions, skills and ways of acting that are often taken for granted, and which are acquired through the activities and experiences of everyday life.
2. However, in light of the 2012 Olympic Games, where women's boxing was included for the first time, this may be changing.
3. Jefferson's arguments are based on the work of the psychoanalyst Melanie Klein.
4. The recent surge in white-collar boxing as a hobby may be changing this fact.

3

The Case of Frank: Respect, Embodiment and the Appeal of the Boxing Gym

Introduction

In this case study, I present Frank. I discuss how he accomplishes his masculinity through embodiment and also why the boxing gym was a huge source of appeal for him. I explore the ways in which he invests in the sport of boxing to overcome structural and personal vulnerabilities, and also how he copes with experiences of prior victimisation in a violent habitus that positions 'respect' as a central theme. I illustrate the ways in which Frank reconstructs himself physically, mentally and emotionally, whereby the sanctuary of the gym contributed not only towards Frank's search for respect, but also his desistance from violence as a young man; the boxing gym therefore allowing him to redefine himself as a boxer rather than a gang member. Having said that, the pro-social mechanisms that have incapacitated Frank in the gym over his life-course are merely temporary, and this is evidenced throughout his narrative, as he discloses personal incidences of violence and persistence in a habitus that respects retaliation.

Frank's story

Frank is 31 years old and has boxed since he was 12. Growing up in the UK as a young black male in the 1980s in an area of deep social exclusion, Frank immediately disclosed that he "[doesn't] trust many people". He was a little cautious about talking to an interviewer: "I don't really want to go on record, but I'll do it because you seem cool". Considering I had been hanging around the boxing gym for a few weeks now, and the boxers had got to see my face and know my name, I managed to convince Frank that I was not a 'fed' (police officer), and he agreed to share his story with me.

Boxing gyms are particularly noisy places, and the use of a dictaphone was not proving fruitful over the loud hip-hop and rhythmic pummelling of the punch bags. I suggested a café a few doors down from the gym and it was there, over a can of Coke, that I asked Frank to tell me his story. I told him to start at the beginning and take me up to the present day, and he began by saying that his "schooling wasn't great", and that he had been expelled from various primary schools. It was "around the age of 12 years old" that Frank realised that most of his problems "stemmed from anger issues and fighting", and as a result the gym became a source of appeal for him.

Being out of school and part of a single parent family, Frank mainly lived with his father and his brother, yet, considering his father was at work during the day and Frank was expelled from school, he was often left to "his own devices". He resided with his aunt during the day, a mile or so out of his residential area, and "hung around with kids who were not in school" close to her home. In fact, his first experience of boxing was with these young people, who were also excluded.

The boxing gym was run by a trainer who had been in the area for a long time and was used to seeing young men come and go, but Frank remembered the trainer telling him he had a "good punch". This made Frank feel good about himself, and think that he "could be a boxer one day". However, it was not until Frank walked into the ring and participated in some sparring that he realised boxing was more difficult than he had first anticipated, as he recalled "blowing all over the place like a fucking feather". Nonetheless, as the other young men drifted away from the gym, unable to compete with the physical demands of the sport, Frank continued to attend. Spurred on by the encouraging words of the trainer, and the belief that maybe one day he could be a boxer, Frank turned up to the gym most days.

The gym was in close proximity to his aunt's house and not near his permanent address. Therefore, in spite of his dedication, Frank stopped attending when he returned to mainstream education closer to his home. Furthermore, Frank disclosed that certain members of the community where he permanently resided were not happy about him associating with other young people from a different area, as at the time they were seen as rivals to gang factions in the local area. This was a cause of concern for Frank, as during his teenage years who you associated with, and the area you belonged to, formed part of a cultural identity that many young men were ascribing to:

> 'Where you came from mattered back then more than it does now in some ways, there was no way I could hang out with my mates from my auntie's house and live at my dad's, no way.'

Frank was warned to "stay away and stop chillin' with those guys", otherwise he would be "putting [himself] in an awkward position". As a result of these threats, the boxing gym that he had start to attend was no longer an option. Regardless, Frank still had a desire to box, and he disclosed that it became more important now, particularly as a result of these threats:

> 'When you got beef like I had, it makes you wanna learn to defend yourself better, you know what I'm saying? I wanted to keep on boxing because I liked it, but also because I needed it!'

Frank therefore sought out a gym closer to home and began attending frequently after school, distancing himself from friends in the local area, and also those he met at his aunt's house. He began to attend the inner-city gym where we first met, and has continued to come here for the last 19 years. It is here that Frank trains younger members, while simultaneously maintaining his physique to facilitate his occupation as a bouncer. In fact, maintaining his physique was the important element in Frank's story, and a theme that would recur throughout my research. It became particularly evident in Frank's story after quite a brutal sparring session. When I asked Frank if he was in pain after suffering a broken rib, he begrudgingly replied that he wasn't, and that it was "nothing", and the only thing troubling him, was the fact that the injury reminded him that he was "mortal" and he "hated" that thought. He then proceeded to tell everyone he had broken his rib, and parade his injury around the gym as a symbol of masochistic pride and endurance. Indeed, the words that jumped out of the conversation for me were "mortal" and "I hate it"; from that point onwards, I came to realise that most boxers do not see themselves as humans – they see themselves as infallible machines, projecting an image of indestructibility.

I wanted to unpick Frank's original motivation for boxing as a result of this conversation. Was it a sense of immortality that Frank desired? Or was it because he 'needed it' to defend himself against threatening behaviour in the community? I chose to return to the question: "Tell me the story of how you became a boxer". In the method of narrative interviewing it is important to grasp the full complexity of the story told. Therefore, I asked Frank about his time at primary school, as he disclosed in the first five minutes of talking, that "anger issues and fighting" were the main cause of his schooling problems:

DJ:	You said you were angry when you were younger, when you first started boxing, can I ask what it was that was making you angry at the time?
Frank:	Looking back on it now, probably a combination of a lot of things, maybe someone pissed me off, or another kid had disrespected me or something.
DJ:	Yeah.
Frank:	Coz as a kid you're trying to find yourself, and growing up in this area you've got to stand your ground.
DJ:	Stand your ground?
Frank:	Yeah, you've got to be a strong character, you've got to be strong, you can't let people bully you around, because you become that guy, that victim ...
DJ:	That victim?
Frank:	Going through childhood there was a tendency, or there was potential for me to become that victim.

This was a sore point and one that Frank found difficult to disclose. The idea of being a victim was so abhorrent to Frank, that he would do almost anything in his power to avoid it, making me think that Frank's reference to immortality was a way to defend against annihilating feelings of victimhood. This is not dissimilar to Jefferson's analysis of Mike Tyson, and his summation that Tyson's exterior presentation of hardness was in fact a way to disavow any sense of softness or victimhood. Moreover, the fact that Frank referred to his school experience as "that victim", led me to think that he may be trying to put some distance between himself and the victimising experience, by referring to "that" victim – "that" which does not belong to me. This allowed Frank to hold his experience at arm's length, thus helping to reduce feelings of shame and humiliation (Winlow and Hall 2009).

When trying to probe Frank further, especially regarding his unwanted anxieties around being a victim, he referred to how "alpha males" would "capitalise on it straight away". When I asked Frank to clarify his point, he summed it up by saying they would "smell fear". I felt it important to reach an understanding of the term 'alpha male' from Frank's perspective, as this was an interesting reference point, and also at odds with the term 'victim'.

DJ:	What does the term 'alpha male' mean to you?
Frank:	For most people it explains the fact ... someone who's self-assured, confident, ermmm ... and self-assured and confident, and I'd say someone who doesn't take much shit.

This seemed a strange answer, but evident from Frank's perspective that 'alpha males' are men who can defend themselves, "someone who doesn't take much shit", and also someone who would "retaliate when the time came". Conversely, a self-assured, confident male might be more apt at "taking shit", whereas someone who was riddled with self-doubt might see enemies everywhere. It started to transpire from Frank's story that the appeal of boxing was part of a strategy to deny being a victim, to avoid being bullied, and to develop, in his mind, a persona that "doesn't take much shit". For Frank, the way to achieve this was to invest in his physical capital via the medium of boxing.

As the conversation ensued, Frank seemed to soften and open up a little more, as he admitted to "not being the toughest of kids". He admitted that boxing was a form of defence, and disclosed that prior to joining the gym, there were times when he would fight and get his "arse kicked":

DJ:	Was boxing a form of self-defence for you?
Frank:	Yeah, didn't like the fact that 'I got it' [beaten up] – it could bug for me for days, weeks, you know what I mean?
DJ:	Right.
Frank:	The fact I'd lost meant learning boxing for me was like a skill and made me more of a fighter. Boxing helped as well as people respected me more.

From this small excerpt, we can ascertain from Frank's narrative that the fear of losing a fight – and becoming a victim – could produce unwanted thoughts and feelings after the event that could plague him for weeks. Accordingly, Frank invested in the sport of boxing to make him more able to fight, more able to defend himself against potential attacks and, in some respects, more able to eradicate the shame and humiliation that could replay in his mind after the offending incident. It further transpired that Frank felt more respected when able to defend himself, particularly in an environment that values retaliation as a method of maintaining respect.

As the narrative further unfolded, it became clear that Frank associated the concept of respect with the concept of being feared. This was not uncommon among those who boxed, as the word 'respect' was something that was mentioned frequently and exalted to the point where losing or gaining respect became a matter of life or death. This notion of 'respect' became a key theme and a turning point in the research, as something that was evident in nearly all of my interviews. What I learnt from these men was that their definition of respect meant the ability to intimidate and command fear. This was one of many strategies to accrue respect, especially in a milieu that values retaliation as respectful behaviour. When asking Frank what respect meant to him, and how boxing somehow made people respect him more, he said:

> 'The fact that I boxed when I went back to school at the age of 13 my physique looked good, even at that age, right you know, I'd get the respect. Even the older kids would be like "there's boxer" and they wouldn't call me by my name just "boxer".'

The fact that even now other young people refer to him as "boxer" still bolsters Frank's confidence, and he said it has been instrumental in motivating him to maintain his physique right up to the present day. Returning to Connell's (1985) point that masculinity emanates from men's bodies, I would tentatively assert that Frank's good-looking physique, in his mind, was part of a strategy to accrue and maintain respect in an environment that valued these things, further evidenced by his commitment and dedication that has lasted, so far, for 19 years. Indeed, by investing in his physical capital, Frank was not only able to ward off any potential attacks that could threaten his sense of masculinity and render him a further victim, but also, more importantly, able to reconstruct himself from the subject position of 'victim' to that of 'boxer'. This chimes with Jefferson's (1998:18) work yet again – the ability for boxing to transform young men with histories of bullying into 'compleat destroyers'.

This is further evidenced from early on in his life with Frank's reference to the older children at school not calling him by his name anymore, indicative that the identity of 'boxer' was vastly important to him. He swelled with pride when he told me this part of his story, as he talked of how he would "get respect now" for being known as 'boxer' and not as 'Frank'. When I asked Frank how he felt about being called 'boxer', he replied: "It felt nice, better than being bullied".

Frosh (1997:72) interprets the concern of boys and men with body size and muscularity as representing some kind of 'estrangement' from their bodies: 'They are striving to make their body the instrument of the will, to be honed and worked upon so that it will be able to achieve what is expected of it.' In Frank's case, his body became part of his identity – a visual representation worthy of consideration and respect, and also as an outward defence mechanism to avoid being a further victim of bullying. This investment in physical capital as an antidote to being bullied was an important investment for Frank – so much so, that he distanced himself from this concept with almost disgust, therefore withdrawing his previous reference to being bullied:

> 'I would not say I was a bullied child in school, I wouldn't go so far as to say I was bullied, but that all stopped when I started boxing anyway.'

Frank qualified his statement with how "that all stopped" when he started boxing. Arguably, Frank had constructed himself a new identity as a 'boxer', one with an investment in physical capital that even the "older lads respected". Indeed, this reconstruction and investment in boxing became part of a strategy for Frank, as he searched for the respect that he felt he lacked as a young boy. In his eyes, this was achievable through the medium of boxing. It is this element of his story that I turn to next.

Battle wounds: Frank's search for respect

Many of the issues that Frank raises in his narrative of growing up in a socially disenfranchised community, chime with Elijah Anderson's (1999) *Code of the Street*. According to Anderson, this 'code' is a reciprocally understood way of living – a set of prescriptions and proscriptions for behaviour in communities where other institutions and codes have failed. Frank disclosed that in his community they are deeply suspicious of authority, and that the police "only ever come round 'ere when looking for gang bangers". Anderson claims that this code was particularly inherent in inner-city black communities with inherent socioeconomic decline. This contributes to a strong sense in the community that they are 'on their own', especially regarding self-protection and self-defence. Accordingly, members of these communities must take personal responsibility. Frank illustrates this in the following excerpt:

> 'Around here you respect someone you fear. It's not necessarily the fear element but the combination of things - don't fuck with that guy because this is what he might … what he's gonna do! He's a moneyman, he got cash, and he got boys to back him. So if someone got cash but ain't willing to defend it then he's a pussy innit? You understand?'

When I probed at the respect/fear equation, Frank seemed perplexed, and I sensed an air of patronisation as he explained what he meant:

DJ:	Do you think respect and fear are the same thing?
Frank:	I think they can go hand in hand definitely.
DJ:	So why would you respect someone you feared?
Frank:	Hmmmmm, let me give you an analogy. Did I respect my parents when I was born? No, because there was times when I was disobedient you know what I'm saying? But when they beat the shit out of me I feared them didn't I?

This allows us a glimpse into how Frank associates 'respect' with 'fear' and 'obedience' – however achieved – as the use of violence by his parents developed a sense of fear in Frank that he saw as a mark of respect for them. As Frank grew up, he alluded to still respecting his parents, even though they "don't give me an arse wuppin' no more", but maintained that it was because of the beatings that he originally developed a sense of respect for them. From this, I tentatively assert that Frank sees violence as a way of gaining respect and maintaining a sense of fear in others. Additionally, the area where Frank lived in his younger years was, as he put it, "somewhere you had to be on your toes" – a place he alluded to as being somewhat tense; somewhere that required a sense of vigilance. It seemed that Frank's investment in physical capital was not only part of a strategic response when in school and family environments, but also a cultural one, particularly in a habitus that placed an onus on violence as a defence mechanism.

Frank not only demonstrates how violence is used to protect one's self and one's assets among his community, but also resorts to the disparaging word "pussy", when describing someone who isn't willing to resort to violence . Often used among men, the word 'pussy' denotes weakness, femininity, and an ability to shaft with impunity. Used in this derogatory manner, the slang term for a woman's genitalia, 'pussy' simply means 'not masculine'. To refer to someone as a 'pussy' is often viewed as emasculating, a further indicator that the individual is somehow not behaving accordingly in particular cultural environments. Moreover, while being disrespectful of women, the word 'pussy', when used in an emasculating way, can often be seen as a mark of disrespect. For some men, this is worthy of a counter-attack:

> 'You can respect someone because of the position they're in, but they can retain that respect, you can retain that respect for them through violence yeah. You can't fuck with this guy, he ain't a pussy, you can't rob this guy, because if you fuck with him he's gonna kill you.'

It started to become starkly obvious that Frank viewed violence as a way of instilling fear in others, seeing violence as a defence mechanism against victimisation, and also as a method of gaining respect. Frank was able to gain his idea of respect, often talking of "wanting to be strong", "wanting to physically hold [my] own", and through the sport of boxing he was able to achieve this:

DJ:	For you, is boxing a way of getting some respect?
Frank:	Definitely, kids that would go and train I'd get respect from them - my peer group I would - coz of my physique, I was well oiled man, so that peer group get respect from them, for being competitive in that peer group yeah.

The nature of most sports is inherently competitive. According to Messner (1990), successful competition in the rule-bound structure of sport is a major platform for male identity and their relationship to wider society. Thus, we can see from Frank's recollection of being a young man that competing, and having a good physique, was an important factor in his peer group.

I would argue that it was also a way to maintain status among "kids that would go train", as in any hyper-masculine context, hierarchies based on muscularity and strength will be evident. Moreover, Frank disclosed that his good physique "boosted his self-esteem" and gave him a "bit of kudos" in the community; whereas I would argue that Frank's idea of kudos was intermingled and confused with what he perceived as a sense of fear. If Frank could instil fear in others, then he was unlikely to come under attack, and this was his modus operandi.

In Frank's mind, his muscular physique, and the ability to use it in force-occupying ways, allowed him to convey an impression that he would not tolerate victimisation.

This is not uncommon in communities such as the one that Frank grew up in, communities that prioritise reciprocal respect and arguably adhere to what Anderson (1999) refers to as the 'Code of the Street'. This code is an unspoken allegiance between community members that unequivocally gives pre-eminence to the defence of one's reputation and the maintenance of respect. More interestingly, notions of respect defined by Kant (1964) and Sennett (2003) describe respect as being worthy of consideration; and conversely, notions of disrespect as being unworthy of consideration. Seen in this light, notions of respect – and the facets that it conjures for men in communities such as Frank's – are very important, informing ideas of self-esteem.

Frank's peer group were a source of conflict for him, as the 'gang' factions becoming apparent in the area at the time worried him. Having now left school, "going down that road" put Frank in a vulnerable position to conform to the group expectations. Without disclosing specific details, Frank lifted his shirt to show a scar that he referred to as a "battle wound". This was about 10cm long and evidently a stab wound. When I asked for the story of the scar, he became vague and talked about how he sought refuge in the boxing gym to escape the "drama outside" and the "options that go with that".

According to Frank, the 'options' open to his peer group during that period were: "Prison, death, or a shit job". He disclosed that a lot of his peers had fallen victim to either imprisonment or gang violence.[1] Matza (1964), among others (see Cohen 1955; Cloward and Ohlin 1960), refers to this worldview as a sense of 'fate' or 'blocked opportunities theory', thereby discussing how men growing up in disadvantaged areas usually perceive themselves as having limited options. In short, these theories argue that individuals in specific subcultures fatalistically experience themselves as object and effect rather than as subject and cause. In Frank's case, a sense of fatalism was apparent when he disclosed what options he felt were available to him and his peers. It was only with the security of the boxing gym that Frank felt that he had opportunities; opportunities to be the "next world champion", and because of this he dedicated all his time to pursuing this "dream".

In order to pursue this goal, Frank trained on a daily basis, distancing himself from a peer group who were otherwise involved in street violence and antisocial behaviour. The newly discovered peer group in the boxing gym developed a sense of camaraderie among those attending, and Frank felt that he had found a "new crew".

Wacquant (2004:68) writes that '[b]oxers relish the fact that they share membership in the same small guild, renowned for its physical toughness and bravery', as they revel in the enjoyment of knowing that they are different from others. Perceived as fighters, boxers glory in this title, as it not only comes with a sense of satisfaction and pride for those who participate, but also adds to the element of danger and masculine prestige contained in the image.

Additionally, for Frank, the competitive element of the gym also served as an incentive, as he believed that it "drives you to be better than what you are". He argued that it was imperative for young men to be competitive, as it "helps you develop as a man". When further trying to unpick Frank's reasoning behind the appeal of the gym, he stated that:

> 'It's what's promoted to young men isn't it - for the reasons I've stated - a man should be strong and should be able to defend his family.'

Again, Frank refers to the word "defence" as a reason to engage in boxing, arguably basing his argument on a cultural expectation of masculine performativity, particularly in a habitus that takes defence very seriously. By making reference to this cultural expectation – what is promoted to young men – he demonstrates Connell's (1995) point that to maintain dominance and respect, men must not become subject to the will of others. Frank further believed that men should be manly and women should be feminine, and therefore justified violent behaviour as a natural recourse for men:

> 'There are certain career paths that are directed towards men, boxing is a career path directed towards men more so than women, because it's naturally a manly sport, and it's not a women's role to go do that, just as it's not a women's role to go die on the battlefield.'

Aside from the references to 'natural manliness', I found the idea of boxing and its comparison to "the battlefield" an interesting analogy, as the military – like the boxing gym – is a further site for the performance of a certain type of aggressive hyper-masculinity. In other words, the ethos of both these arenas is one that promotes endurance, strength and physicality, and therefore chimes consecutively in Frank's mind as a comparative career choice that reinforces masculinity and marginalises women. Moreover, the other common denominator linking the boxing/military connotation is the sanctioned use of violence, and I posed this dichotomy to Frank:

DJ:	What war and boxing have in common is violence is it not?
Frank:	Yeah, you have to see boxing as a life and death situation, I mean, what's the next stage from knocking someone out? It's taking their life isn't it?

This answer was aggressive, and the fact that Frank referred to boxing as a "life and death situation" led me to believe that Frank's investment in the sport was of great importance to him. Again, I couldn't help feeling that for Frank, boxing was a defence mechanism for staying safe, hence the "life and death" analogy. Frank further disclosed that boxing "forms his character"; without it, he feels "lost", discussing how absences from the gym and taking time out from training lead to a sense of vulnerability for him. When not training, Frank feels "undisciplined" and inevitably finds himself "down the wrong road of smoking and drinking":

> 'I feel it in myself - I need to train, otherwise fuck knows what would happen.'

Seemingly, from Frank's narrative he obtains a certain sense of morality and physical purity from his training, but when I pressed Frank further, trying to explore his deep-seated need to train, he discussed how it made him feel "secure" in himself. I asked him if there was ever a time when he did not feel secure, and he said when he is not fit and when he was a teenager. I tried to get to the bottom of what being "secure" meant to Frank, and identify if there was anyone, or any situation, that made him feel particularly vulnerable.

Frank reported fearing attack from "everybody" as he disclosed how he started as a bouncer and doorman "working the doors at 18" and had to "put up with loads of shit from everyone" in this position. This sense of paranoia was evident in Frank's overall demeanour. When we walked back to the gym after our interview, we nearly found ourselves in an altercation with a group of drunken males, who Frank presumed were "eyeballing" him. Fortunately, the situation did not escalate, and Frank refrained from "fuckin' them up". This was slightly worrying, as Frank had already disclosed he "worked the doors", and this seems like an environment where drunken males are commonplace. I felt that Frank's occupational choice was interesting, and a source of insight into further exploring Frank's understanding of violence.

Boxing and reconstruction of the self

It was evident from Frank's narrative that his identity as a boxer (and subsequently a doorman) played a huge part in who he is as a human being. Comments heard throughout the gym – Frank as 'boxer', Frank as 'doorman' – gave him his status, his power and his control. Frank had built his self-confidence both in and outside the gym, and carved both of these identities on the successful employment of violence, both of which reinforced each other. Hobbs et al (2003:222) identified that: 'Most bouncers emerge from social environments that embrace the potential benefits and rewards of violent conduct'. Frank was no different. He came from a social environment where violence was seen as a solution to a problem. In his disclosures he justified his violent behaviour towards anyone he felt "disrespected" him:

> 'I'm not one to start trouble, but I'll finish it if I have to, you get me?'

Frank's original desire to box was never made explicit, yet it somehow seemed a necessity for him now, as he expressed his "need to train". I sensed that this 'need' was not just one of physical purity, but also one of power and control. Indeed, Frank gains a sense of identity through being both a boxer and a bouncer, and his investment in both these identities is of great importance to him. The appeal of the gym lies in Frank's reconstruction and maintenance of an identity that allows him to accomplish his masculinity in line with cultural mores, while creating distance between a younger self who "wasn't the toughest of kids". I never unearthed the story of his battle wound, but I expect the scar to be shown on a regular basis, as this formed part of Frank's story and his transition from victim to boxer.

As Theberge (1991:124) writes: 'Successful images require successful bodies, which have been trained, disciplined and orchestrated to enhance our personal value'. For men like Frank, success came from embodiment – his sense of personal value – arguably explaining his "*need* to train" and his sense of shame or guilt when not doing so. His body became the source of his identity; it created a distance between the victimhood of his teenage years, and later became a source of income and power in his occupation as a bouncer. Not only did the scar form part of Frank's trajectory, but it also evidenced his "toughness", his "hardness",[2] and further demonstrated his willingness to be able to withstand pain. Connell (1995:53) posits that: 'Bodily experience is often central in memories of our own lives, and thus in our understanding of who and what we are'.

These signifiers become vastly important for men like Frank, as they not only serve as defence mechanisms in environments that value shows of strength, but also contribute towards accruing respect and status for those in possession of both physical and social capital. Additionally, Frank was able to reconstruct himself sufficiently enough to obtain a career as a bouncer in the night-time economy; contributing further to the status and power he now had in the gym environment. For Frank, bouncing was a "laugh" and a "way to pay the bills", and he often discussed how he liked the environment of both gym and door as places where the "boys hang out!"

Winlow et al (2001) posit that 'bouncing' becomes important for certain men for a whole host of reasons, and is generally perceived as a way to earn money, while further investing in long-established violent reputations. Furthermore, the 'cumulative knowledge of where and how violence is situated in relation to both culture and the self, provides the primary skills, and indeed the essential and pre-requisite cultural triggers for the choice of bouncing as an occupation' (Winlow et al 2001: 224). Indeed, Hobbs et al (2003) posit that the logistics involved in the working environment of the night-time economy leads to a heightened sense of violence, and this is often coupled with men's gendered and class-specific cultural socialisation. For men like Frank, it is arguable that the profession of door-work is not just about the competency required for the profession, but a knowledge of the inner workings and cultural mores of contemporary urban violence.

With this in mind, and the constant threat of potential violent encounters forming part of one's occupation, it is no surprise that Frank feels a sense of paranoia. For Frank and his colleagues, professions such as bouncing, when amalgamated with violence, paranoia and gender/class focal concerns, view violence – both actual and perceived – at the very heart of door-work. Violence provides a framework for notions of respect (Neff et al 1991; Butler and Maruna 2009), and this is vastly important to men like Frank – men who have been subjected to previous violent attacks, and who also inhabit daily environments where violence is an acceptable solution to a problem.

This is not an uncommon thought. Work by Wolfgang (1959), Luckenbill (1977), Katz (1988) and Toch (1992), among others, suggests that violence is a compensatory measure when certain individuals feel their identity is under threat – in particular, individuals who have been sensitised to shame (Gilligan 1996). Gilligan theorises that violent self-images – images that are underpinned by self-narratives – are constructed by feelings of shame and insecurity. He proposes that violent men tend to summon and engage in violent physical altercations as a way to defend against the psychological anxiety of being shamed and humiliated. This, in turn, restores feelings of power and control to the self, and rectifies the self-imagery that one will not tolerate disrespect and the shame that coexists. For Frank, the shame of repeat victimisation was so abhorrent, that he would do everything in his power to avoid any future recourse.

Therefore, violence forms part of their cultural make-up, a strategy and a resource in maintaining respect and avoiding shame. Boxing contributes to this maintenance and avoidance. It forms part of the strategy that not only allows Frank to employ its physical benefits in the maintenance of his 'respectful' reputation, but also proves useful in his chosen occupation as a bouncer.

Summary

In this case study, I have looked at the appeal of boxing, using Frank as an example of how men accomplish their masculinity through embodiment and sport. Furthermore, I have examined the investments that men like Frank make into reconstructions of self through the medium of boxing and physical capital, while demonstrating that the gym can be a source of comfort for those who have experienced personal violence in their daily lives. However, the logic of respect that is ingrained in the habitus of both gym and street overrides the incapacitating elements of the boxing gym, as Frank not only confessed to being attuned to incidences of violent retaliation, but also physically demonstrated his capacity for it, when we were returning to the gym after our interview.

I conclude that the appeal of boxing for men such as Frank lies in its ability to hone and craft identities that are concomitant with accruing respect and commanding fear in others. These elements of respect and fear – and how to maintain them – are ingrained in men like Frank, and employed as a defensive structure in the avoidance of further shame and humiliation. Identities that are classified as 'respectful' are crafted in the gym environment for the majority of men who attend, and can be transposable across both gym and street. This becomes counteractive to the desistance-promoting elements of the boxing gym, as the identities honed take precedence over the pro-social mechanisms that the gym can provide.

These themes will be further discussed in the next chapter, as we turn our attention to Eric. He also demonstrates how the appeal of boxing is rooted in a sense of reconstruction, both physically and mentally, and how these signifiers are somewhat impervious to desistance from violence and actually more finely attuned to a persistently violent habitus.

Notes

1 Almost identical to the words of Pinklon Thomas, the 1985 WBC heavyweight champion: "Without boxing, I'd be selling heroin, dead, or in jail" (cited in Hauser, T. (1986) *The Black Lights: Inside the World of Professional Boxing*, New York: McGraw-Hill).

2 Hardness not being dissimilar to 'machine-like' or 'cold, hard steel' – references commonly found in combat films and men's advertising.

4

The Case of Eric: Self-Violence, Boxing and the Damaged, Emasculated Body

Introduction

In this case study, I demonstrate how Eric embodies his masculinity through the medium of boxing, and how he strives to accomplish masculine ideals that prioritise domination, violence, endurance and winning. I will argue that the accomplishment of these ideals can – and does – lead to injury and anxiety for Eric, as I consider how injuries and violence are thought of as commonplace in the gym environment and how these are negated through fear of emasculation.

I will argue these points by illustrating Eric's career in the sport of boxing and how this impacted on his life-course and relationships both in and outside of the gym. I begin with Eric as a small child, discussing his first experience of injury and violence and, subsequently, his first experiences with boxing. I follow this with his narrative of winning the Light Middleweight British title, and finish with his present story as a boxing coach ten years after relinquishing his belt. Throughout the case study, I present Eric's subsequent understanding of violence and why boxing was initially appealing for him, particularly as he has been participating in the sport for over 30 years.

Eric's story

Eric's was the first face I saw when I entered the gym to begin my research, and I came to realise over the six months that I spent in the boxing gym, that Eric *was* the gym. He spent every day there, training the professionals, encouraging the amateurs and scouting for further talent. At 51 years old, Eric looked good, with his sculpted torso and his enviable ability to do hundreds of sit-ups. Boxing gyms have implicit hierarchies, and the trainer's past victories and titles place them at the top. Their photographs adorn the walls, and belts and trophies are usually on display for all to see. Much of the discussion centres on the trainer's heyday, and this serves to encourage the dreams and aspirations of the younger men in the gym. This is not dissimilar to Wacquant's (2004:35) observations: 'In both layout and adornment, the gym constitutes something of a temple of the pugilistic cult by the presence on its walls of the major fighters, past and present, to whom the budding boxers from ghetto gyms devote a selective but tenacious adoration'.

Exalted to heroic status, the coach becomes the mentor, the sage and the executioner to these young men, who so desperately want to make it to the top of the boxing pyramid. It is with this status that the coach commands the gym, whether in the choice of music to be played as the pugilists rhythmically hit the bags, or the berating of members if they owe any money for unpaid training. The trainer cracks the jokes, commands the attention, and is fundamentally the eyes and ears of the boxing gym. Indeed, everything related to the gym – from its lack of finances, to the men's salacious gossip – is passed through the coach, sometimes in pursuit of his wisdom, at other times simply just to spread rumours.

Although boxing gyms are competitive environments, and Messner (1992) would argue that men's friendships are impoverished by competition and aggression, I would align with de Garis (2010) and argue that there is a specific cohesion within the gym. The men who attend are generally quite friendly with one another, and the trainer is most certainly the lynchpin. However, Messner (1992) argues that the intimacy created within masculine sports is a '*covert intimacy*', an intimacy that is characterised by *doing* together, rather than mutual talk about their inner lives. Indeed, the intimacy is created by talk of external facts: football, community relations, and diets. Therefore, inner lives are rarely discussed. When they are discussed, it is usually a cursory nod to a small issue, or a perfunctory remark about a partner or recent friend's general misgivings. This is not to say that intimacy is not allowed in the boxing gym. In some respects, it is a very intimate environment. However, the intimacy is controlled and managed, and the men carefully choose what they say and to whom, especially if they feel they may experience humiliation or judgement as a result of sharing a tale of vulnerability. Having said that, the relationship between coach and student is slightly different, and the familiarity shared between them is akin to that between father and child.

Messner's (1992:232) argument is therefore convincing, when he suggests that 'male friendships fit into an overall system of power', particularly as the trainer is the one who either makes or breaks friendships and careers. Accordingly, men flock to the trainer with almost cultish abandon, further supporting the work of Wacquant (1995b:81): 'Trainers often become surrogate fathers to their understudies, devoting inordinate amounts of time and energy to resolving love affairs, financial difficulties, and other private quandaries'. Most certainly, the trainer is the pivotal member in the gym, as he not only teaches the young boxers how to punch, but he also mentors them, 'fathers' them, and repairs their physical capital with icepacks, plasters and soothing encouragement.

The beginning of a boxer: Eric's trajectory

When I asked Eric to tell me the story of how he became a trainer, he took me back to his birth. Born in 1961 to Jamaican parents, the first thing Eric disclosed was that his parents thought he was not going to survive. Born with "under-developed lungs" and acute asthma, Eric was given the last rites less than 24 hours after his birth. Surviving the night, and pulling through, Eric grew into a young boy believing that he was "a very sickly child", and therefore not capable of doing much. Under medical care throughout his childhood, Eric was instructed to participate in sport as a way of benefiting him,[1] and it was through the doctor's advice that Eric began his long career in sport. School sports became a starting point for Eric, and it was through the 1,500 metres that Eric demonstrated his "determination to win".

"Never in class, and always kicked out for messing around," Eric said he left school with only a few qualifications, mainly in metalwork and other technical craft skills. Having left school, and devoid of the structure and daily routine it provided, Eric began to create his own excitement. Among his group of friends, Eric was the quieter one, so when his friend showed up in a stolen car, he "didn't know what to do, I suppose". Succumbing to the influence of friends, and worried about their opinions of him if he did not, Eric went along for the ride. It was only after the police caught him and he got a "good leathering from my dad" that Eric realised he needed a new distraction. With encouragement from his mother, a few qualifications, and a regret for not trying harder at school, Eric left the surrounding area and applied for an apprenticeship in the north of England. Then in 1977, he first walked through the doors of a boxing gym.

Still presenting with "severe breathing difficulties", Eric struggled to keep up with the other pugilists in the gym, and the stronger boxers would leave him wheezing by the side of the road as he did his best to fit into a new city and a new sport. With his aforementioned "determination to win", Eric was not swayed. He carried on running and showing up to the gym every week. However, being away from his childhood sweetheart, who Eric had married upon leaving school, proved too difficult, so he returned back to his original neighbourhood to start a family and to settle down. With an apprenticeship in welding under his belt, and a taste for boxing, Eric signed up to the gym that in the future he would come to jointly own with Marcus, the other trainer in the gym.

Eric continued to box on an amateur level throughout the late 1970s and started a family with his long-term partner. Engineering during the day and attending the gym in his spare time, Eric developed a "wicked punch" and won his first 11 fights as an amateur by knockout. It is with this punch and reputation that Eric was offered the opportunity to turn professional. Not everyone was as pleased as Eric regarding his choice to turn professional, as it meant a full-time career in the sport, with little chance of ever "making it big". Eric's mother, who had always been Eric's "rock" refused to attend any of his fights, as "she thought it was crazy and barbaric and completely unnecessary". She never understood the concept of "men just pounding each other in the head". However, Eric was determined to disregard his mother's opinion of boxing, and decided: "To box to the best of my ability, train hard and not fool around". Here began Eric's 30-year career in boxing.

Physical capital and the boxer's means of production

To be successful at professional level, a boxer must thoroughly commit and place themselves under the aegis of the gym in a monastic fashion. Known to sleep in the gym, Eric, among others, would lock themselves in overnight to be able to train when the other men would be at home with their families. This dedication to the sport is, according to Eric, what "separates the winners from the losers".

Eric's dedication was self-destructive. Having started his professional career and succeeding in winning his first few fights, Eric began to increase his training regime to the point where it would affect his asthma. Finding himself unable to sustain the demands of the ring, Eric would secretly use his inhaler between rounds and "to this day, nobody knew I was suffering, nobody ever said anything". Indeed, this idea of suffering became a common theme in Eric's narrative, as he navigated his way through a tumultuous boxing career that has now left him permanently scarred.

Boxing is a body-centred sacrificial universe. Joyce Carol Oates (1987:5) could not have been more perceptive when she said: 'Like a dancer, a boxer "is" his body, and totally identified with it'. Boxers' bodies are obsessive organisms, templates and instruments of their lives – their whole existence pivots around the sculpting, moulding and manipulation of the body. Pierre Bourdieu (1986:241) referred to this concept as 'accumulated labour' – the appropriation of social energy in the form of reified or living labour. From Bourdieu I borrow the term 'physical capital'.

Much like fixed capital, physical capital has inherent structural limitations, including a life expectancy. As Emmanuel Steward from the world-famous Kronk Gym in Detroit put it: 'The body is like an automobile, it's got so many miles in it and that's it' (in Halpern 1988:278). Boxers like Eric are entrepreneurs in physical capital; they transform the value of their bodily investment into social capital in the form of recognition, titles and financial rewards. The body becomes the boxer's means of production, the somatic entity that transforms itself into monetary value through constant appropriation. For boxers like Eric, however, this sense of dependency on their body and its inherent temporality can have catastrophic effects, particularly when no longer meeting the demands of a sport that places emphasis on physical capital. Wacquant (1989) identified that boxers carefully manage the investment of their physical assets over time. Yet for Eric, being eager to please and worried about "keeping-up" regarding his "breathing difficulties", this proved not to be the case.

It is not just for the obvious fiscal rewards that boxers invest so heavily in the sport. By using Eric's case, among others, I will argue that this investment in physical capital and social capital is not only imbued with a sense of recognition at a structural level, but it also operates at a deeper, psychic level for some men who participate. In short, boxing becomes a very personal activity for some men – so much so, that when they lose or become too injured to box, feelings of unworthiness or loss creep into their psychic make-up.

To unpick the reasons why Eric physically scarred himself for the sport, and to unearth the psychic investment that he had resting in boxing, we must return to his childhood and the concept of being a "sickly child", as this was something that Eric would return to time and time again in his narrative. There was a sense of ambivalence with

Eric, as in one moment he identified greatly with sickness, arguably almost enjoyed it, yet at other times he regularly worried about it. The fact of being given the last rites at birth was something that stuck with Eric, and it was with this "fighting spirit" that he found himself in a situation that went against his better judgement regarding his physical wellbeing:

> 'I remember going into my first pro-fight, and I wasn't very happy as I had injured my hand in sparring a few days before I was due to have my pro-debut. I went to the doctors and they told me something had gone and maybe it wasn't such a good idea that I fight, and should rest it until it healed. I kept on training, and the hand was still hurting - every time I threw a punch. The pain! I didn't really want to fight this guy because of my hand, but because of all the "fuss" that everybody had made, arranging the fight - saying I would beat him, I went against my better judgement and fought.'

This judgement call may have left Eric with a trophy, but it also caused him a scaphoid fracture so serious that a surgeon told Eric that he would never box again. When I asked Eric how he felt about the latter, he said he "had no regrets", and to my surprise, he told me how he had continued boxing as soon as the plaster cast was off his right hand. Using the left hand as a substitute, Eric was back in the gym within two months, continuing to box against the advice of his own surgeon and his own better judgement.

Thus, Eric's investment in boxing, as well as being a way to acquire physical capital, also grew to self-destructive levels, as he often overrode his own sense of personal safety. To attempt to understand why this was the case, we must delve deeper into his story.

"Think you're a big man, do you?" Eric's relationship with his father and the appeal of the gym

Eric was always close to his mother. He was named after her deceased brother, who had died in childbirth, and this was something that Eric felt he had to live up to. Eric was one of six children, and it was "from birth that my dad took an instant dislike to me, and that never subsided until I became a 'big man' and I was British champion". Eric felt his father's dislike for him throughout his life, and it was only through succeeding at boxing that his dad started behaving differently towards him. According to Eric, "It was too late, as he had already made me feel that way towards him, that no matter what he did or said I was never going to change the way I felt". What led Eric to this conclusion lies at the heart of his investment in boxing, and it was not until one Saturday morning, while watching football on the television, that he realised just how much his father disliked him:

> 'I remember this particular day, I must have been around 13 or 14 and was watching Grandstand on TV. I was intently watching as I loved sport at the time, and my dad was saying something to me whilst drinking this can of lager. You've probably done it yourself where you are watching something and not really paying attention to what they're saying and all I remember is that can of beer hitting me on the side of the head and I was on the floor shaking and thinking, "What's all this about?"'

It transpired that Eric's father tried to strangle him that day, while screaming at his son: "You think you're a big man, do you? Then fight with me." It was only through the intervention of Eric's mother that he said he had escaped.

Eric: He jumped on me and was choking me, I thought that was it, I thought it was over. My mum came downstairs and dragged him off in the nick of time.
DJ: Otherwise he would have killed you?
Eric: Oh absolutely. He has tried to kill me a few times in anger.

This was revealed to me in the fourth interview I did with Eric, and it explained a lot about his process and investment in boxing. Previously, I had thought that Eric boxed to a destructive level to prove something to himself and others about being classed as a "sickly child", but it further transpired in this particular interview that Eric also boxed to defend himself against his father's murderous rages, as he expressed how he was "terrified of his father", until he "knew how to land a good one and see a man sleep".

Indeed, Eric made sense of his father's violence through the idea of him being a "sickly child". In Eric's mind, it justified his father's behaviour, by saying that not only was it cultural – being first-generation Jamaican it was somehow permissible – but that his own sickness as a child diverted his mother's attention from his father, and this resulted in his father harbouring a "jealous hatred" for him. I expressed that this must have been extremely difficult for Eric and he agreed. Yet, the inherent lack of care for his own body found him justifying his father's behaviour with a strange ambivalence:

> 'It was hard, but if you don't know any difference you just take it, but growing up was miserable, he was very strict and ruled the house with the belt.'

Eric believed he was the only one to suffer the wrath of his father. He was convinced that his childhood illness was the source of disdain, and yet, throughout the long conversations I had with Eric, it transpired that his father also beat and hospitalised his younger brother, threatened Eric's mother, and sexually abused his sisters. It was a harrowing tale of familial abuse. It was only once Eric had left school and begun his apprenticeship away from the family home that he discovered boxing, and when he returned back to the neighbourhood, he confronted his father, safe in the knowledge that he could defend himself:

> 'I remember one time when I came home to visit my mum, and I was lying on my bed with my brothers. We could hear the banging of my dad coming up the stairs, and we glanced around real quick to make sure everything was tidy as he was a bit military. He comes into the bedroom and he has an angry face, it was obvious he was looking for someone to pick on. He comes over to me and starts hitting me in the chest, I'm trying to keep my cool and I can see my brothers aren't going to do anything. There is only so much I can take of this as he is hurting me, and I am not taking this anymore, I jump up and scream, "Right this is the last time you put your fucking hands on me, come on!"'

From this excerpt, we can glean that Eric had found the strength to retaliate, his experience of boxing had contributed towards a new line of defence. It had provided him with the confidence to stand up to his father, to become a "big man". Accordingly, Eric associated this idea of being a "big man" as being willing to fight, and also as a way to gain some form of acceptance from his violent father. Yet, underneath all that bravado, Eric felt "afraid", his father "scared him shitless". However, Eric was determined to never let "him put his hands on me again", and standing up to him that day "changed my life surrounding him". Eric disclosed that this was the last time his father attacked him, whether that was attributable to the retaliation, or simply because Eric moved out of the family home remains to be seen. Yet somehow, the display of violence that Eric showed to his father became a turning point in Eric's life. Eric further disclosed that the only time his father showed any acknowledgement that Eric was his son, was when his photograph was in the local newspaper, having won the British title the night before in front of a packed audience. Only then did Eric's father proclaim any love or care for his son:

> 'Well when I became champion he was proud. He would say: "This is my big boxing son, my son be a boxer man."'

Now that Eric had secured the British title and therefore demonstrated his "toughness", his father became intent on showing the community just how tough his son was. For Eric, this recognition was "too little, too late":

> 'My father would try and parade me up and down the street. I would think: "I'm not under any illusion here, I'm not letting it go, I know why all of a sudden you like me, it's because I make you look good!"'

At this point, and in receipt of the British title, Eric had proved all that was necessary to his peers in terms of his boxing prowess. Yet this deep-seated hatred for his father never subsided, as Eric had no qualms in stating that he "hates him to this day" and is "glad he's dead".

Boxing therefore came to be the only facet of Eric that his father accepted, whereby his demonstration of "toughness" through acts of violence won his father's respect. However, boxing, while providing a medium to obtain masculine honour and respect, did not come without its own pitfalls, as Eric struggled to reach the pinnacle of his career and father's acknowledgement. The bodily sacrifice and psychological problems this caused Eric throughout his journey produced their own set of problems, as he found himself struggling not only for acceptance in the family home, but also in the local boxing fraternity.

The boxing bulimic: Eric's bodily destruction for a sense of acceptance

In the gym, there was a collection of fighters who all began their professional careers at the same time, and Eric said he felt "part of something big". He felt like he "fitted in". Post-injury and with extensive surgery to his right hand, Eric began to box professionally again, developing his left hand to the point that "it became my signature punch, and left many a man sleeping on the canvas". However, underneath this bravado was an insecurity that would haunt Eric, as he found himself struggling to meet the expectations of his trainer and to keep up with the physical demands of a professional career. For Eric, this sense of "fitting in" and acceptance became a huge investment for him.

Turner (1984:112) writes: 'Successful images require successful bodies, which have been trained, disciplined, and orchestrated to enhance our personal value'. Further, Bartky (1988:77) believes that disciplinary practices are representational means for establishing a 'structure of the self', and that a sense of self as distinct and skilled is critical to the establishment of a secure and stable identity. For men like Eric, it is easy to see and hear in his words how the manipulation and appropriation of his corporeality became his personal value, and how his sense of embodiment had a destructive outlook that took self-harm, pain and endurance as a focal point.

> 'I remember fighting that kid on the wall up there, on that photograph above you, that was a big night, I was tipped to win. And would you believe it? I messed my weight up.[2] My weight wasn't good. I was messing around eating and in the end, I had to make myself sick! A lot of people don't know that, you're the first person I've told that I did that.'

Almost with a sense of shame, Eric seemed to be embarrassed that he had resorted to self-induced vomiting to lose weight. When I asked him why he went to such lengths, he returned to the idea of "not wanting to mess up, not wanting to let people down". This seemed like a common theme in some of Eric's decisions based on physical health, and it seemed that he would rather self-harm and abuse his body, than cope with a sense of failure or loss of expectation placed upon him by his peers and trainer. Wiley (1989:227) calls boxing: '[a]ssault and battery with deadly weapons called the fists of man'; and this assault can leave irreversible damage on one's own body and that of competitors. Eric seemed to disregard this idea, putting his body through damaging practices such as bulimia and self-harm. Indeed, Eric was willing to sacrifice his physical health for the sake of acceptance and occupational success. This wasn't just about occupational success; there was a deeper level of investment, based around Eric's sense of identity and personal value, that led him to this bodily abuse. I would argue that this was a destructive method, whereby Eric was able to accomplish his masculinity and to gain acceptance from others for doing so.

Boxing is distinct, in that it is the only sport that purposefully aims to inflict physical damage upon one's opponent. It might not be the sport with the highest rate of injury[3] (American Medical Association 1983), but it is the only sport in which the body is specifically employed to intentionally inflict pain on another. Messner (1990:211) writes: 'The body as a weapon ultimately results in violence against one's own body'. I would argue that an inherent lack of care for one's own body has to be present, to allow for the violence against it to prevail.

Wacquant (1995a) claims that boxers come to conceive of physical corrosion as part of the pugilistic order of things, an acceptable price to pay, and one that they believe they can significantly minimise through hard training. This would certainly form part of the argument in the case of Eric, as being in the company of men with similar dispositions allowed for the flourishing of a culture that thrives on endurance and bodily pain. Furthermore, Goffman (1959:85–102) states that the 'government of the body is a collective enterprise requiring team-work'. For Eric, the appropriation of his body was not only his responsibility, but also the responsibility of his peers and trainers. It was with this expectation and need for acceptance that he found himself sacrificing his health for the good of the gym. Indeed, the surgery on his fractured scaphoid was still apparent. Eric said: "It never got better, I just learnt to cope with it" as he navigated his way through his professional career. Regardless, not everyone was sympathetic towards Eric's injury, least of all his trainer. Eric said:

> 'Sometimes my trainer could be quite harsh towards somebody with an injury, he was of the notion that "you'll be alright get on with it" that type of thing. He just didn't have time for it. He would say: "Don't be soft", push me in that direction, he just wasn't very sympathetic to people who had injuries.'

This was an interesting point in Eric's narratives, and I felt this was the crux and justification for Eric's bodily abuse. It became apparent in Eric's story that the coach "was a winner who bred winning into you and he bred hard work and determination"; and that any weakness – be it injury or otherwise – would not be tolerated in his boxing gym. This became a bone of contention (literally) for Eric, and ultimately the reason why he left this particular gym, as he found himself unable to cope with further abuse from a man who was also collectively referred to as "dad".

Eric:	He used to call me horrible names.
DJ:	Such as?
Eric:	A wimp – all kinds of horrible things – saying that I didn't want to fight, that I didn't have any bottle. Because I had an injury he wasn't very sympathetic towards it, and you can ask any of the lads and they will admit that he could be a bit horrible.

It seemed from Eric's story that the escapism he found in boxing merely replicated the horror at home. Eric endured the abuse from his trainer, as he had to endure the abuse from his father, and I found it interesting that he potentially craved acceptance from abusive men. By investing in masculine discourses that demonstrate toughness and working through pain, Eric was able to obtain the acknowledgement he so desired, but this came at a price – in Eric's case, it was his physical safety. I therefore posed the question to Eric whether or not he thought that his trainer had his best interests at heart? Eric felt that he did not, even going so far as to say that:

> 'This is what people were saying, but I ignored it, I believed in him 100%, even though at the time he used to give you a hard time.'

Regardless of this, Eric endured the abusive relationship with his trainer and continued to be successful under the chosen gym. However, during the preparation for the highly anticipated British championship, Eric's mother became seriously ill. Hospitalised due to a stroke, Eric's mother started to deteriorate rapidly, and Eric found himself juggling palliative care with pugilistic training. Two weeks before the big fight, Eric's mother passed away, and he said he "didn't grieve in the way you normally would for a parent":

> 'I didn't grieve. I didn't have time. I had to take care of the funeral and train for the fight in two weeks so I had a lot going on. I was angry but I was keeping it in, I wasn't letting it out because I was training for the fight, and I knew if I trained hard for this fight I could win! So I put away all my grieving problems and just got stuck in and trained hard.'

It later transpired that Eric was to lose the "fight of his life" this time. He put this down to weight loss, attributable to stress and the toll of his mother's death on his mental state. Indeed, the pressure to win cost him his health, both physically and mentally:

> 'The emotions that I was fighting with were, "I've got to do this. I've got to do this." My mum has just passed away and this is the biggest fight of my life and I've got to win! My mum would have wanted me to win.'

Ironically, his mother never wanted Eric to be a boxer; yet now, after her death, Eric constructs the idea that his mother would have wanted him to win. I would argue that this construction was merely a justification for his deep-seated need to prove himself, and to be accepted, in spite of the berating from his coach for having an injury. Moreover, if Eric could win the British title, then his entry into the coveted Boxing Hall of Fame would be guaranteed, and with that would follow acceptance from his father, trainer and peers. As it turned out, Eric lost that night, and even though he went on to win the title in the end, he believes now that he should never have stepped into the ring that first night:

> 'I was no longer thinking boxing strategies, I was thinking just knock him out! I had this red mist raging over me, and my trainer is driving me on to go out there and knock him out! I kept thinking whatever he tells me to do I've got to do it. The fear of me losing the most important fight of my life when I've just lost the most important person in my life made me reckless.'

It was only after the loss of the fight that "the real problems started" for Eric. He disclosed feeling "angry, hurt and an overwhelming sadness", and that he found it hard to distinguish whether that was attributable to the loss of the fight or the loss of his mother:

> 'I was devastated as you could imagine. I didn't want to box again. I thought this is it. I've had enough. I got beat in the most important fight of my life. My mum has gone. And I remember being out on the rooftop and walking to the edge and looking over and thinking I've had enough.'

What prevented Eric from suicide that day was the thought that his mother would have classed the attempt as "the easy way out". I found this to be of significance in Eric's narrative, as it again demonstrated his external locus of evaluation, when determining his sense of self-worth. It seemed that for Eric, what people thought of him was more important than what he thought of himself. This external locus thus provided him with the justification to train instead of to grieve, to injure himself permanently to avoid "making a fuss", and to tolerate abuse from significant others in the form of fatherly figures.

This was to change, however, when Eric confronted his trainer, just as he did his father previously. After his suicidal feelings, and with the desire to "take another shot at the title", Eric found himself the brunt of his trainer's aggression for the last time:

Eric: Things started to change, and my trainer said something to me at the time that made me not want to be here anymore.

DJ: What did he say to you?

Eric: He said: 'You could have been a good fighter, you could have been a great fighter, if you had more balls'.

DJ: Really?

Eric: He said, I could have been a better fighter [if] I had had more balls, a bit more bottle about me, and I went home that night and I cried. I was devastated. It could have been anything else but the fact that he said I didn't have 'balls', after everything I had been through and telling me I had no 'heart', that's out of order, it was an insult to me as a man, you know what I mean?

The concept of 'heart' in a boxing gym is not necessarily one of a physical nature. To have 'heart' is to imbue a sense of physical toughness and courage, 'an uncompromising sense of masculine honour, and an expressive stress on personal performance and style' (Abrahams 1970). For Eric's trainer to say that he "had no heart" was received by Eric as a direct attack on his masculine honour and, in Eric's words, "it was an insult to me as a man". 'Balls' in this sense of the word refers to a man's testes, and the concept of having 'balls' is to represent a strong sense of masculine courage and virility. For Eric's trainer to say if he 'had had more balls' signifies that he thought Eric was cowardly and feminine. To be perceived as having 'no balls', therefore, signifies that you possess feminine qualities and lack sexual potency – qualities that are associated with subordinate masculinity.

Connell (1995:54) writes: 'The constitution of masculinity through bodily performance means that gender is vulnerable when the performance cannot be sustained – for instance as a result of physical disability'. Therefore, Eric felt that his masculine gender performance came into question as a result of his injury and loss of the British title. This was enough of an insult for Eric to leave the gym and never return, until his trainer died a few months later.

Not only was this an insult to Eric's corporeal gender performance, it symbolised his place in the hierarchy of masculine order. According to Connell (1995:54), the institutional organisation of sport embeds definitive social relations. Competition and hierarchy among men, and exclusion or domination of women, are social relations of gender that are both realised and symbolised in bodily performances – 'the performance is symbolic and kinetic, social and bodily, at one and the same time, and these aspects depend on each other' (Connell 1995:54). Accordingly, Eric felt disempowered by his trainer, not just on a somatic level, but also on a deeper cultural and psychic level.

The boxer's 'heart' and the controlling of a monster – Eric and violence outside the ring

Having left the gym as a result of the trainer's insults, Eric found himself "lost" and "unsure of what to do with myself". Resorting to labouring on a building site to "feed the family", Eric started to reconstruct his sense of masculinity through physical labour. A few months later, Eric got offered a chance to start boxing again under a different trainer. "Needing to fight [as] I had no fucking money and couldn't turn it down", Eric entered the ring for the first time in the six months since his old trainer had died. With a "different outlook" and "feeling better about my mum and stuff", Eric agreed to another fight for the British title. As he was "not fighting fit", Eric became worried that he would "let people down", and once again, dieting and training became Eric's obsession. With little time to re-orientate himself with the world of professional fighting, Eric found himself having to lose 4 pounds in 24 hours to make the weight for the second title fight. Anxious at being overweight, Eric disclosed that he resorted to his bulimic habits, and "knowing he had to do it", he sat in a sauna overnight to "dry out" and lose the extra pounds he needed to be able to step back into the ring:

> 'I was due to get £600 for that fight and I was skint, I knew I had to do it. So I sat in the sauna all night sucking ice

> and making the body sweat. I lost 3 pounds that night but I was ill, seriously ill.'

Again, this seemed like another example of abuse that Eric inflicted upon himself to demonstrate a sense of masculine determination. The destruction that Eric was willing to subject his body to manifested itself in Eric's psychic make-up, as he reinvested in the sport of boxing, and re-entered the pugilistic world within which he so desperately desired acceptance. Interestingly, Eric's phrasing in his description of making "the" body sweat as opposed to making "my" body sweat, chimes with White and Sweet's (1955) work around pain and disembodiment. They reported that patients almost universally describe pain as 'it' as opposed to 'I', and that the painful body is often experienced as something foreign to the self. Leder (1990:77) would go so far as to say: 'To experience the painful body as merely an "it", that which is separate from the essential self, yields some relief and re-establishes one's integrity in the face of an overwhelming threat'. In Eric's case, this would certainly make sense.

Eric eventually won the British title he so desperately wanted, and his entry into the boxing elite was complete. With this experience, and almost 20 years in this social world, Eric retired from the sport as a contender, and turned his hand to coaching. Working in the gym that he left some years ago after the disagreement with his trainer, Eric found himself in the position that his deceased trainer had abused when Eric was a young boxer. Determined not to make the same mistakes, Eric sought young boxers wanting to turn professional, with a sense of instilling his learning and success into the next generation of pugilists.

I was interested in what part of Eric's narrative was pertinent to him, and what elements of it he would be inculcating in the young boxers now under his tuition. Interestingly, it transpired that what was pertinent to Eric was the same issue that his previous trainer had berated him for:

Eric:	Trying to teach somebody a bit of heart, a bit of courage can sometimes be difficult. I remember a part of my career, I wouldn't say I was lacking heart, it was just a little bit lacking aggression, the aggressive bit was lacking.
DJ:	Is that essential for boxing?
Eric:	I'm talking about that killer instinct, the ability to hurt somebody beyond all reason.

From the preceding excerpt, it seemed that Eric associated 'heart' with 'heartless' – a way to secure and confirm courage, by demonstrating aggression. I felt that Eric learnt his aggression as a result of wanting to fit into the boxing fraternity, as he disclosed that he had sessions with a sport psychologist to help him develop this "killer instinct". Indeed, Eric felt that he had too much compassion within the ring, and this was an interesting point, particularly when he referred to himself as a "controlled monster".

This is reminiscent of the work of Jack Katz (1988:243), when he discusses the masculine metaphor of 'heart' as the 'readiness to take action', contrasting with that of the feminine image of 'losing self-control'. For Eric, I would argue that this "controlled monster" performance was a further way to secure his masculine identity, as a result of being told that he had "no balls". More importantly, I wanted to find out whether or not this "controlled monster" reared its ugly head when outside the ring:

DJ: Did you ever find this killer instinct came with you outside of the ring?

Eric: No. One time. One time I nearly knocked somebody out, but he was taunting me and being a cheeky bastard.

We can see that Eric immediately denied the transfer of aggression from the ring to the street, yet, the more we talked, the more I got the impression that it most certainly did. Eric justified this response as a "disrespectful" act. According to Eric, the man in question insinuated that Eric was not worthy of his British title, and inferred that his career would be soon over, as he "had too many sick days". This enraged Eric, as it was reminiscent of his trainer's berating comments, and indicative of Eric's lack of self-belief and subsequent disembodiment. Eric had invested so much of his identity into the winning of a British title, that any threat to this achievement was immediately seen as a threat to his identity.

Eric justified his aggression outside the ring in defence of his fragile newfound identity, just as he had neutralised his father's aggression in the past. Zimmerman (1998:90) argues that identities are 'transportable', and that these identities are enacted when relevant to a situation. For Eric, as with many of the men in this sample, it transpired that issues of identity and disrespect were classified as the most important precursor to violence. Eric's low self-esteem meant that issues of disrespect became heightened – and therefore defended against – at any cost.

Moreover, the abuse that Eric had suffered as a child chimes with recent work by Baglivio et al (2015) and Wolff et al (2017) into adverse childhood events, and the relationship that childhood trauma can have on future violence perpetration. Baglivio et al (2015:230) state that 'the proximal effects of childhood trauma include an increased risk for delinquency, fighting, dating violence, and carrying a weapon, as well as mental health issues such as substance use and conduct disorders, and suicidal ideation and attempts'.

All this considered, it would seem that Eric's experiences of domestic violence created a hyper-vigilance to feelings of disrespect, not uncommon in men who have experienced abuse and humiliation at the hands of others (Gilligan 1996). This hyper-vigilance, coupled with the physical abuse, fits with the adverse childhood events matrix developed by Felitti et al (1998). This matrix suggests that for children who experience a myriad of cumulative adverse events in childhood, the likelihood of delinquency and violence in later years is increased. So much so, that between 75 per cent and 93 per cent of youth entering the youth justice system have experienced some type of trauma, in comparison to 25 per cent to 34 per cent of the general population (Costello et al 2003; Evans-Chase 2014). While this may not necessarily be the case for Eric, having never been incarcerated, it does demonstrate the negative impact that childhood abuse and trauma can have on the psychic underpinnings of men involved in violent social worlds. (For further discussion, see Gadd 2000, 2002).

The logic of violence: transposable attitudes from ring to street

Identities became a focal point in boxers' narratives, as I listened to stories of violence both in and outside the ring. Spending significant amounts of time in the boxing gym, allowed me a glimpse not only into boxers' professional lives, but also into their personal lives. In between rounds, and over lunch, the men would discuss football or their own families, and with that, Eric frequently discussed his son. Relaying tales of how Eric Junior "couldn't control his temper", and "he doesn't know where he gets it from", Eric would discuss with me how he worried for his son and the influence of local gangs in the area. I tentatively asked Eric whether he thought he was in any way influential in Eric Junior's bad temper:

DJ:	Do you think it might have anything to do with you being a boxer?
Eric:	I don't know where he gets it from, he has some aggression issues, but I can only think that he is of the age now were I can't go get the belt and whack him no more.
DJ:	Really?
Eric:	Yeah, I give them a slap before they say anything, because I know that if I don't threaten them with violence and just be the nice guy with all talking, then they are not going to respect me and tell me the truth.

It transpired from Eric's narrative that he also "ruled the house with a belt", and while he argued over the course of our many interactions that he "wasn't a strict parent" like his father was, it did become apparent that he had inherited some of his father's traits. It seemed, from Eric's narrative, that he also viewed violence as a solution to a problem; particularly ones that may have involved a confrontation with those who Eric felt had been disrespectful towards him. It seemed that the past humiliations of his father's murderous rages were still bubbling under the surface, leading him to re-enact the same methods as his father, to ensure that his children respected him and always told him the truth. Hall (1997), Winlow (2001), Hobbs et al (2003) and Winlow and Hall (2009) argue that men who carry with them ingrained visceral dispositions towards violence, are products of socialisation in climates of aggression, domination and insecurity. Therefore, Eric came to value violence and its rehearsal at the centre of his own self-identity.

Moreover, the core logic of respect – being defensive in nature – can act as a justification to react impulsively in its defence and maintenance, and in some cases encourage men to respond aggressively to what they perceive as a threat. Interestingly, Winlow and Hall (2009), in their psychosocial assessment of male violence, argue that revisiting an event becomes a crucial process in grasping the essence of the now; and according to an individual's subjective memories of past humiliations often means that violent men address unfolding social interaction as a means of taking control of painful memories.

Accordingly, this allows for men to rewrite the past and to emancipate themselves from previous failures, therefore maintaining and ensuring respect and the identity that goes with it. In this case, Eric's violence against his own children and the retaliatory messages he transmitted in the gym to his younger professionals allowed him to rewrite the past and to take control of his painful memories. Furthermore, the masculine discourses that Eric became complicit in, now dominated his overall thinking, as he not only embraced the culture of the gym as a way to distance himself from the emasculating concept of once being a "sickly child" and "not the toughest of kids", but also as a way to craft a new identity as someone who "doesn't take any shit from no-one no more".

Summary

From the case study presented in this chapter, I argue that Eric suffered an abusive childhood that haunts him to this day. Seeking out boxing when freed from the abusive environment of the family home, Eric saw an opportunity to invest not only in his social capital (when training for an apprenticeship in welding), but also in his physical capital, to help ward off feelings of vulnerability and to defend against future attacks. Seeing himself as a "sickly child" led Eric throughout his life to believe that this was the reason for his father's abuse, and I would argue, a contributory factor in the further abuse of his body through sacrificial and unhealthy pugilistic practice –what psychoanalysts would refer to as repetition compulsion.[4] Moreover, the masculine discourses inherent in the boxing gym provided a medium through which Eric could accomplish his masculinity in line with masculine sporting ideals. The aegis of the gym therefore allowed Eric to prove to himself and others that he was capable of overcoming his fear, through enduring and investing in physical capital enhancing routines.

With this "determination to win", Eric crafted an identity of a champion – so much so, that when his newfound identity came under threat, he retaliated with violence, and/or plunged into suicidal thoughts of unworthiness and loss. This sense of unworthiness was something that Eric struggled with throughout his career, as he constantly strived for acceptance, whether in the eyes of his father or the eyes of his trainer. Indeed, Eric psychically and physically invested in the sport of boxing to such and extent, that he maimed himself in the ring to avoid "making a fuss" and upsetting his trainer.

This lack of care for his own body contributed to Eric going against his better judgement throughout his boxing career. A sense of craving for acceptance, and a constant need to prove himself, led Eric to risk his body in performance, ultimately scarring him both emotionally and physically for the rest of his life. Once his entry into the elite world of boxing was complete, and his father no longer viewed him as a punching bag, Eric's identity as a "sickly child" started to become a distant memory. Having said that, threats or perceived incidents of disrespect could somehow upset Eric's fragile identity as a boxing champion, and lead to potentially violent outbursts in the defence of his ego, further demonstrated by his story of how he wanted to "kill" a fellow boxer, when he taunted Eric about his "sick days".

Researchers who are focused on the occurrence of aggression posit that some individuals feel a psychological need to engage in violence, when they feel that their identity is being threatened (Wolfgang 1959; Luckenbill 1977; Katz 1988; Scheff and Retzinger 1991; Toch 1992). Gilligan's (1996) work on shame and violence suggests that violent recourse is a way to destroy vulnerability, a way to defend against feelings of shame.

Therefore, for men like Eric, they are thought to use aggression as a compensatory measure to boost a dwindling ego, and/or their social status (Young 2002). In this case, Eric, who was unsure of himself to begin with, and subjected to ridicule and humiliation throughout his early life, has arguably been left with the view that his earlier identity as a sickly child was worthy of abuse. It was only when he became "a big boxer man" in his father's and his trainer's eyes that he held any feelings of self-worth and positive self-affirmation, thus developing a tenacious relationship between boxing and his ideas of self-worth.

As a result of this relationship, any personal slight or perceived incidents of disrespect not only fractured Eric's sense of identity, but also triggered aggressive outbursts in the name of it. More importantly, Eric saw no problem with this, as he neutralised his violence outside the ring and 'denied victim status' (Sykes and Matza 1957) to his son and others who challenged him. This was because he felt that his "respect" and personal consideration were in jeopardy, and therefore excused his behaviour as simply "not taking any shit from no-one no more". Moreover, Eric's reasoning and justifications for violence are further complicit in masculine discourses that not only employ the body in the pursuit of winning, but also view violence as a viable solution to a problem when outside the ring, commonly seen in the work of Kreager (2007) and Messner (1990).

These particular sporting discourses therefore reinforce the logic of street-based violence, when they suggest that men should be able to defend their honour regardless of the cost to themselves (Goffman 1967; Katz 1988; Neff et al 1991; Anderson 1999), and should also be able to endure a beating at the hands of others if necessary (Winlow 2001). For men like Eric, their understanding of violence becomes intertwined with discourses that speak to violent retaliation, and those that recommend the employment of the body in the domination of another. These recommendations become heightened for some men, particularly those, like Eric, who are predisposed to shame (Scheff and Retzinger 1991; Gilligan 1996). Finally, this can be counterproductive when assessing the impact that boxing has on desistance from violence, as the rewards proffered in the maintenance of masculine identities of this nature override men's abilities to desist, particularly when faced with threats to their self-identity and self-worth.

In the next chapter, the themes discussed here are interrogated further through the case study of Leroy. Leroy's story discusses boxing's appeal as a mechanism to avoid shame. It tells the story of Leroy and his upbringing in a 'hard' working-class environment that valued toughness and respect. With a violent boxing father, Leroy talks of boxing as a way of life, and the ways in which intersections of class, working-class habitus, and violence mould his life. His story further reflects on how boxing can be employed as a form of 'physical capital', and how the prestige that comes with 'hardness' can be used to overcome feelings of shame, stigma and vulnerability.

Notes

1 Whether the benefit was to Eric medically, in terms of his asthma, or whether it was psychological in terms of him combating his overarching belief in being a "sickly child" is questionable.

2 Weight is a contentious issue in any boxing gym, as 'making weight' is imperative to fighting in your category – heavyweight, lightweight, and so on. Yet some practices, such as 'drying out' to lose weight, are seen as very unhealthy; starving your body of water for 24 hours is common, as are extensive periods in saunas to 'dry out' before weighing in for competition.

3 Boxers commonly like to point out that sports such as horse riding and Formula One result in more injuries among participants than boxing, and this is a substantiated claim. However, the aim of the latter sports is not intentionally to inflict bodily injury, as it is with the sport of boxing.

4 Repetition compulsion is maladaptive behaviour that individuals re-enact, by placing themselves in situations where events or feelings will most likely be repeated. Freud 1975 referred to this as *The Daemonic Drive to Repeat*.

5

The Case of Leroy: Shame, Violence and Reputation

Introduction

This chapter describes the case study of Leroy. It looks at the original and enduring appeal of boxing for him and also its relation to his early home life, including his relationship with his father. I discuss Leroy's upbringing in an environment surrounded by violence, and offer insights into how this may have contributed to Leroy's understanding of violence. I conclude by discussing whether or not the sport of boxing has any influence on the way he views and employs violence in his everyday life.

Leroy's story

Leroy was a professional boxer of British descent. He was relatively small and stocky in appearance, and his shaved head and tattoos added to his overall demeanour of a fighter. He was in possession of many trophies, and his photographs also adorned the walls of the gym. Yet Leroy did not boast of his success like other men in this book, nor did he chide the amateurs, which was common practice among the professionals. He was a sensitive interviewee and also slightly nervous: he constantly checked in with me with regard to his answers being "right" and seemed anxious about what I thought of his ability to communicate. This became apparent throughout the interview, as he disclosed that he was "street-smart but put a piece of paper in front of me and game over". In fact, Leroy seemed quite concerned about his ability to communicate with those he perceived as "cleverer" than him, and he often referred to himself as "thick" and incapable of doing anything other than boxing. He left school without any qualifications after long spells of truancy and "just signed on", until he "got picked to fight for England and made it".

Leroy grew up in a relatively deprived part of the city with his parents and sister. His dad was also a professional boxer and, according toLeroy, he could often be seen out drinking and being "Jack the Lad on the beer after the boxing". A dominant but absent figure in Leroy's life, his father often disappeared for days on end, even fathering another child with a local woman. Leroy's primary relationships were with his mother and sister, who he claims are his "best mates", going so far as to say that his sister "would back me up on anything". Being three years older thanLeroy, his sister adopted the role of caregiver and substitute parent, and Leroy often referred to his sister as "always looking after us as a kid and stuff". Being raised in a pub as a younger child, Leroy talked of being surrounded by aggression:

Leroy:	My dad liked to drink didn't he, you know what I mean, but he wouldn't even know he used to hit me, he would have forgot. There's things … there's things … like with my mum and all that. I lived in a pub didn't I, I've seen my dad crack guys and all that, I've seen guys snap pool cues and start belting each other whilst I've been sat there. I've seen it all.
DJ:	Right.
Leroy:	I lived in the pub for just over a year it was, it was from nine years old till ten. It was bad. We had a dog, a pitbull, and that used to be involved in the fights, all sorts, it was bad.

He referred to his dad as "different" and "strong" – strong in the sense that he never saw him "back down or admit to being wrong". Leroy described not being frightened of anyone but his dad, and when he found himself in altercations with the police as a teenager, he would plead with them to take him anywhere but home:

> 'As a kid when I was getting into trouble, I wasn't scared of the police or nothing. When other kids would go "shush" here's the police, I would think I'm more scared of my dad! I wouldn't want 'em to take me home to my dad. If we did mad things and the police would come, I would be like "please listen, don't take me home yeah?"'

Leroy's story of boxing began with him not being at all interested in the sport. He talked of his dad being a journeyman – a 'stand-in' for professionals who drop out of fights at the last minute, rather than cancelling the show and losing money. Journeymen step in and fight, regardless of whether they win or lose (for a portrait of the journeyman, see Schulian 1983). As a result, Leroy witnessed his father "broken" on numerous occasions after boxing matches, and this originally discouraged him:

> 'Seeing my dad come home with black eyes and all that, you know as a kid, and I would say: "what's up?" And he'd been beat, or he'd won, you know … it just wasn't something that I took to as a kid or anything. I know some things go over your head as a kid … He never used to be just like "come 'ere", or give us a hug or anything. He was too strong.'

This seemed like a good point to ask Leroy to tell me the story of how it was, growing up with a dad as a boxer, as from the outset his father seemed like a strong presence in his life:

DJ:	Tell me the story of how it was for you growing up with your dad being a boxer.
Leroy:	As a boxer? Flippin 'eck! My dad used to have … That's how I was known as a kid, my dad just boxed. You know what I mean? He used to come home like I said with black eyes and things like that. I was just different you know, because my dad was always in training. And when he boxed he was out and that was it, so I didn't really see my dad. When he was training it was always "shush get out of the house", we had to be quiet. But I am sort of like that with my kid now. Whereas at the time I was thinking … but now I know, now I have a kid myself, so saying now to my kid you have to be quiet helped me understand where my dad was coming from.

Understanding where his dad was "coming from" proved to be important, as Leroy was still confused why his father behaved that way towards his family, especially as his father "never remembers the beatings". According to Leroy, his father often asks him and his older sister what they "remember most about being a kid". Leroy humours him and just tells him "nice things", to keep him from "feeling guilty", therefore "avoiding any more drama". Leroy justified his dad's behaviour throughout the interview as being symptomatic of being a boxer, and excused his lack of care and affection as inherent, especially due to his grandfather also being absent and abusive:

Leroy: With my dad it was different, he used to tell me about my granddad, he died now, but he used to be like 'you come here' and give my dad the belt, 'what's that for' my dad would say, crying, 'before you do anything' he'd say. You know proper old school and all that. Some of that was in my dad when we were kids. I've got another brother because my dad is with another woman, so stuff like that. We were just different. I have a kid now, but I didn't see my dad all the time … now that I've had my little lad, I think it sort of opened my dad's eyes a little bit because he loves my son to bits.

DJ: So he's a granddad?

Leroy: Yeah he is the granddad now. I just think because my dad is strong, it is hard for him to say sorry if you know what I mean. In certain situations, you know, I've had a few cracks off my dad …

Leroy rationalised his own father's behaviour, by portraying the abuse as "being in" his father and handed down via a paternal lineage. This hereditariness was not uncommon among the men in the gym, and echoes the literature on young men who view domestic abuse as normative behaviour (Spatz Widom 1989; Mullender et al 2002; Gadd et al 2014). In some respects, Leroy saw the abuse as a form of "tough love". Being known as the "kid whose dad boxed" contributed to Leroy's reputation as a young adult, and he disclosed that on most occasions "people would leave me the fuck alone on the estate". However, once the family had moved off the estate and into more comfortable middle-class surroundings, Leroy soon discovered that his dad's boxing career negatively impacted on his schooling. At this point, I felt it important to ask Leroy about his school days, as he referred to himself as not being particularly "academic", and it was during his last years of school that he took up the sport of boxing:

Leroy: We moved to the outskirts of town, and I moved school and all that, and obviously at that age I didn't know anyone, it was hard. When I moved all my mates were still in the previous town, but I used to go and see them. I knocked about with some lads, I still see them now, they come to the gym, they used to box and they said: 'why don't you come boxing?' This was in my last year of school and they said: 'come box, your dad boxes'. It all started from there really, then it changed everything, because I'm not academic me, and I thought … I used to watch boxing and all that, and when I was just leaving school, I thought what am I going to do? And I thought I'm going to box, that's it I'm going to box. Then I was asking my dad loads of questions, watching tapes; getting out all my dad's old tapes. I just loved it. It changed everything. It changed me that was it.

DJ: How did it change you?

Leroy: I wasn't going out with my mates, you know, when they were all going out drinking on the streets, I wasn't doing any of that. I was going home to get up early in the morning to go running. It changed everything. All my mates eating rubbish, it started at my last year of school and everyone was eating shit and I was like 'no, I'm not having it'.

DJ: You said you weren't particularly academic, how was school for you then?

Leroy: I didn't like it. Honestly, I couldn't do anything. Maybe coz the school I went to at first has been shut down now, that was a crazy school. Cars used to get blown up all the time and everything, you used to get robbed walking down the street at night-time or whatever, you know when you're just mooching [hanging out] as a kid. Then I have gone to this other school, which was proper Catholic. Any mither [trouble] and that was it, you got detention or had to pick up litter. It was just mad. When I moved schools, I had no friends, so I was just sort of different.

DJ: Different?

Leroy: Yeah definitely, I got suspended and everything, a few times for fighting in school, but I was not boxing at the time when this was going on. They used to have one yard on this side and one on that side and I used to cut through. Something happened, someone said something, and it all started like that. I started fighting with one of the older lads, I was in the third year and he just came up to me and I started fighting, saying that I thought I was 'hard and all that' … but I was getting done for things because my dad was a boxer … you know what I mean? There were things going on in school, and I obviously wasn't as academic as other kids, they had different backgrounds to me, I think they were a bit wealthier; that was my perspective anyway. They had better clothes than me and everything, they were a bit more well- off and I was different in that way. I don't think they understood where I was coming from, you know, the teachers and all that …

From this account, we can see that Leroy feels a sense of difference; he refers to this difference on more than one occasion within the first ten minutes of the interview. Arguably, the difference hinges upon his father's occupation and Leroy's ambivalent feelings of inadequacy and protection as a result. Clearly, for Leroy the image of his father was inexplicably bound up within his image of 'difference' at school, compounded by a move from his original place of education to a different one, where any sign of misbehaviour was immediately penalised. Moving from an area where his previous school was nostalgically described as "crazy", Leroy felt judged among his new school peers.

This new school instilled a sense of inadequacy in Leroy, as he described those who attended as "wealthier" and "in better clothes than me". Also, the kudos placed upon Leroy as a result of his father's occupation was not forthcoming in the new school, as he found his peers challenging, as opposed to fearful and compliant. Without friends and "back up", Leroy felt isolated, and the power he once wielded in the previous school and on the estate as a result of being the son of the "local famous boxer" began to diminish. He further described the teachers as not understanding where he "was coming from", and I detected a sense of loneliness in Leroy, as he recounted feeling "less academic" and "from a different background". He described this as:

> 'It wasn't like the other kid's mum and dads and all that. That is why it was hard for me at school, because they were with their mum and dads and I was just like .... I wasn't out looking for sympathy, but I used to think: "you lot are just different to me, you lot have had a silver spoon ... so for me, I used to do mad things to get money and stuff ... pinching things, things like that. In that school people had Sprayways and North Faces [designer labels], so that's getting sold. Then mobile phones started to come out ...'

Leroy's sense of inadequacy in relation to his dad's career and his family's lack of wealth permeated into his feelings of isolation and envy. In new school surroundings, Leroy started to equate success with affluence and academic ability; attributes that he admittedly was without. Additionally, his fragile sense of self-worth came under attack, as he sensed his difference from other children and their parents, thus "doing mad things" to either attract attention to his loneliness or to create legitimate wealth through illegitimate means. Feeling this sense of difference due to the school move, Leroy talked of how his dad "tried to better us by moving to this area", but described the process as "gutting", therefore leading to periods of absconding. Leroy described how he "would get on my bike and fly back to the estate", where he could "feel at home with people who get me, people who are like me".

Originally being born into a "working-class household", Leroy fondly remembered growing up on the council estate with his mother and sister, whereas hisfather was described as "hard" and "unpredictable", and Leroy would talk of his sister running up the stairs to hide, when she heard her father was due home:

Leroy:	Me and my sister would be messing about, having a laugh and that, and my mum would say 'your dad's coming home in a minute', my sister would leg it up the stairs scared shitless.
DJ:	Right.
Leroy:	Like, some people talk about their past, about being a kid and it being a laugh and everything. I had a laugh with my mates, but some things ... I think I only got to see my dad proper when he has had a fight and got some money, and then he would

> buy us something. But apart from that he would be out on the piss and everything you know what I mean. So that now he's the granddad, I mean my granddad probably did the same with him when he was a kid, it's probably all he knows, but I don't want to be like that with my kid. I'm with my kid every day and that, but my dad … flippin' 'eck, I was a kid …

Being with his son daily was important to Leroy, as he talked of reading to him every day and "fighting at top level to give him everything he wants", whereas Leroy only ever saw his father sporadically and then he "usually passed out pissed on the chair". This led Leroy to talk of wanting to create a "different scenario for my little lad", and while "being out for a bit on the piss after a fight and that, I still come home to my little lad every night". While not always present in the family home, Leroy's father became very well known in the surrounding area, and the local community apparently "respected the family name".

Winlow (2001:23) describes how being a 'local celebrity would meet the desires of most "hard" men'. I would argue that Leroy's father fits the bill. Indeed, the cultural importance of a family name is exceptionally strong among working-class males (Winlow 2001:23), and in this respect, Leroy's family name became synonymous with boxing and also violence, especially when his father was employed as a local pub landlord. Leroy argued that: "not every family could run a boozer on a rough estate", and felt that it was during this time that his father was at his most violent and unpredictable:

> 'Obviously because he was drinking a lot, my dad was at his worse when we had the pub. He would scream at us all the time, and swing for us. He had to be like that though, because if people thought they could take the piss, they would. People from the estate knew not to kick off but if we got some out-of-towners in then it would kick off.'

Leroy described how his father would employ his mates to sit at the end of the bar and "back him up if it went off"; paying them in "free booze" and "lock ins", which comprised copious amounts of drinking outside of licensed hours. The pub became renowned as a "proper dodgy gangster pub", and Leroy's dad assumed the mantle of local "hardman" with ease. The pub therefore became a site for Leroy's father to further establish his identity in the community, and he ruled over the estate by engendering a sense of fear and respect among its residents. Leroy would describe how people would generally be overly polite to his father, or simply "cross the street when they saw him coming".

Winlow (2001), among others (see Katz 1988; Feldman 1991; Hobbs 1995; Hall 1997), describes the 'hardman' as a man dedicated to violence, with first-hand knowledge of its historical and cultural potential, thus 'marking him out from others whose daily strategies feature the avoidance of conflict' (Hobbs 1995:51). For Leroy's father, daily conflict was a part of everyday life. Leroy describes how his dad "enjoyed the buzz of it, he loved to drink and ruck you know what I mean, that's why being a journeyman suited him; he got paid for fighting!"

More to the point, Hall (1997:466) describes in vivid detail the cultural practices associated with cultures of hardness – visceral cultures – and argues that these cultures of hardness are durable, visible forms that are ubiquitous and reproducing in their effects in working-class institutions and milieus. These practices 'manifest themselves as sporadic, unpredictable actions of intimidation and violence, erupting constantly'. Leroy's father fitted this mould and imbued a sense of hardness, not dissimilar to Hall's or Winlow's description of the 'hard lad' – disenfranchised from the 'neo-capitalist pleasure dome' (Hall 1997), permeable for those not on the margins of mainstream commodifying practices.

Working-class habitus and boxing

Leroy's father was an absent, violent man, who capitalised on his aggressive style of behaviour to earn a living as a journeyman and also as a pub landlord. Violence was an integral theme in the childhood of both Leroy and his father, and has evidently played an essential part in forming their adult identities.

The identities of Leroy's father and subsequently of Leroy are 'situated around a cultural frame of tough, resourceful masculinity that transcends both economic epochs and generational responses to communal problems' (Hobbs 1995:29). This is evidenced by Leroy's father's immediate and violent response to any "kicking off in the boozer", and by Leroy's ability to enact violence and "switch it on when need be".

Leroy junior bore his father's name with a sense of status and respect. When on the council estate and among like-minded friends, Leroy would gain kudos as the son of a boxing champion, disclosing that he was "never one of those kids that got robbed walking down the street at night time". However, when faced with a different set of peers, those who attended his new school and who were not necessarily familiar with Leroy's father, Leroy felt inadequate and judged for his father's occupation. He often found himself reluctantly fighting, to defend the honour of his family name – no longer in a habitus where the name carried a sense of fear for those who heard it. Moreover, it began to represent difference and disrespect for Leroy, as the family name became equated with "roughness". Being known as the kid whose dad boxed came to symbolise something less than admiration in Leroy's new school surroundings – and it made him feel "different". "Getting done for things because my dad was a boxer" began to take shape in Leroy's narrative, as he relayed anxieties about moving areas and changing schools:

> 'I got pulled to one side one time and the teacher was saying ... one of my dad's fights was on the news one time, it had kicked off in the audience. It was massive and that was my dad's fight, that. Obviously, my misbehaving in school wasn't particularly me, I think in certain situations the teachers just pinpointed me out all the time because of my name. I got pulled to one side one time and they were asking me: "what's going on at home?" But I think they were just different, you know the way I was brought up with my parents, and the way they were brought up with their parents. That school wasn't me you know what I mean. It just wasn't ... All the way through that school, all the way through I wasn't meant to be in that school.'

Leroy constantly reiterates his difference in "that school" and sees himself as incompatible, based on his father's occupation as a boxer and on his own class positioning being at odds with the other children. As a result of the televised incident referred to in the last quotation, and a perceived sense of "difference", Leroy began to misbehave seriously:

Leroy: I think because of the news bit, I think it just got all out of proportion from there, you know what I mean. Obviously, my dad made the news with the boxing and all that because the fans have kicked off, all hometown lads. But from then on school wise, it was different.

DJ: Different how?

Leroy:	I wasn't like proper naughty or anything but things went missing a lot. A teacher's purse went once and straightaway I was blamed!
DJ:	Right.
Leroy:	Yeah and I was like 'it wasn't me sir', 'but you got seen walking down the corridor Leroy', and I was like 'and?' I got detention that day and had to go isolation or something, and I'm coming out of there and funnily enough a teacher's purse got nicked ...
DJ:	Right.
Leroy:	Because of the news bit, I think it just got all out of proportion from there, you know what I mean ... I knew older lads didn't I as well, people who never did anything, just sat in the house, so I would chill with them instead of going school.
DJ:	How long did you do that for?
Leroy:	My mum and dad still don't know I did that, yeah they don't know I did that. I did it for a bit, I did it enough so if letters came to the house my big sister would always sort it. We are good mates me and my sister you know.

Leroy's sister obviously bore the same surname as their father, yet did not internalise the same sense of pressure or ambivalence that Leroy did. Leroy put this down to her leaving the new school after six months and not really having to deal with the aftermath of the incident making local news. Yet it is arguable that Leroy's sister felt less pressure than Leroy did, when it came to "defending the family name".

When Leroy did attend school, he said he felt "disrespected", as teachers would refer to him by just his surname. Leroy interpreted this as disrespectful and as a further reference to his dad's reputation:

> 'I used to say things or ... I used to say to teachers you can't say that ... as they would say things like "oi [surname]" this that and the other, and I used to say: "I've got a first name!" "Stop answering back" they'd say, and I'd be like I'm not behind the door I know what you mean you cannot go around saying things like that, I know kids give lip, but they can't be speaking to people like that, whereas I used to get done for it all. The other kids would be saying: "I can't

> believe you just said that" and I'd say: "I'm not being cheeky or ought, I'm telling them to treat me with some respect".'

Leroy felt persecuted at school for his father's violent legacy, and I would go so far as to say that Leroy, like others in the sample, was hyper-vigilant to issues of disrespect. This is evidenced in his narrative, when he refers to "getting done for it all", and how the teachers would refer to him by his surname only. In fact, Leroy disclosed only "getting on" with one teacher; he was the sports teacher and therefore familiar with Leroy's father's occupation:

> 'One teacher he was alright, he was a sports teacher, he was alright with us, but he wasn't there long. I think because he knew my dad was a boxer and had seen my dad's fights, he was alright with us.'

This was the only connection that Leroy discussed having within the school, as sport was a common discussion point and a potential bonding element in the relationship with his teacher. Leroy's mixed feelings about his father's career became apparent as he felt that the sports teacher admired his father's occupation, whereas the other teachers were repelled by it. By developing a bond with the sports teacher, Leroy started to feel accepted in the school. However, when the teacher left after a year, Leroy began to truant seriously. Because of this loss of attachment, and the allegations of stealing from other staff members,[1] Leroy decided that he had had enough and never went back. Not attending school in the final year gave Leroy plenty of time on his hands, and this is when he first started to box. Discouraged by his father in the beginning, Leroy started to attend the local gym with his older friends. Having been told that boxing is "hard" by his dad, Leroy inevitably threw himself into the sport wholeheartedly:

> 'It's probably one of them; when your dad says no, you say yes. If he had of said "yeah go do it", I probably would have said "no I'm not doing it". It wasn't the fact that somebody says - "don't do it", I just liked it, I enjoyed it, you know feeling good about myself after the gym and that. It was when I am sparring with kids who have already had ten fights and I'm getting the better of them that I thought I should be doing this.'

"Feeling good" about himself was the most important thing to Leroy at that time, and ironically, he chose the sport that defined his father and that had subsequently labelled him as the "rough kid". Nevertheless, the determination shown by Leroy in his first year of boxing gained him a place on the England team, an event he described as "proof that I was capable of something, proof that I was worthy". Leroy went on to become a national champion.

When asked about any regrets to do with truanting from school, Leroy said he did not care, and could not do "anything other than boxing because I got fuck all else going for me". This led me to believe that Leroy was not as confident outside the ring as he was in it. Coupled with his ability to disparage himself academically, I would suggest that Leroy invested in boxing to overcome his feelings of both vulnerability and low self-esteem. Additionally, I would argue that boxing was familiar territory to Leroy. As much as he shied away from the sport originally, having seen his dad "broken" on numerous occasions, the visceral habitus[2] (Hall 1997; Ellis et al 2017) of home life and his rejection by his new school peers directed Leroy into an occupation that sat comfortably within a social world and an environment where violence was a 'cultural expectation' (Wolfgang 1959). This cultural expectation therefore made Leroy as famous at boxing as his dad was at being the local 'hardman'.

Truanting from school, and hanging out with the older lads, allowed Leroy to hone his boxing skills in the local gym, and also reinforced his status as the local hardman's son, thereby creating a further distance between the middle-class children due to sit their exams at his rejected secondary school and Leroy's sense of self-esteem regarding these. The boxing gym became Leroy's "sanctuary" – a common narrative among young men who struggle at school or in environments where they do not necessarily feel safe. Accordingly, the gym often becomes an "island of stability and order" (Wacquant 2004:31), when their lives become complicated or disjointed.

The dedicatory approach to the gym, as a result of the routine and order it provides, detains and incapacitates young men. In Leroy's case, it stopped him "from drinking on the streets with his mates and getting into bother", further valourising Hall's (1997:465) arguments that "visceral cultures consist of punctuality, sobriety, conscientiousness and the other respectable working-class virtues". In truth, the habitus and masculine discourses pervading the gym environment are not that dissimilar from the environment that young men say they wish to escape. While no longer stealing from peers and teachers, Leroy disclosed that he would not be afraid to "call upon his dad and his mates", if he ever needed to.

As Anderson (1999:94) observed in his study: 'violence was not always used, but always a possibility'. Indeed, Leroy understood that, as suggested by Hobbs et al (2003:223), 'violence possesses a multiplicity of meanings within working-class cultures that elevate its importance in everyday life' As a result of growing up with a father like his, Leroy was complicit in what Hobbs calls these 'traditional images of masculinity and violence that are played out from within networks based upon the family' (Hobbs 1995:108). Leroy was not afraid to harness the cultural environment and the violent inheritance that defined him and his father, as it not only allowed Leroy to "call upon the firm", but also facilitated the transformation of cultural capital into *pugilistic* economic capital (Bourdieu 1977:183; Wacquant 1995a).

Shame, stigma and class

Leroy was a vulnerable and likeable character. We spent hours talking about his life, both formally and informally, and when he had the reassurances that his story would remain anonymous, he relaxed and opened up. His relationship with his father was at the root of Leroy's vulnerabilities and identity, and he was often referred to as 'junior' in the gym, as most of the other members "remembered his dad's heydays". Leroy would rather forget his dad's heydays, as these were the times when his father was at his most absent and abusive, evidenced by his memories of seeing his father with "black eyes" and being told to get out of the house, which for a small child I can imagine was very unsettling. Due to his father's reputation – and subsequent news reports berating the fighting among his father's supporters – Leroy was unable to escape the shadow of his father's name and reputation as local 'hardman'. While this worked for Leroy on one level – protecting him within a violent milieu that saw young men being robbed – it also worked against him, when he had to change areas and school.

Citing differences due to wealth and family upbringing, Leroy clearly felt different in his new peer group, even resorting to stealing to accrue status within an environment that he perceived as wealthier than his – particularly those designer labels and cultural artefacts that young people aspire to own. Paul Willis (1977:39), in his classic study *Learning to Labour*, states that 'shortage of cash becomes the single biggest pressure' in young men's lives, as it provides evidence of their ability to 'make it in the real world', proving their 'essential nature' as 'males'; a practice that reproduces a specific type of white working-class masculinity.

Struggling academically was also something that Leroy discussed, as he talked of other children's parents being different and encouraging, whereas he felt his parents took no interest in his school record. It is not uncommon among working-class boys to view academic achievement as emasculating (Willis 1997). I would argue that Leroy felt more comfortable in adopting a traditional white working-class mentality that places onus on manual – not mental – labour (Willis 1997).

I would further argue that Leroy adopted a more manual occupation such as boxing, not only because of structural determinations but also due to low self-esteem surrounding his intellectual and academic abilities. Leroy constantly referred to himself as "not academic", even calling himself "thick" on numerous occasions. Indeed, the internalisation of the guiding habitus facilitated a withdrawal into an informal world of boxing and truancy for Leroy, as he developed what Willis calls a 'differentiation from authority', and rejected the mental labour of qualifications for more manual masculine occupations commonly favoured among Willis's 'lads' (1977:65). The impetus to box was also an additional mechanism by which Leroy could manage both the stigma accruing to him via his father's reputation, and the attendant vulnerability he felt in his younger home life.

Until Leroy discovered boxing for himself, he believed there was "fuck all else" going for him, and in this case, it would be easy to attribute his decision to box as simply a way of gaining status. Yet Leroy's decision to box was more about feeling good, to mitigate his feelings of low self-worth, while being subject to social determinants that dictated that masculine manual pursuits were appropriate for working-class lads like him. As Willis (1977:174) states: 'structures which have now become sources of meaning, definition and identity provide the framework and basis for decisions and choices in life'. This view of cultural forms and reproduction, according to Willis, is part of a necessary dialectic of reproduction that inevitably condemns a good proportion of working-class kids to a future of manual work; in Leroy's case, it would certainly ring true.

In *The Hidden Injuries of Class*, Sennett and Cobb (1973) discuss the ways in which shame and class intersect. They argue that working-class men feel that because of their class and occupational positioning, they are not accorded the respect they deserve. This lack of respect translates not only as the fault of others – particularly those in power, such as teachers and bosses – but also as a subtle wound; a self-inflicted one, whereby young men perceive their class positioning and lack of opportunity as partly their fault. Sennett and Cobb postulate that respect is largely based on individual achievement and the sense that one's individual success is linked to personal identity, an identity that is individualistic and remarkable.

In the broader church that is the sociology of emotions, shame manifests itself as chronic low self-esteem. Sennett and Cobb write that young working-class men carry this burden, as their talents (or lack of) do not allow them to stand out from the masses. Thus, for young men like Leroy, education, rather than being a source of personal and cultural growth, provides only shame and rejection. It creates a divide between those young men who will succeed and those who are doomed to fail. In Sennett and Cobb's words:

By the time children are ten or eleven the split between the many and the few who are expected to "make something of themselves" is out in the open … [the mass of] boys in class act as though they were serving time, as though school work and classes have become something to wait out, a blank space in their lives they hope to survive. (Sennett and Cobb 1973:82–3).

Alongside feelings of shame came a change of school for Leroy, as his networks of support among his friends became uprooted and his father sought to better his family's lifestyle with a change of area. This is evidenced by Leroy absconding from his new home and cycling back to the council estate, where he felt more accepted and supported for his father's occupation, rather than being judged and shamed for it. In his new school, fighting and stealing became a way for Leroy to stake a claim when he felt inadequate, particularly when older boys would approach him, asking if he thought he was "hard" like his dad. Leroy was quick to lay blame at the feet of other boys, yet I sensed that Leroy was equally responsible for the violent altercations, as part of a systematic defence mechanism designed to conceal feelings of inadequacy and also to uphold the "family name". Moreover, this was supported by the further conversations I had with Leroy, when he would state that: "attack is the best form of defence".

Aggression and fighting are part of 'accomplishing masculinity' for some young men (Messerschmidt 1993). I would argue that Leroy's aggressive responses were most certainly a way to maintain his masculinity, but also part of a systematic defence against vulnerability and shame – shame as a result of his own academic ability, his father's occupation, and a marked difference between the visceral habitus of the council estate he fondly grew up on, and the middle school where he felt judged and "different". 'Even students with the right answers must deal with having the wrong accent, clothing or physical appearance', writes Scheff (2000:91) in *Shame and the Sociological Bond*. For Leroy, school was a vale of shame.

Leroy's vulnerabilities presented themselves in the form of intellectual ability and wealth, which became exacerbated with a change of school. Leroy's "difference" became heightened, as he perceived himself as being vulnerable to attack from both pupils and teachers. "Not knowing where I was coming from" evidenced his sense of loneliness, as he found himself without friends and subject to hostile taunts from other children not "respecting the family name".

The appeal of boxing, therefore, facilitated the maintenance of the family name as "hard", while also allowing Leroy to achieve monetary success, when he felt there was "nothing else" he could do. Employing the only resources available to him, Leroy felt that boxing was a way to prove he was "good at something" and "worthy". The fact that Leroy referred to boxing as "changing everything" is a direct reference to how he invested in the sport for reasons other than just enjoying it, and "beating men who had already had ten fights" allowed Leroy to feel a sense of achievement that he felt he lacked in other areas.

This rings true with Cooley's (1922:184) historical work into the 'looking-glass self', which implies that the social nature of oneself refers directly to emotions of pride and shame. Cooley sees self-monitoring in terms of three steps: 'A self-idea of this sort seems to have three principal elements: the imagination of our appearance to the other person; the imagination of his judgement of that appearance, and some sort of self-feeling, such as pride or mortification' (Cooley 1922:184).

For Leroy, the self-monitoring required to overcome shame with emotions of pride was sacrosanct, and therein lies part of boxing's vast appeal. The sweet science is not only structured to replace shame with pride, but is laden with discourses of triumph and glory. For Leroy, this was the perfect antidote to feelings of low self-worth.

By participating in boxing, Leroy was also able to develop a relationship with his father, as he talked of "getting out all his dad's old tapes" and "asking him loads of questions". Leroy seemed to now understand where his dad was "coming from", as he found himself asking his own son to be quiet in the house. Furthermore, to quote Ellis et al (2017:8)Leroy was potentially able to 'psychologically rehabilitate' his own image of his father and justify his aggressive behaviour towards him as a child as ultimately a positive learning experience (Hobbs 1994; Winlow 2001).

Nevertheless, he was keen to distinguish himself from his father's drinking and violence, and made excuses for it under a misguided genetic theory of paternal lineage. Leroy believed that his father's abuse was indicative of what Winlow 2012 suggested as a 'cold realism', whereby the father figure and the surrounding narrative are constructed in a way that violence is instrumental in the battle for dignity, honour and self-respect. Moreover, the abuse of young sons by their violent fathers is often justified as a necessary preparation for the cold realism of life on the margins, and a life subsumed by unrelenting competitive individualism and physical dominance (Ellis et al 2017). Leroy's formative social environment and experiences of violence allowed him to draw upon cultural resources when necessary. I argue that recruits to the profession of boxing carry forth forms of cultural capital that reflect their socialisation as contemporary working-class men, acutely conscious of their physicality and drawing on violence and its negotiation in their everyday social world (Hobbs 1995; Winlow 2001; Hobbs et al 2003).

Violence was an integral part of both Leroy's and his father's life, with physical resilience and competence in relation to male-on-male violence (see Connell 1995) being considered a crucial concern and ideal within working-class masculinities (see also Willis 1977). According to Winlow (2001), class is a key tool in understanding both the social and cultural determinants of violence and its meanings to participants. For working-class males such as Leroy and his father, violence is often an aspect of their cultural environment and inheritance. So much so, that it has a major influence on their social and cultural understanding of everyday life (Hobbs 1995; Winlow 2001).

For Leroy, violence served as a resource to be called upon at any time, his "dad's firm" just being a "phone call away". Granted, while Leroy did not necessarily engage in day-to-day violence, as his dad had done in his "heyday", his gendered and class-specific cultural socialisation led to a heightened sense of violence that allowed for him to understand the complex interactive preludes and precursors of violent behaviour (Winlow 2001). This, in turn, assisted Leroy in choosing the sport of boxing.

As Hobbs (1995) suggests, the remnants of industrial employment cultures, once stripped of their potential for communal action in both the workplace and workplace-dependent neighbourhoods, have provided an ideal pool of apprentices to the ranks of occupations such as boxing and organised crime. As we have seen in this case study, boxing becomes the ideal vehicle for men like Leroy, and indeed his father – a vehicle to transform the cultural capital of working-class violence into economic capital in the form of belts and titles.

For Leroy in particular, boxing's appeal was twofold: it provided the perfect route into meaningful employment; and it was the perfect vehicle for the avoidance of shame. Boxing allowed Leroy not only to replace the shame of class with all its hidden injuries, but also to construct an identity that veiled the shame with pride, honour and self-respect. Without boxing, Leroy really did think he had "fuck all else".

Summary

Through Leroy's case study, I have interrogated how the boxing gym can be appealing in its ability to provide young working-class men with feelings of pride and honour. Through the accruing and maintenance of physical capital, the act of boxing allows young men to disavow feelings of shame and low self-esteem, and replace them with feelings of pride and self-respect. This is achieved through providing young men with avenues to distinguish themselves, and therefore create social capital through the vehicle of the self.

According to Wacquant (1995a:2) boxers are 'entrepreneurs in bodily capital', and thus able to convert bodily capital into *pugilistic capital*, a form of currency that takes shape in the image of belts, recognition and income streams. Moreover, boxing mimics the visceral habitus that men like Leroy and his father are versed in, thus providing an educational system they can grasp, without having to pass an entrance exam. Accordingly, it keeps them locked in the guiding habitus, whereby violence is a resource that can be called upon at any time.

In the next chapter, I discuss in more detail the appealing nature of the boxing gym, and pull together the arguments presented in the three case studies. Drawing on the stories of Frank, Eric and Leroy, weaved in with fieldnotes from the regular attendees, I examine how the gym is a site of social, physical and psychological reconstruction, and how this forms part of the wider appeal for men looking to create new identities and outlooks.

Notes

1 After the interview had finished and the voice recorder was switched off, Simon admitted to stealing the teacher's purse with his friend.

2 During the industrial heyday – and synonymous with the post-industrial working classes – the *visceral habitus is a form of masculinity that* is grounded in the functional requirements of work in the heavy and extractive industries and service in military conflicts. It further signifies and reproduces social reputation, which is often synonymous with violence and physical cultures (Hall 1997).

6

The Appeal of the Boxing Gym

Introduction

In this chapter, I discuss the themes that emerged from my research, particularly those that relate to boxing's enduring appeal, and also those that demonstrate how the sport can be a fundamental source of masculine accomplishment and status. I begin with a reflection on the initial appeal of boxing for some of the men in the gym, and also consider how that relates to their understanding of why they continue to attend. Furthermore, I discuss how boxing is a response to personal and structural vulnerability for the majority of men in this sample, and therefore present data to illustrate how the appeal of boxing has changed for them over their life-course.

Moreover, I present evidence to demonstrate how these men's journeys throughout their amateur and professional careers have changed, and whether or not there are differences in the reasons why they persist. Indeed, I explore the tension between the straightforward 'surface' reward-statements of men (money, status, fame, health, discipline, and so on) and what are interpreted as 'deeper' motivations, suggesting that the gym is a physical, social but also a psychological space for accomplishing masculinity, and for creating and sustaining self-worth in the face of chronic autobiographical and structural limitations.

Reflections on the appeal of boxing

During the six months that I spent in the field in the world of amateur and professional boxing, it became increasingly evident that the gym was an important and valuable space for the men who attended. The conversations I had with these men, and the time I spent hanging around this inner-city gym, allowed me a brief glimpse into their social world, and thus permitted me access to their worldview. Most of the men I spoke with had a personal reason for participating: some talked of getting fit and losing weight, whereas others talked of boxing being their 'life'. Others perceived themselves as contributing to the night-time economy, or overcoming some form of social, economic or academic barrier.

One of the successful professionals I spoke with proclaimed that boxing, "Proved I was capable of doing something, that I was worthy of something" (Leroy, 32 years old, professional). Coincidentally, this phrase echoes the words uttered by the character Billy Tully in the cult boxing film *Fat City*, when he proclaimed: 'To be somebody, that's what it's all about, to escape from anonymity, from dreariness, if only for the space of a few rounds'. One of the other men I spoke with believed that boxing was a "good thing to channel into" and "if you haven't got anything to put your aggression into, it goes elsewhere – thieving, fighting or robbing" (Ricky, 20 years old, professional).

For others, boxing was an ancillary activity to a career in the night-time economy, providing the physical capital needed to guard the pubs and nightclubs in a metropolitan city. For some men, the boxing gym was simply a place to come and hang out, constructed as a neutral space that remained a place of safety – no matter what was happening in the community outside. Wacquant (2004:31) referred to boxing gyms as 'islands of stability and order', in that they 'protect an individual from the street' and 'act as a buffer against the insecurity of the neighbourhood and pressures of everyday life'. Wacquant believed that boxing gyms helped to regulate men's lives, when disorder and delinquency engulf it, and this was indicative for a significant number of men in my sample. Men such as Marcus, the 42-year-old trainer who grew up in the surrounding community, disclosed how the gang violence that beleaguered the area during the 1990s was "left outside the gym doors for us to pick up after training!"

The majority of the men involved in this research invested heavily into the sport of boxing – and gym life. Professional trainers, professional boxers and various amateurs said boxing symbolised – to them at least – much more than a place where you went to punch a few bags and "let off steam". They spoke of the gym as family, community and companionship. Even when not lacing up gloves or reaching for skipping ropes, men would loiter around the edges, discussing lovers, football and, in some instances, court cases.

Interestingly, some men spoke of the boxing gym as they would a lover and discussed (without being aware) the sensual and erotic pull of pugilism; disclosing how the smell of sweat and the feel of skin contributed to the seduction of the sport:

> 'Once you get the boxing bug, you got it for life I'm tellin' you, you walk up them stairs and you can hear the music and it turns you on you know what I'm saying, gets your blood pumping, you can smell the sweat and gloves, I love that feeling.' (Derek, 32 years old, amateur)
>
> 'Good man on man combat is the best buzz you can have, forget drugs, a good fight is the best buzz, up against the ropes toe to toe.' (Baz, 38 years old, amateur)
>
> 'In the ring where it's all dark outside, and it's just you and him, puts you in a trance, like a form of dancing, and all you can hear is breathing …' (Sal, 42 years old, retired professional boxer and trainer)

These quotes are reminiscent of Stephen Lyng's (1998) concept of 'edgework', whereby participants combine the exhilaration and momentary integration of danger, risk and skill in the experience of boxing. The physicality required to participate in a sport like boxing only adds to the appeal and, according to Lyng (1998), the feeling of danger being averted by skilful awareness is what makes 'edgework' all the more risqué.

Certainly, the physicality required to invest in the sport was a huge draw, as men chiselled their bodies into either money-making machines or defensive structures. The preening and manly display, coupled with the psychological realisationof physical capital, was carnivalesque at times – and, in some respects, grotesque, as some men would approach their bodies with a dysmorphic lens. Put simply, the investment in the body as a structure was extreme. Some men would push their desire for bodily perfection to bizarre lengths, sometimes culminating in vomiting after workout sessions or, as with the case of Eric, starving oneself to "make weight". This perfectionism and endurance were clearly visible for those employed in the professional boxing circuit; however, it could also be seen in men working in the security industry.

Bouncers and professional boxers were at the top of the hierarchy, and this was quite evident in the way the gym functioned. It was not very often that those with professions such as these had to queue for equipment or to wait for a parking space outside – this was due to the respect and prestige placed upon them as a result of their earning a living from the crafting of their physicality. The men in these superior positions also did favours for gym attendees, such as guest lists for nightclubs and ringside seats. Therefore the regular attendees behaved in ways that maintained the bouncers' and professionals' exalted positions. This hierarchy was clearly well established.

Moreover, it became quite clear early on in my fieldwork, that this hierarchy was based on physicality and the participants' capacity for violence, whereby those with the highest rate of physical capital had the most power. Professions that supported or employed physical capital in the day-to-day occupations of these men merely contributed towards this omnipotence. These men existed in a habitus that took violence as a normal part of everyday life.

Thus, the boxing world came to be seen as a site where implicit rules of physical capital and masculine accomplishment governed its smooth running. Indeed, it was seen as a place of excitement, male companionship and ruthless violent competition – and all these factors contributed to its appeal (Jump 2016).

Boxing's appeal: status, fame and action

Goffman (1967:185) explicitly lists boxing as 'where the action is'. According to Goffman, 'action' is a set of activities that are consequential, problematic and undertaken for what is felt to be their own sake (Goffman 1967:185). Action therefore involves the 'wilful undertaking of serious chances' (Goffman 1967:181). Boxing is paradigmatic of 'action', as it is clearly evident that "performers will place money, reputation and physical safety in jeopardy, all at the same time'.

Roger a retired boxing coach, and the oldest member in the gym (at 63 years of age), kindly pointed out this idea of 'action' to me during the warm-up to a professional fight: "It's the only sport where you have two doctors on hand, a resuscitation team on standby, and an ambulance outside". Referring to the injustice and excitement of the game, especially as some investments never pay off, Roger proclaimed that: "Boxing is the only sport where you can do all the work and sometimes never get paid". For example, if a professional gets knocked out in the first round, and therefore becomes known as 'dead meat', it can leave both trainer and pugilist out of pocket. If a fight gets cancelled at the last minute due to injury, the purse can get taken elsewhere. Therefore, men who enter an occupation that depends on the 'willful undertaking of serious chances' (Goffman 1967:181), decisively realign the structure and texture of their entire existence in ways that place them in a unique position to assert their agency.

The majority of boxers in this study felt that by stepping into the ring, they would achieve something forbidden to them outside, whether that is wealth, fame, excitement, or more importantly, a sense of control. Wacquant (1995b:510) writes that, '[i]t is the unspeakable prosaic joys of being caught up in a thickly knit web of tensionful activities' that valorise men and 'imbue their life with élan, drive and significance'. This valour and its subsequent rewards can seemingly be attained under the boxer's own powers; a direct outcome of their individual choice and toils. As Ricky a young professional in the gym once said: "I did this myself, no-one else did it. I was shit at school but looks who's laughing now".

Unsurprisingly, money was a strong motivating factor in the appeal of boxing. Most men talked of "getting out from round 'ere when I make my millions" (Derek, 32 years old). At face value, boxing would seem appealing for simply that reason: a sport that requires little equipment and nothing in the way of academic qualifications. Having said that, very few professionals actually make the coveted million, and many become injured and retire early as a result (Wacquant 1995a, 1995b). Eric, who was discussed in the case studies (see Chapter 4), demonstrates this unwavering appeal for the status and money that comes with boxing success, and the sacrifices that have to be made in order to achieve it. What is surprising is that Eric, and most of the men I interviewed, did not originally begin boxing for financial gain. Yet in order to be successful, they had to adopt the discourses commonly seen in competitive hyper-masculine environments – an approach that exalts invincibility.

Boxing's appeal is not so much a reaction to material deprivation as one might think. It is arguably more of a vehicle for exerting a sense of agency, establishing authority, and remodelling oneself in the world, particularly if those participating felt that other opportunities for success are blocked. Indeed, it was quite common to hear men such as Ricky state that he "couldn't do nothing but box now", having left school with no qualifications or potential job prospects. Whereas men such as Baz (a 38-year-old amateur), felt that boxing gave him a sense of purpose, after struggling to find work and purpose on release from prison: "Boxing saved my life man, if I just had to sit at home all day being on the dole and that, then without boxing I'd go mad, gives me something to do, something to focus on, and I get by with what the social give me."

The idea of the boxing gym being a place of purpose and resolve is common among those who have conducted ethnographies in them (see Sugden 1996; Wacquant 2004; Trimbur 2009). In my study, a vast majority of the men reported that the gym was like 'family', or how they could not imagine their life without the gym and its structure. As much as this may be the case – whereby the gym fosters a community spirit – the moment that men step into the gym, they are fed a steady diet of masculine discourses that exalt the idea of the lone warrior or modern gladiator, which in some respects contradicts the collective attitude to which they attest.

This idea of the lone warrior, which many men reaffirm when they repeat the boxing mantra 'When you step into the ring you step in alone', gives them a platform on which to affirm their valour and their heroic self. This mantra allows for pugilists to escape the status of 'non-person' to which they have been consigned (Goffman 1959:151), and in some respects, it further develops their status as a modern gladiator, fighting against all odds. As the famous *Rocky* posters that littered the gym attested: 'His life was a million to one shot'.

This idea of a heroic self is prominent in combat sports such as boxing. The modern gladiator – triumphant and masculine – reigns supreme, and one way to achieve this perceived image is to invest heavily in body sculpting. Creating physical presence and mass, while at the same time projecting an air of invincibility and insouciance, is seen as imperative to achieving gladiator status among the boxing community.[1] Fearlessness and enduring pain are other imperatives at work in the gym, buttressed by perceived notions of masculinity, and indicative of Sabo's 'pain principle'(Sabo 1986) – the idea that working and playing through pain is an affirmation of masculinity and strength. Indeed, Eric, who we met in the case studies (Chapter 4), often talked of fighting through pain – "I just kept hitting him, I knew my hand was broke but I had to carry on, all the work I'd put in – I couldn't let everyone down" – as he discusses how he entered a title fight with a broken hand, just so he could avoid the shame of pulling out at the last minute and "letting everyone down", including himself.

Certainly, this idea of disassociation with one's body is evident in boxing, with men seeing their bodies as machines as opposed to flesh and blood, and treating them as one might a fancy car – polishing it, checking it and showing it off around the neighbourhood. Yet, on the other hand, they destroy it through obsessive exercise and monotonous drills, all the while convinced that "the harder you push the more you succeed" (Eric, trainer, 51 years old). This monocular view chimes again with Klein's (1990) work into bodybuilding, and the idea that the body is a temple. However, that temple can house a raft of personal hidden anxieties, whereby the muscle simply becomes the physical armour to mask a psychological vulnerability (Fussell 1991). Jefferson (1998:78) also posits that 'hardness' can also be defined as a 'certain indifference to the body', an ability to withstand pain and injury regardless of rationality and consequences. I would argue that this concept drives men to repeat behaviours that they know to be destructive but that they are compelled to repeat.

It became apparent that one of the major appeals of boxing was its ability to allow men to craft their bodies in line with masculine discourses of the modern gladiator, while simultaneously allowing them to escape the reality of their circumstances, particularly those men who were disadvantaged through lack of employment or through criminal records. The gym was viewed as a site of reconstruction, whether that was a new family, a new identity or a new body, and the men in attendance each had their own personal reason for attending. When asking each man individually to "Tell me the story of how you became a boxer", each one, in some way or another, referred to the physical element and to body sculpting as part of their original motivation.

Crafted, 'hard' bodies represented status in the gym, but more importantly, they represented control. Coward (1984:229) claims that a 'body defined is a body controlled'. Those in the gym who could withstand pain such as that suffered by Eric, or those who dedicated their lives to professions that required physical sculpting, were seen as men in control. If a boxer could control his body, he could craft it, thereby demonstrating his competence, his skill, his status. It is a culture that takes physicality as the primary definer of masculinity (Connell 1995). If the men in this study could demonstrate a sense of control over their bodies, then they felt more in control of their lives, particularly for those who felt disempowered by structural forces, such as the job market or the criminal justice system:

> 'Can't get a job coz of my criminal record, so I help out at the gym, Marcus lets me train for free if I mop once a week and sort out the glove box and stuff, helps me save on subs and that, and I get to work out everyday - keep myself in shape, keep myself sane!' (Baz, 38 years old, amateur)

> 'I have to work out otherwise I'd go mad, when my body feels good, I feel good, and it helps my mood.' (Jonny, 19 years old, professional)

Eric felt he had "something to prove", having been diagnosed with chronic asthma as a child, whereas Marcus "needed to train", having left school and merely "hanging on the streets with the boys". Ricky and Jonny felt that being a professional boxer was all they had going for them, whereas Frank sought the sanctuary of the gym to escape the "drama outside". Each of them relied on their physical capital as a means to make money or to reconstruct themselves in a new light. The gym was viewed as the place to do that – a place where they could hone and sculpt a new identity, physically, structurally and mentally. These elements of reconstruction, combined with the control and sense of determinism that boxing provided, contributed to the gym being a site of enduring appeal for those in attendance.

Boxing's appeal: dedication, reconstruction and bodywork

Sacrifice and monastic devotion are touted as the way to achieve success in the boxing gym. Men could be often heard discussing how, if they "put in the work, there's no way I can lose" (Ricky, 20 years old, professional). The professionals, in particular, were vocal about their dedication and determination to win, and Ricky often posed in the mirror-lined gym and bellowed how he was unstoppable, particularly if he "kept training and getting up at 6am to run every day", while also "sparring three times a week".

Jonny, a young professional like Ricky, also disclosed that he would get up earlier than the rest of the professionals to go running, because he wanted to "be the best", and also how "boxing ain't like a job but a hobby you get paid for". Indeed, being the best was everything to these men, and the culture of competition in the gym was widespread. Everyone wanted their photograph to adorn the walls, so they could join the ranks of the professionals before them, or become famous like Tyson, Lennox Lewis or Muhammad Ali. Members of the gym saw success as being achievable through hard work – hard bodily work – and it seemed that the more you were able to do physically, the better chance you had at making it. The trainers encouraged this sentiment, and often joked that they would lock the boxers in the gym and "have a fight to the death to prove who was the best". As would be expected, the boxers absorbed this ethos, and occasionally could be heard placing bets on who would "walk out of the gym alive".

Competition motivated these men. Everyone wanted to be better than everyone else. There was a real fear among gym members of being humiliated or ostracised for being weak, and the boxing gym worked to this hierarchy. The framework was based on bodily success: who can go the most rounds, who can do the most chin-ups in a timed minute, and who has the most feared reputation.

This idea of reputation was also prominent in the gym culture, and there was a tacit understanding, an unspoken code. Trainers were usually in charge. One in particular, called Marcus, collected the money. He exuded a sense of control and command in the gym. His photograph was on the wall next to the ring, and he still embodied the same physical capital as he had done in his earlier days as a professional boxer. This was achieved by countless hours "on the weights", particularly if there was a professional bout due (even though he was not on the bill), and he was known to come in and train during the night.

Appearance and physical bulk were important in this milieu, as were symbols such as cars, tattoos and jewellery.[2] They all seemed to symbolise success for these men, and most of them coveted these symbols, if they did not already possess them. Nonetheless, bodily capital took precedence. Muscles, bulk and endurance seemed to be worth more in the gym environment than any ostentatious asset. Men dieted obsessively, particularly if there was a fight coming up, and there was always a queue for the scales, as men lined up to check their daily weight. Food and nutrition were discussed regularly, and it was not uncommon to hear how men would starve themselves prior to a bout. Drying out was also another technique, whereby men would starve themselves of water to lose a few extra pounds prior to weighing in. Not making the weight was a real fear, because that meant that the fight could potentially be cancelled, and the purse taken elsewhere. Hence, men equated bodily capital with financial gain. For many, this bodily manipulation and destruction felt like the only way to succeed. Bodies became these men's prized assets, and yet, underneath the bravado and valour, there was a deep fear of injury and/or death.

The somatic culture of the boxing gym formed part of a wider masculine discourse that informed men on how to behave, how to endure and, most importantly, how to be male. It embodied competition, fearlessness and lack of intimacy, commonly seen traits in masculine sporting discourses (Sabo 1986; Messner 1990). Additionally, it further served to create a gulf between what it means to be masculine and what it means to be feminine, as men relied on 'biology ideology' (Lorber 1993) and notions of the stronger sex to assist in the making of their masculinity. As Matthews (2014:12) states in his ethnography of boxing: 'ideas about biology were used to explain difference between men, thus enabling a "scientific" explanation of caricatured and stereotypical notions about "outsider groups"'.

Boxing's appeal: competition and the accomplishment of masculinity

In the gym, men invested in traditional versions of masculinity that evoked gender binaries and ideas of a stronger sex. For example, quite a few of the members seemed perturbed at my presence, or acted as if I simply was not there. In my opinion, this was to maintain a sense of gender difference, as boxers constantly distanced themselves from anything classified as feminine. Femininity in this arena implied softness, maternity and vulnerability, and this was to be avoided at all costs.

As a result, the construction of boxing became one that depended heavily on binary oppositions, especially those between men and women, arguably supporting essentialist claims to exclusivity. Work by Woodward (2004) supports this claim, discussing how boxing remains forever rooted in a binary logic, and is therefore constructed around a resistance to any rhetoric of gender transgression. These theories were illuminated in my research, as men openly discussed their disdain for women's boxing:

> 'Nah man, I'm not into that. Women should be admired and appreciated as opposed to bust-up and beaten.' (Marcus, 42 years old, professional trainer)
>
> 'I'm a traditional man me, don't like women fighting and that, I should be the one to protect them not the other way around, know what I'm saying.' (Frank, 31 years old, bouncer and amateur boxer)
>
> 'If women wanna box then let 'em, they'll soon go back to pilates when they realise how hard this is ...' (Baz, 38 years old, amateur boxer)

Women were discussed in ways that construed them as opposites – fragile and maternal – and a lot of the men did not believe that women should box. This dualistic thinking pervaded all aspects of the sport, not only in the gym but also in the national press at the time. Amir Khan, one of Britain's best-known boxers, was also not in favour: "'deep down I think women shouldn't fight, that's my opinion. When you get hit it can be very painful ... women can get knocked out'" (*The Guardian* 2012).

Boxing might present as being traditionally masculine, yet the inclusion of women's boxing in the Olympics of 2012 was a historical moment when this traditional version may have been challenged

Regardless, this was worrying for some men in the gym during the course of my research:

> 'For women, boxing is too physical. Women shouldn't box because of their wombs and everything. Women are a lot different than men. I would rather they didn't do it.' (Marcus, 42 years old, professional trainer)
>
> 'Women's boxing in the Olympics? Are you having a fucking laugh?' (Baz, 38 years old, amateur boxer)

It became imperative to the success of this research, to explore the ways that men constructed meanings associated with gender and violence, and how this positioned them both structurally and subjectively. All too often in this research, men in the boxing gym could be heard speaking in ways that asserted dominance of women and each other. On more than one occasion, I heard references to "pussies", "girls" and "bitches", with the former being the most common – and the most likely to provoke retaliation. This is because it refers to a woman's genitalia, and in the male homosocial world of sport, it becomes an emasculating term that serves to separate the weak from the strong. To be classified as "someone's bitch" in this hyper-masculine arena also relates to masculine discourses surrounding sexuality, and literally means to get "fucked" by one's opponent – in the sense of being beaten as opposed to penetrated. This term was mainly spoken by the professionals and in reference to an upcoming opponent's presumed defeat. For example, Ricky stated that he was "going to make him my bitch", and then proceeded to laugh along with the other boxers.

Known as 'banter', this idea of joking around in the boxing gym was actually a proliferation of discourses in the gender order, and ultimately, a perpetuation of men's dominance over women. Curry (1991) discusses how insults and jibes are a kind of verbal jousting and are representative of men's friendships in sporting cultures. Klein (1986) posits that many of the men in his study of Mexican baseball players used jokes and jibes as 'weapons'. Messner (1992) also argues that relationships between teammates are characterised by an 'antagonistic cooperation' that is predicated on competition and domination. Through the medium of language, male athletes can bond, while concomitantly keeping intimacy at arm's length. It is usually at the expense of others – women, gay men and ethnic minorities – and this was evidenced not only through verbal interactions in the boxing gym, but also through the choice of music men chose to train to. Misogynistic hip-hop was usually played, and the trainer regulated the choice of music. His taste in music could usually be relied upon to have derogatory terms directed at women and gay men, and all too often had references to violence and revenge in the songs.[3]

Competitiveness was inherent in the gym, and successful competition regulated men's relationships with the world and each other. Competition among men develops hierarchy, and is deeply embedded in social structures of gender, race and class, especially with the cultural meanings accorded to masculinity (Willis 1977; Messerschmidt 1993; Jump 2017). Marcus, the prominent trainer in the gym, illuminates this point, as he stated that "competition breeds competition" among men, and it was this factor above all others that maintained his interest in attending.

According to Connell (1995:54): 'Men's greater sporting prowess has become a theme of backlash against feminism, as it serves as symbolic proof of men's superiority and right to rule'. In linking embodied constructions of masculinity in structural concepts of patriarchy, Connell (1983:27) suggests that it is through a combination of both strength and skill that this is possible: 'what it means to be masculine is, quite literally, to embody force, to embody competence'. It is through a combination of strength and skill that the body can be symbolised as masculine, and arguably, nowhere else but in the discourse of boxing can this be so readily harnessed (Woodward 2007; Matthews 2014).

Connell (1995:54) writes that 'sport has come to be the leading definer of masculinity in mass culture', and for the men in this research it was certainly a method of accomplishing and reaffirming their masculinity. However, in the boxing gym, violence or the capacity for violence also formed part of men's gendered identity, and aggression and violence shown in the ring were permissible, whereby injuries had to be conceded as being part of the game. Messner (1990) discovered that men 'naturalised' their capacity for aggression and violence in sport, as the rewards and prestige placed upon athletes who demonstrated it in the pursuit of winning reinforced and created contexts in which violence became normalised (Smith 1974; Vaz 1980; Matthews 2014).

In the boxing gym, superfluous violence was rewarded with masculine kudos, and this was reinforced by nicknames such as 'Hardcore', 'Ruthless' and 'Ice' (due to the cold-heartedness shown in the ring). Indeed, men who demonstrated cold-heartedness or lack of empathy were seen as hard guys, and this lack of empathy was consistent throughout the gym, as men seemed intent on inflicting as much pain as possible in the pursuit of winning. Black eyes and cut lips would be worn with pride – because as much as losing is frowned upon, the *way* you lose is just as important. Men who lost with valour or demonstrated heart (courage) in the ring were not viewed as negatively as those who were knocked down or who threw in the towel.[4] To surrender or give up was viewed as emasculating, as much as not being able to withstand pain or defeat.

Wacquant (1995a:496) refers to this as 'the specific honor of the pugilist' and relates it to that of an ancient gladiator – a refusal to concede or back down. As previously mentioned, Sabo (1986) refers to this as the 'pain principle', a concept with huge significance in terms of the structure and value of the boxing world. Any boxer who quits in the middle of a fight is branded with the mark of infamy and suffers a kind of symbolic death, as non-compliance to the principle of pain can result in ostracisation, and reduces those who concede to 'pussy' or 'bitch' status; pejorative terms that relate to feminine softness and inferior sexuality.

The subjective understandings that men have in relation to aggression and violence are observable in the boxing gym. Among the men in this study, identities were often predicated on violence and its potential enactment. Often, violence was used as a weapon – in combination with language – and without being openly aware of the success of the professionals, one quickly understood who was revered and who was feared.

Tattoos were also symbolic in the gym, as they acted as further trophies in men's successful quest for body modification. Interestingly, Sanders (1989) refers to this as 'permanent bodily alteration' that allows one to redefine one's identity and position in social classifications. Most of the boxers' artwork comprised religious iconography with quotes that held religious meaning, even though none of the participants ever disclosed being religious. The quotes usually related to endurance-promoting mantras or to their relatives' names – usually the children of the men themselves, further promoting their virility and sexual potency. More than one member had a pair of boxing gloves tattooed onto their arm. When asked what his tattoos symbolised, Ricky (20 years old) replied: 'I pray to the god of boxing, me mate'. Wacquant (2004:100) stated in his ethnographic work that: 'The gym is to boxing what the church is to religion, becoming a boxer, training for a fight is a little like entering a religious order'. Indeed, men rose early on Sundays to run, and many took the ethos of boxing as seriously as they would a faith.[5]

Like religion, the homology of boxing is predicated on the notion of sacrifice, as it is widely believed in boxing circles that the more you sacrifice, the better chance you have of winning and ascending into the highest ranks. The notion of sacrifice in boxing reinforced a sense of control among men, as they invested in sporting discourses that proclaimed that 'without pain, there is no gain', thus sanctioning and perpetuating wider masculine structures that dictate that success is predicated on competition, endurance and bodily capital. As James Gilligan (1996:96) writes in *Violence: Reflections on our Deadliest Epidemic:* 'People will willingly sacrifice their bodies if they perceive it as the only way to avoid "losing face"'.

> 'The fight is won in the gym, not in the ring, coz the fight is with yourself, and when you walk into that squared circle knowing that you have given up everything to win, then you win.' (Marcus, 42 years old, professional trainer)

> 'I knew I just had to keep hitting him, if I could just keep doing that then I had a shot at winning, I wasn't gonna stop.' (Eric, 51 years old, trainer).

This mentality of competition being inherent in boxing further perpetuated men's decisive triumph over their own bodies (Connell 1990), serving to reinforce discourses that talk of physiques only having meaning when deployed in the act of winning. The will to win, or 'fight with yourself', did not merely arise from personal 'drive' – familiar words often bandied around in sport arenas – but more from a social structure of sporting competition that serves to perpetuate a gender order in which it resides comfortably.

In order to properly conceptualise the masculinity/boxing relationship, it is important to stipulate that most men enter this social world already aware of their gender identity and positioning. Judith Butler (1999) posits that gender is merely 'performance' and always in a developmental process that unfolds in a social context. The boxing gym thus proved to be a fascinating context in which to examine the performance and unfolding of masculine gender identity – particularly as it is distinguished from femininity, which is construed as its psychic opposite. Yet enactment was often contradictory, as this traditional masculinity was also haunted by frailty and failure; the sculpted, hard male body that largely contributes to discourses surrounding traditional masculinity always has to negotiate the frailty and failure that characterises boxing (Woodward 2004).

While not necessarily appealing, the masculinities that are carved out in this sport are always contradictory, vulnerable and fractured. The risk of injury in boxing is so high, that the ability to degenerate from beautiful to grotesque is a slippery slope that boxers are more than aware of (Woodward 2004). As (Connell 1995:54) posits: 'The constitution of masculinity through bodily performance means that gender is vulnerable when the performance cannot be sustained – for instance, as a result of physical disability'. More often than not, this idea was evidenced through boxers' stories detailing suicidal thoughts, when unable to perform due to injury. After suffering defeat as a result of a broken wrist, Eric (see Chapter 4) stated that he felt as if he had lost his "ability to be a man", and also described feeling suicidal at the time. Sal a prominent boxer, now a trainer, detailed this sense of vulnerability after a street attack that left him in a wheelchair for six months:

> 'The assault stopped me turning pro - it was my dream - so I went through all the usual, feeling suicidal you know, I didn't have anything. It sounds dead shambolic but until that happened I was living with a Page 3 Girl [glamour model] and had a Sierra Cosworth [sports car]. You know, I was living the lifestyle - sports cars and fighting at the top level, then when that happened, it was just like hmmmm. I hit rock bottom.' (Sal, 42 years old, retired professional boxer and trainer)

With these vignettes in mind, it is fair to state that the appealing elements of the gym are related to the masculinity that could be achieved through 'bodywork' – through physical capital and commitment to the pain principle (Sabo 1986). This was further supported by heteronormative banter, and a psychological distancing from anything classified as feminine. Physical hardness was valourised, as was mental toughness. Men demonstrated their capabilities in these areas by investing in competitive bodywork and endurance tests. Additionally, money, status, fame and muscle all contributed to the appeal and masculine discourses inherent in the gym culture, further allowing for men to perform their masculinity in conventional ways.

Woodward (2004:7) posits that: 'Boxing invokes hegemonic masculinity'. This is further expressed by Joyce Carol Oates (1987:72), when she writes: 'No two men can occupy the same space at the same time, boxing is for men, and is about men, and is men'. What is crucial in both Woodward's and Oates' accounts of male boxing are the competitive, hierarchical masculinities it fosters. Masculinity involves more than a series of iterative gendered actions, as masculinities enacted at the gym are also embodied. They involve a strong investment in traditional corporeal masculinity (Connell 1985, 1995) – traditional in the sense that muscle size, heterosexuality and the ability to 'risk the body in performance' (Feldman 1991; Lyng 1998) are classified as the ultimate indices of manhood and hardness.

Accordingly, the appeal of the boxing gym is grounded in a sense of hardness. This is evidenced by famous names such as 'Iron Mike Tyson', or 'Hands of Stone Duran' – boxing pseudonyms that evoke a sense of hardness, coldness and industry. To say that one boxes, is to say that one is hard; it is to say that you are made with materials that are infallible and not easy to break. This sense of hardness coexists with a sense of manliness – a sense of industry and toil – reminiscent of working-class masculinities and their associations with heavy industry and visceral cultures (Bathrick 1990; Hall 1997; Winlow 2001).

In short, boxing as an occupation carries weight in masculine working-class communities. These are communities built on the use of the physical body as a method not only to negotiate one's masculinity, but also to negotiate one's income and social standing. For the men in this study, who predominantly heralded from these cultures, boxing was a conduit for accomplishing masculinity, when other channels seemed blocked. It served as a career option for the talented among the sample; and for others, it acted as a safety net, when chaos and disruption threatened to enfold their lives.

Indeed, boxing's appeal is a combination of both these things: a masculine homosocial world that reinforces gender binaries; and a reinforcement of working-class habitus ideals that the majority of these men were familiar with. It is thus appealing for these very reasons – money, status, fame and action – and the ability to craft physical capital, when the potential to accrue social capital is somewhat limited. The boxing gym is therefore viewed as an important site for men, and one that encapsulates a host of meanings for those who attend.

On a deeper, perhaps less conscious level of understanding by its participants, it is further used as a site that allows men to overcome some form of personal or structural vulnerability, and it is to this fascinating element that I turn next.

Boxing as a response to personal and structural vulnerability

One of the most important themes in the masculinity/sport equation is the overall relationship that men have towards intimacy. As de Garis (2002:100) has argued, boxing is appealing because it provides a site of acceptable 'somatic intimacy', that allows for 'cooperative sharing which is intimate, shared and familial'. For some men in this study, boxing provided 'brothers' and 'second fathers' in the shape of peers and trainers. Boxing therefore demonstrated an emotional attachment through terms that clearly speak of the protective and nurturing functions it possesses for them, while providing a safe place to express feelings of friendship, companionship and camaraderie:

> 'Don't know where I'd be without the gym, it's like family to me.' (Jonny, 19 years old, professional)
>
> 'I come to the gym on Christmas day to say a prayer for Paul [deceased trainer and former father figure] before I go home to my other family.' (Marcus, 42 years old, professional trainer).

In the main, however, participation was also fractured by an inherent sense of competition and a fear of intimacy and femininity. Messner (1990), among others (see Chodorow 1978; Rubin 1982), argues that these levels of intimacy create ambivalence, and while craved and accepted in the rule-bound structure of sport, the attachments formed also constitute a major threat to psychological boundaries around fragile masculine identities (Chodorow 1978).

Gilligan (1996) claims that males tend to perceive vulnerability alongside the possibility of violence in situations of close affiliation, and interestingly, the majority of men in this piece suffered some form of violence, usually at the hands of their fathers. This ambivalence towards intimacy therefore became inherent in most of these men's social interactions, including their sporting experiences. While men expressed companionship in familial terms, there was always a perceived distance that protected the boxers from becoming too intimate – too vulnerable.

> 'Boxing teaches you that you're on your own in life, it's the same as the ring man, when you step out, you step out alone, and when you go down you go down alone.' (Marcus, 42 years old, professional trainer)

Conversely, de Garis (2002:97) posits that: 'The gym is a "safe" place to express intimacy because the textual representations of boxing as masculine and violent deter allegations of weakness or femininity'. In my study, men refrained from discussing any intimate concerns, unless it provided a further opportunity to buttress a sense of masculine pride and reinforce their standing in the gender order. Women were often the targets of the men's intimate concerns, as participants would openly discuss chastising their wives and girlfriends for any form of challenge or complaint.[6] One of the professional boxers, recently separated from his partner, often talked about the arguments he had surrounding childcare, and he could be counted on to disparage his partner as a result. He felt that it was a woman's job to care for their child, and struggled to comprehend that childcare was also his responsibility, particularly when it affected his "training schedule".

In the boxing world, individuals' roles and separate positions in hierarchical structures are determined by competition in a clearly defined system that governs interactions and relationships. In the boxing gym, members would push the boundaries to gain any advantage over an opponent, but would always demonstrate regard for the rules in the game. Messner (1990) posits that this is part of a system, or code of conduct, that places safe boundaries around their aggression and their relationship with others. To not have these rules in sport – particularly boxing – would result in chaos on both physical and psychological levels, as there would be an 'incredibly frightening need to constantly negotiate and renegotiate relationships' (Messner 1990). Nevertheless, intimacy *in* the rule-bound structure of sport feels relatively safe to those who participate, and in some respects the boxing gym provided a relatively comfortable context in which to develop a certain kind of relationship with other men.

However, forms of interaction in this gym were devoid of *visible* emotion and were therefore rarely authentic. This was evidenced by one participant, Derek, disclosing that when he was diagnosed with testicular cancer, he felt unable to discuss this with other gym members, and as a result, he left the gym for over two years until he had recuperated. This undoubtedly reinforces Connell's earlier words (Connell 1990) around how disabilities and illnesses contradict the constitution of masculinity – so much so in this case, that Derek felt unable to disclose his cancer to his gym peers. As a result of Derek's experience, it seemed that intimacy was only permissible when it perpetuated discourses in the gender order. This was more than evident in the gym. Those members who breached this tacit agreement were chided and referred to as "pussies", particularly if the situation under discussion involved altercations with female partners or other men who did not box.

There was an unspoken code in the boxing gym, which dictated that members should not carry their daily trivialities into the gym with them, and least of all vocalise any sensitive issues in relation to love, work or family obligations. This was constantly reinforced with verbal cues that shouted: 'Leave your personal shit at the door', and posters displaying text that stated: 'Discipline involves the mind as well as the body'. Indeed, Wacquant (2004:37) posits that: 'Everything takes place as if a tacit pact of nonaggression governed interpersonal relations and ruled out any topic of conversation liable to threaten this "playful form of association", hamper the smooth functioning of daily individual exchanges, and thereby endanger the specific masculine subculture that the gym perpetuates'.

However, most of the men interviewed in this piece spoke fondly of the gym, and many discussed how boxing had acted as some kind of salvation; usually salvation from crime, but more often than not, salvation from vulnerability. For these men, vulnerability took the form of divorce (although this was rarely discussed) or re-entry after periods of imprisonment.[7] Yet more often than not, this sense of vulnerability tacitly focused on the prevention of repeat victimisation. Notably, most men in this study had suffered some form of physical or emotional abuse throughout their formative years – either through familial abuse or peer bullying – and at least eight of the ten men interviewed disclosed that physical violence had been present throughout the lives from an early age:

> 'It was crazy, the whole thing was crazy. I could write a book about living in that environment. There was a situation that I will never forget, and my brother will never forget it either because my dad beat my brother so bad that he nearly killed him. And you know why? Because he forgot to polish his boots for work.' (Eric, 51 years old, boxing trainer)

> 'Errr it's difficult to say things about my dad. The "tough love" that he showed me growing up you know, as an ex-marine. I don't know. I feared him. I feared him. I think there is only me and my brother on our street who didn't have a criminal record, and I think that's part of being hit and the fear of my dad.' (Sal, 42 years old, retired boxer)

> 'My dad liked to drink didn't he, you know what I mean? But he wouldn't even know now that he used to hit me, he would have forgot.' (Leroy, 32 years old, professional boxer)

> 'Did I respect my parents when I was born? No. Because there was times when I was disobedient you know what I'm saying? But when they beat the shit out of me, I feared them then didn't I.' (Frank, 31 years old, boxer)

For these men, violence had been so diffused throughout their lives, or had taken such similar and recurring patterns, that it had simply become part of what life was like for them. The violence was emotional and physical, and more often than not involved the father. Only one of the participants had no further contact with his father, while the remainder seemed to accept their father's abuse as simply a way of life, with Frank stating that, "It never did me no harm, toughened me up it did". Interestingly, most of the respondents took up the sport of boxing in their early teenage years, when the abuse was at its peak, and *every* one of them believed that boxing had played a significant role in the formation of their identity.

From an early age, violence formed part of these men's habitus – an aspect of inherited culture in their daily lives that almost goes without saying. Indeed, this habitus of violence operated on a deeper level than rational ideology and became embedded in their sense of self. Moreover, boxers are required to understand the complex interactive preludes and precursors of violence, and this, combined with practical occupational considerations, allowed violence to become entrenched in these men's self-concepts.

This is clearly the case in the habitus of boxers, as many have already incorporated violence into their own sense of self. Accordingly, when faced with conflict, violence becomes confirmed and underlined as both an obligation and an expectation (Tedeschi and Felson 1994). The men in this study defined themselves with violence – saw it as part of their everyday life – so much so, that some participants would return from road-running, having been involved in an impromptu street fight and with no comprehension that this may be illicit:

> 'I'll bang that cunt out if he talks to me like that again, sat on the wall like a dickhead outside, while I'm in here trying to get ready for next Saturday's fight.' (Jonny, 19 years old, professional)

This identity as a 'fighter', shaped men like Jonny, and also acted as a crutch in times of personal danger and uncertainty. Ricky, another young professional, defined the outlook of a fighter as someone "more than willing to physically fight if the occasion arises". He described himself as a "fighter at heart" and was prepared to "physically fight anyone you put in front of me". It later transpired that the reasons why he chose to hone this identity was as a result of being small when he had to move to secondary school:

> 'Most people understand that if they are scared of you they won't push you, they won't mess around with you, they won't annoy, they won't test you. You know what I mean?

> They won't take the piss out of you; you know what I mean? If they are a bit wary of you, they will move onto the next person so they don't have a real fight on their hands. That's why I did a lot of my fighting; it was to make a statement at secondary school. Basically, I'm not a big lad so it was more a "don't fuck with me kinda thing". And it worked. Errr, quite quickly, you saw other kids getting dragged about in the corridors and all that. No-one used to drag me.' (Ricky)

Boxing therefore became attractive to such men, as it not only spoke a language they were already familiar with, but it also acted as a physical defence mechanism, when their lives became unreliable, disrupted or threatened. Sullivan (1950, 1953) called these defence mechanisms 'security operations', a way to reduce feelings of psychological anxiety when confronted with events that threaten one's identity. Defence mechanisms consist of thoughts or behaviours aimed at returning a sense of security and power to the ego (Sullivan 1950); thus, engaging in confrontations is thought to be one such 'security operation', as individuals can challenge another's behaviour or assertions towards them. These confrontations allow men to draw upon an inherited cultural framework that places violence central to their own sense of self, and to use it as a personal resource that informs and advises social interaction and performance (Hobbs et al 2003).

Seen in this way, feelings of inadequacy can be defended against by enacting violence, as individuals attempt to defend a specific self-image, so as to avoid feelings of inferiority and weakness. Behaving aggressively can be an especially important defence mechanism for individuals who feel that access to alternative ways of demonstrating their social worth is limited (Gilligan 1996; Bourgois 1996; Anderson 1999). This was an important point in the research. For men like Ricky, boxing not only "paid the bills", but it further allowed him to invest in physical capital – he could deposit muscle in the bank as well as money. This depositing mechanism contributed to the eradication of feelings of low self-worth associated with financial and masculine insecurities. In fact, a lot of the men in the gym reported starting out from a limited structural position, confirming this appealing aspect of the gym. This idea is further compounded in work by Andrew Tolson (1977), when he suggests that the accomplishment of masculinity is formally based in the attainment of a wage.

Whereas regular attendance at the gym more or less guaranteed Ricky's wage, it was the gruelling workouts and his muscular frame that gave him a real sense of power. This is because his muscular frame eradicated a sense of fear and inferiority. As Ricky attested earlier, the muscular armour that boxing produced, protected and defended him against others, when he was at school. Similarly, for men like Eric, the original appeal of boxing resided in his need to "prove himself", and later in life became a way to stand up to his abusive father. For Frank, boxing's appeal resided in his need to "escape the streets", and it ultimately carved him out a career in the night-time economy. For men like Sal, and many others, boxing was a way to establish a new identity, as his story told of bullying taunts at school as a result of being overweight:

> 'I was the fat kid weren't I? All that shit with my dad made me find safety in food, wasn't until I started boxing that the weight started to come off, then the bullying stopped! Ha!' (Sal, 42 years old, retired professional boxer and trainer)

Undoubtedly, the boxing gym provided a place of security for the majority of men in this study. It became, in Wacquant's (2004) words, 'an island of order and stability' for those who attended. The gym provided structure and companionship to men both young and old from the surrounding area, while acting as a place of salvation when "things were bad at home" (Leroy, 32 years old). Some men discussed how some of the trainers had become father figures and significant others to them in times of need, and also how having a purpose and structure in their lives had distinguished them from other young people hanging around on the streets:

> 'I walked into the gym, and my coach was there, he has been at the gym for 55 years now, and we basically just developed a relationship from there, I became part of the family.' (Sal, 42 years old, retired boxer/trainer)

> 'I stopped going to school in the end … didn't bother with my exams or anything, my life became about boxing, it changed everything I did, because I'm not academic me, and I thought … I used to watch boxing and all that, and when I was leaving school I thought what am I going to do? And I thought I'm going to box - that's it - I'm going to box.' (Leroy, 34 years old, professional)

It was also common to hear how boxing had "saved" men's lives, and without it they believed they would have either been "in jail" or "dead", with some of the men who had been previously imprisoned stating that boxing also "kept them out":

> 'Started boxing in jail, nothing else to do like, it helped me stay focused when I came out, stay away from the scene and all that - start over.' (Baz, 38 years old, amateur)

> 'If I hadn't started boxing when I did I reckon I'd be dead by now, either that or in jail for something serious.' (Ricky, 20 years old)

In the main, however, each of the participants interviewed demonstrated some form of vulnerability, an anxiety relating to a previous or potential violent attack. For many, their life story was one in which they experienced problematic family relationships, became involved in criminal activities, felt stigmatised and excluded, and doubted their abilities outside the realm of boxing. In describing their childhoods and lives, many of the respondents appeared to be struggling with memories of major family disruption – violence, in particular, was reported as an issue – and this resulted in feelings of betrayal, distrust, insecurity and inadequacy. Others recalled being rejected by parents and significant others, and many of these men reported feeling abandoned and abused, which led them to feel unsure of their social status and/or self-worth:

> 'When I was at home I had to be a soldier, I'd say my dad didn't have a son - he had a soldier. I got love off my mum, but my dad was in charge and that was just the way it was. So what I got from the gym was men who knew how to fight - knew how to look after themselves, but could let that "toughness" be something else. They just looked after me, gave me [a] hug, spoke to me like an adult and cared for me. Whereas my dad, he served 22 years in the Marines - tough love - he's just that kind of man.' (Sal, 42 years old, retired professional boxer and trainer)

> 'Having a dad as a boxer, seeing him come home with black eyes and all that, you know as a kid, and I would say: "What's up?" And he'd been beat, or he'd won, you know … it just wasn't something that I took to as a kid or anything. I know some things go over your head as a kid …. He never used to be just like, "come 'ere", or give us a hug or anything. He was too strong.' (Leroy, 34 years old, professional boxer)

> 'Paul the trainer was my second dad, he picked me up off the street and turned me into a professional. He's dead now, and not a day goes by that I don't think about him and everything he did for me.' (Marcus, 42 years old, professional trainer)

Boxing and the significant others present in the gym therefore provided a medium to alleviate both Sal's and Leroy's anxieties. By providing an activity for both these men to invest in, it allowed them to replace feelings of weakness with feelings of pride, valour, competitiveness and self-worth. For men like Sal and Leroy, becoming a boxer meant becoming somebody.

Boxing further provided opportunities to convert physical capital into financial capital, when other avenues were perceived as blocked. Marcus often spoke of how boxing and his coach gave him "a chance", as prior to boxing he had:

> 'Never been nothing, never done nothing, just hanging on the streets with my boys.' (Marcus, 42 years old, professional trainer)

In the main, feelings of powerlessness associated with being a victim of abuse, or structural disadvantage, led some of the men to attempt to resist and/or replace these feelings of powerlessness and victimhood with feelings of power and control. This idea, in their eyes at least, could be obtained by overcoming another in the ring, or accruing trophies and belts that proved they had 'made it'. Physical force among these men was regarded as a 'natural' drive, a way to secure rewards, particularly those that seemed unobtainable by more conventional methods (Cloward and Ohlin 1960). As Ricky often stated: "I'm a fighter at heart". Indeed, this idea of violence being 'at heart' – and therefore beyond the responsibility of the individual – was characteristic of boxers as a social group.

As a result, boxers were not only well equipped to respond in the face of perceived threats, but also felt obligated to respond socially to an apparently biological compulsion. This was often used as an excuse for violence, as it located it in a seemingly 'inevitable frame' (Rubinstein 1973). The men in this study further believed that boxing was their 'way out', but I sensed it was also a way to not 'look in'. Therefore, boxing allowed men to bury fear behind walls of muscle, and invest in a discourse that repudiates intimacy. By shunning this intimacy, and investing in discourses surrounding competition, bodily endurance and virility, men were able to distance themselves from the idea of 'victim' – the feminine other. They were able to create a space that allowed them to dictate what level of intimacy was permissible, whether that be 'sparring' (de Garis 2002) or simply having somewhere to 'hang out'.

In terms of genuineness, the intimacy was staged. It never deviated from the masculine script. It merely replicated intimacy that one might see outside the gym, confirming and maintaining their position in the gender order. Indeed, vulnerability meant 'victim' to most men in this research, and having adopted this subject position previously in their lives, most made sure that they would never return. Boxing therefore allowed men to invest in both bodily and structural discourses that eradicated any sense of vulnerability – so much so, that presenting themselves as invincible became embedded in their psychic economy; it became written in their mind as well as on their body.

Summary

I have discussed in depth how the appeal of boxing encompasses many different elements for those who participate. I have presented data that reflects on boxing's enduring appeal from a structural perspective in terms of money, fame, status and action (Goffman 1967), and have examined how the gym came to be seen as a medium by which to obtain all of these.

I have then outlined how the gym was viewed as a place of reconstruction, a site of development for men in both structural and embodied terms, as men consistently employed the sport of boxing as way to craft both a body and a self-concept that fits with an overarching masculine ideal – an ideal that is transposable between both gym and working-class habitus mores, from which the majority of these men herald.

Finally, I have illustrated how these men's journeys have changed, and how boxing is not merely a response to material and structural deprivation, but also protects and ensures the prevention of repeat victimisation. Boxing acted as an 'island of stability and order' (Wacquant 2004), when delinquency and disorder threatened it. This could either be structural constraints, in terms of class, race and gender, or through the prevention of further victimisation via parent or peer physical abuse.

Thus, boxing carries a host of different meanings for different participants. These meanings, while portrayed in a serious manner, also reflected a hidden anxiety – an anxiety inherent in masculine sporting cultures that threatens the structure of the male self (Messner 1990; Kreager 2007). Physical identity via the 'production of bodies' (Wacquant 2004) was culturally sanctioned in the gym as a way to achieve success; yet, the notion of sacrifice was less about control and free will than about the management of anxiety.

To invest as heavily as the men did in this study – classifying boxing as their 'life' – led me to believe that something *more than* investment in bodily and structural discourses motivated these men. Jefferson (1998:78) posits that: 'It is about representations of the masculine body *and* their psychic underpinnings; for without the latter it is impossible to comprehend how masculine body imagery has sufficient affect to be reproduced across the generations'. Indeed, with each participant in this study, a sense of vulnerability and hyper-vigilance towards violence was present. Boxing somehow served as a defence mechanism against this, whereby investing in the very masculine discourses that combat sports perpetuate, men were able to defend successively against feelings of anxiety, vulnerability and femininity.

The masculine identities forged in the boxing gym were a process of establishing boundaries around traditional masculinity and dealing with some of the anxieties that beset masculinity. Boxing therefore became subjectively ingrained in the fabric of these men's lives – "the boxing bug" – as one professional described it, almost disease-like and difficult to relinquish. Furthermore, boxing had a certain *romance* to it that cannot be explained away by ecological antecedents and financial difficulties. The 'route out of the ghetto thesis' (Bourgois 1996; Wacquant 2004) became too simplistic and overdetermined, as the investments made by the men in this research went beyond structural discourses surrounding poverty and just 'making millions'.

I therefore argue that the investments made by these men in the sport of boxing ran deeper into their psychic make-up than mere lack of career opportunities. In truth, it formed part of their identities as fighters and as boxers, ultimately helping to construct a new sense of self more in line with exalted masculine ideals – a self that could never be shamed or humiliated again, and least of all victimised.

Notes

1 Not dissimilar to Katz's (1988) work on 'being alien – not being here for you', as a way to create fear among others.

2 Feminist theorists, such as Faludi (1999), would argue that symbols constructed around celebrity and consumerism portray a 'crisis of masculinity', characterised by the replacement of a culture of useful production with a culture that is ornamental.

3 Artists such as Buju Banton and N.W.A. were among the play-list.

4 See headlines describing the defeat and retirement of Ricky Hatton: *The Guardian* (2012) "'I couldn't have done more.'– Ricky Hatton Retires with Pride', Sunday 25 November.

5 Alcohol was also off limits during fight training, as were sexual relations.

6 Reminiscent of the work of Holdaway (1983:122), when he discussed some of the views held by the British police: "If it wasn't a girl we would just thump her".

7 For a full discussion of boxing and re-entry, see Trimbur (2009).

7

Desistance and Boxing: The Ambivalence of the Gym

Introduction

In this chapter, I present the findings from my research and discuss in detail how participants viewed and engaged in violent behaviour. I do this by considering how violence has been present throughout these men's lives prior to beginning boxing, and also how the sport speaks to their identities in terms of an attendant culture of respect that evokes and traps some of them in habits of responding to violence. I argue that boxing, while incapacitating, offers nothing by way of cognitive transformation (Giordano et al 2002), as the identities of these men are too heavily invested in violence. Achieving status and being respected, combined with the hyper-masculine discourses present in the boxing gym, overrode theories of incapacitation and pro-social development. I present data to support these arguments.

I begin by discussing findings in relation to boxing as a site of incapacitation, followed by evidence suggesting that the gym only incapacitates men for the time that they are there, and does not wholly contribute to a change in violent attitudes when they are outside this setting. For some, then, boxing arguably creates as many (if not more) opportunities for extra-gym violence than those prevented by incapacitation in the gym. Controversially, boxing can often be more criminogenic than desistance promoting. If not delivered alongside person-centred approaches with adequately trained staff and conforming peers, boxing can do more harm than good. This is not always the populist view, and I appreciate the good that boxing can bring. However, I feel it is important to unpack the assumptions on which the proposed benefits of boxing are based by which boxing has often rode roughshod upon. It is all well and good to suggest that boxing teaches discipline and respect, but for whom and for how long? I address this question in this chapter.

The gym can be a site for pro-social development, and I reflect this point in a discussion around the gym's capacity to produce significant others in the form of peers and trainers. I demonstrate how trainers and peers can bond an individual to the gym, and that this element does have the potential to influence attendees' attitudes in both positive and negative ways. Notwithstanding, I present data to suggest that issues of status and respect take precedence among men who box, and that these concepts are vastly important to the men in this study – more so than the pro-social elements of the gym and its members.

Lastly, I discuss the ways in which the men would consistently justify both actual autobiographical violence and potential theoretical violence, using the boxers' core moral neutralisation techniques. This suggests that they had neither accepted responsibility for their acts, nor effected cognitive change in a way consonant with a secondary form of criminal desistance.

Boxing as a site of incapacitation

Incapacitation is commonly defined as restraint. It is a rationale for punishment, and renders convicted offenders incapable of committing further crimes over specific timeframes. Imprisonment is the most common method of incapacitation, yet electronic tagging is also considered incapacitating. Having said that, it is not just incarceration or the restriction of freedom that incapacitates one's time; sporting activities that divert individuals away from crime, at times when they may otherwise be involved, is also a popular method.

Since the 1960s, participation in sport has been articulated in several UK government policy statements as a form of positive incapacitation, and viewed as a vehicle for reducing crime and drug use among young people (Smith and Waddington 2004). Indeed, it was (and still is) proffered as a space and an activity that would engage young people at times when they otherwise might have been engaged in criminal or delinquent behaviour.

As discussed in Chapter 2 many organisations and charities offer meaningful activities to young people on the fringes of the criminal justice system, and this is not to be scoffed at. Yet, we need to transcend these *ad hominem* statements of how boxing saved men from lives of crime, and really unpick the processes by which the sport does this. I am under no illusion that boxing can – and does – offer young men a route out of criminogenic environments, yet when coupled with classic desistance literature, this is not always clear-cut.

Undoubtedly, boxing is a great 'hook for change' (Giordano et al 2002), yet how much further it can contribute to the desistance process is open to question. Giordano argues that hooks are essential for desistance, yet the cognitive transformative aspects that Giordano's theory requires for a more secondary prolonged period of desistance, is not fully realised in the sample of men in this present study. We can only presume that boxing as a 'hook for change' does not have a strong enough 'projective element' for men to direct their present and future concerns towards (Giordano et al 2002:1055 (emphasis in original)). Put more simply, for a 'hook' (that is, boxing) to be a successful inhibitor of crime, there needs to be a successful pro-social future outlook. In other words, the gym itself has to be a pro-social environment that steers young men into more positive desisting attitudes. This is what Maruna (2001:575) might refer to as a 'redemption script' – 'a story to redeem themselves of their past and to assert a meaningful future'. Boxing, with the best intentions, is not always capable of doing this.

In truth, voices in the gym resonated more with 'condemnation scripts' (Maruna 2001:575) – scripts that spoke of 'nothing left to lose', and a 'focus on happiness through consumption and material gain', as witnessed in the narrative of Ricky. Ricky discussed at length his desire to own the big house and the car, and to make the "mega bucks", while pointing out his lack of agency and ability to do anything but box.

Eric spoke of having "nothing left to lose", as he punched his way through pain to stardom, all the while living in fear of losing the fight money or letting the trainer down. This fight was more personal than professional, and the prestige awarded to men like Eric was equally as psychologically affirming as it was monetary. More importantly, the culture and habitus of pugilism does not always lend itself to the 'walking away' ethos of anti-violence sentiments seen in the 2019 #knifefree Home Office campaign. I would go so far as to say that trained fists are a mere replacement for a blade – potentially less damaging, but the same output.

Nonetheless, incapacitation theories remain relevant for aiding desistance. The most popular and most widely cited example being the Midnight Basketball programmes created in the US in the 1990s (see Hartmann 2001). The proponents of this scheme created the diversion specifically to incapacitate young men during the period between 10pm and 2am, when violent crime was at its hourly peak (Hartmann 2001). Yet, evidence for any effectiveness was weak, and the scheme lacked any kind of coherent and evidence-based theoretical rationale. It represented, at best: '[a]n immediate, practical response to a perceived social problem' (Hartmann 2001:353). Based on this assumption, it would seem that sport just occupies one's time, rather than consciously seeking to change one's attitude. It is therefore arguable that incapacitation theories, while relevant, do not offer a full explanation when it comes to understanding a process of change in criminality.

I argue that due to the sub-cultural ascetic dedication of boxing, incapacitation theories only work by absorbing men's time, and not necessarily as a positive restraint. During the course of this research, I observed that men would attend the boxing gym whenever possible, usually in the region of three times a week for amateurs and five times a week for professionals.[1] In fact, men would spend at least nine to ten hours a week in the gym and would fanatically devote their time to the sport. Regardless, in their personal lives outside the gym, attitudes and behaviours were less sacrificial, as the men in this study often reported that they did exactly what they liked outside the regimen of sport:

> 'In the gym I'm dedicated, I do what I'm told you know what I'm saying, outside I do what I like, ain't nobody out there who's gonna tell me what to do - only my trainer gets to do that.' (Jonny, 19 years old, professional boxer)

Boxing incapacitated these men on a regular basis and, taken at face value, it could be argued that their behaviour when in the gym was respectful and legal. Notwithstanding, my interest lay in their overall understanding of violence, and it became imperative to assess how they understood their own behaviour both in and outside the boxing gym. When in the gym, men would behave according to the rules. These rules ranged from waiting for your turn to be called to spar, sharing the equipment fairly, and not fighting outside legitimate sparring. The men adhered to these rules and the gym functioned like a well-oiled machine, with men tacitly obeying the guidelines and functioning as part of an overarching system. Interestingly, no one person was responsible for dictating the rules, yet the pugilists seemed to understand how the system functioned – in a way that was not dissimilar to Durkheim's theory of 'organic solidarity' (Durkheim 1973).

In the ring, boxers were expected to demonstrate courage, or "heart", as it was often referred to. This use of "heart" usually involved dominating opponents and psychologically "breaking them down". Yet outside the ring, there was an expectation of courteousness and patience as the men would politely wait for equipment, or patiently hold punching bags, while other men took their turn. Not once did I witness the breaking of any rules such as those stipulated earlier. It seemed as if the men complied with each other in this implicit Durkheimian system of interdependence and specialisation. Nevertheless, I soon came to realise, that the same principles did not necessarily apply in the outside world, or outside the realm of sport, and a more agitated, less patient, actor would begin to emerge.

Take Ricky, a young, 20-year-old professional, who had been in the gym since a teenager. Having been brought to the gym by his uncle for "anger problems", Ricky often referred to himself as a "natural born fighter". He felt that he made a good boxer, as a result of being a "scrapper" all his life, and that a violent upbringing gave him "grit" – the ability to withstand pain. Ricky often discussed how he would get involved in altercations when out with his mates. He discussed one particular incident with glee, an incident that had occurred after he had gone out to celebrate his "big win" the night before:

> 'A handful of lads we know are in this club we have gone to after the fight, they are all in one clique; one group. I've gone to the toilet and he started there in the toilets, just for me being a boxer you know what I mean? Because if they can beat me up they can say "I beat Ricky piece of piss", and if they don't, they can say "well what did you expect he's a boxer". Anyway, I've had to crack him before he cracked me because it's gonna go off! You can see it in their eyes and you're better off getting the first shot in so they go straight to sleep and you can get off sharpish.'

From this account, we can see that Ricky was committed to violent behaviour, as this was just one of many incidents that he disclosed. This predilection for violence is particularly evident when Ricky confessed to, "throwing the first shot" after a "big fight". Another incident that Ricky disclosed was part of a discussion we had at the side of the ring, clearly outlining the story of his friend, who was about to be attacked in a restaurant:

> 'We've had a few and I'm sat at this table, my girlfriend was there too. Some lad is staring at me from this other table, so my mate goes over and asks him what his problem is? I see this lad squeezing his bottle in his hand dead tight, so I run over and hit him - pow!'[2]

As the stories unfold, Ricky maintains that he behaves in this way to ensure victory and minimise injury, stating that it is important to "get in there first". I would argue that Ricky's act of violence was a strategy to maintain his identity and perceived respect as a boxer, as well as demonstrating his ability to win both in and outside the aegis of boxing. Indeed, Winlow (2001:45) has attested that, 'the maintenance of honour supplants all other concerns', and I could not agree more. Jack Katz (1988:130) often cites violence as a 'magical transformation' that 'brings comic-book symbolism to life'. I would go so far as to say that the sensuous attraction of violence was particularly heightened after Ricky's "big win".

In the confines of the gym, Ricky would never be faced with such a scenario, as the hierarchical structure dictates that as a professional he is at the top, and therefore respect is a given. Accordingly, Ricky does not have to demonstrate his potential for violence, as the structure of the gym supports his dominant, respected position. Outside these walls, Ricky feels as though "everyone wants a pop", and maintains that he has to be "on his guard" most of the time, demonstrating a hyper-vigilance to violent attacks common among the men in this sample:

> 'It's the same as school right, you gotta prove to others that you won't take no shit, you know what I'm saying? I went on the defence straight off when I changed schools to let people know that I wasn't someone to fuck with.'

According to Winlow (2001), a subliminal hierarchy is formed among certain groups of men, especially those who are attuned to incidences of violence. Such individuals will therefore place themselves in a pecking order, and use their knowledge of violence about others as yardsticks for competition and violent wagers. This idea was evident and transposable across both sites of gym and street, as men would literally gamble on who was the 'toughest' and 'who had beat who' previously. The men often came to the gym already familiar with this measuring tool, demonstrated by Ricky's quote. I would suggest that most men attuned to the habitus of the gym are versed in this particular language of violence.

However, when not surrounded by peers in the gym, Ricky would disclose that growing up was "tough". Changing schools was a traumatic experience for Ricky, so much so that he was excluded not long afterwards, and referred to a pupil referral unit for emotional and behavioural difficulties. It was at this point that his uncle decided to take him to the local boxing gym, and Ricky had been there ever since. As his uncle was "well-known", Ricky found that he did not have to "prove himself" to such a degree when first starting boxing, as the reputation of his uncle preceded him. Accordingly, Ricky was treated with a degree of "respect" for demonstrating violent potential by proxy:

> 'My uncle's well know innit, so when I came here I got respect straight away, he knows Eric and Marcus from back in the day, so I knew I would be looked after and that.'

Common among men such as Ricky, working-class males will acknowledge the appeal of violent capability (Winlow 2001). This was evidenced among gym members in an almost salacious fashion, as young teenage amateurs could be overheard discussing who they thought was the most dominant:

> 'Ricky is fast man though, he's got a wicked cross that's gonna wipe out Danny's, I'm tellin' you he's the hardest here after Frank coz he's sick!' (Elliot, 16 years old)

> 'I wouldn't fuck with Marcus, even now.' (Carl, 16 years old, amateur)

In much of the existing literature, this culture of competition and honour is often stated as being a justified reason for violence (Katz 1988; Scheff 1994; Anderson 1999). Blok (1981:435) recognised the latter in his work on Sicilian men: 'It thrives in certain peripheral subcultures of "men in groups", in bars, dockyards, prisons, and the premises of organised crime, where rank and esteem are largely matters of sheer physical force.' Blok also recognised that the concept of honour is intimately linked to physical force, and this largely pervades arenas such as the military and sport. In this regard, Ricky often felt that he had to defend his honour and position as a boxer with physical force – "the first shot" – to ensure the continuation of respect for his profession and his reputation, regardless of the consequences.

Seen in this light, it could be argued that 'respect' is a very short-lived phenomenon, and therefore quite a fragile attribute to maintain. Daly and Wilson (1988) point out that:

> A seemingly minor affront is not merely a stimulus to action, isolated in time and space. It must be understood within a larger social context of reputation, face, relative social status, and enduring relationships. And in most social milieus a man's reputation depends in part upon the maintenance of a credible threat of violence. (Daly and Wilson 1988:174)

To maintain this illusion of credibility for men like Ricky and Jonny, it involves constantly remaining vigilant to issues of perceived 'disrespect', and thus maintaining their position in the hierarchy. This is especially important for the professionals, as their reputation at the top of the hierarchy must be maintained to ensure continuation of respect and honour. This is also noticeable for the amateurs, yet their emotional psychic reality differs, in the sense that theirs is driven by a desire to be included in the higher echelons of the hierarchy. In the world of boxing, one way to do this is to demonstrate hardness and honour.

This idea of identity and honour is specifically linked to the world of boxing for many reasons. Participation in sport is not only seen as validation of a certain kind of masculinity (Connell 1995), but further relates to the prestige and power of the national state to which it belongs. To say you fight for England is a huge statement among the boxing community, and many of the young professionals aspired to utter these words. For Leroy, his idea of himself changed when he got picked to fight for England. Prior to this, Leroy was consumed with envy and feelings of inadequacy, struggling to accomplish his masculinity at a new school. Getting picked to fight for England proved he was "worthy of something", and this was partly related to the status and prestige that were now bestowed upon him by other males in the gym:

> 'The younger kids coming in here have seen my face around town, on posters and that, so I get that respect, also my dad's a boxer so my surname adds to that you know what I'm saying.'

Indeed, fighting prowess became a badge of honour for most young men in the gym and they wore it with pride. Boxing was more than a few rounds in the ring for most; it forms them physically, while simultaneously moulding their identity and fuelling their social status inside and outside this setting. The association with the gym and the prestige that accompanied being a boxer contributed towards Ricky's, Leroy's and Jonny's sense of self-worth. Furthermore, it ensured that these men's honour remained unchallenged and therefore they were fixed at the top of the pecking order.

Arguably, it is maintaining their honour – above all other concerns – that traps these men in an attendant culture of respect, and locates boxing in a tightly knitted web of criminogenic attitudes and behaviours. Having said that, boxing does have wide-reaching benefits, in as much as it postpones or incapacitates men when they may otherwise be involved in delinquent activity, and it is to these arguments that I turn next.

Boxing as a form of pro-social development

As previously stated (Giordano 2002), boxing can be a superb 'hook for change', and in some respects, its sole attraction is the honour and respect bestowed on any man or woman prepared to step into the ring. It is not my intention to give boxing a 'bad rap', nor is it my intention to discourage anyone from trying it. I am merely offering a more balanced viewpoint that challenges the common tropes. Without question, I champion the sport's ability to offer young people an avenue for positive change. In this section, I outline the benefits of boxing, and its miraculous ability to create community and to foster pro-social attitudes among some young men.

Evidence suggested that these men seemed to temporarily change in pro-social ways when they entered the gym. Comments could often be heard how the space "relaxed" men, gave them "time-out", and allowed them "to chill" with their peers without fear of "trouble" or "beef". This is contradictory to previous arguments, and I believe that the gym acted as a place of safety for its members, because the implicit hierarchy was already established. As well as the maintenance of competition, aggression and violence, men in the gym could feel relatively at ease without experiencing a constant pressure to maintain the illusion of respect that they battled with outside of its walls. As Winlow (2001) attests, the pecking order was already confirmed.

The trainers were mainly responsible for the gym's cohesion and established hierarchy, and they set the tone of the gym. Eric and Marcus ran the gym as a business, but they often referred to it as a "family". This is not uncommon in sport, particularly in boxing gyms. Wacquant (2004:69) keenly observed that the emotional attachment to one's gym, which boxers readily compare to a 'home' or a 'second mother', is testament to the protective and nurturing function that boxing possesses. Accordingly, both the boxers and the trainers developed strong attachments to one another, and the cohesive nature of the gym assisted in the cultivation of mutual respect for each other's position and craft. Marcus was always quick to point out that boxing gyms "allow anyone in", and at one point he offered to drive me around the city, to prove that they were spaces of multiculturalism and acceptance.

Undoubtedly, boxing gyms offer some form of safety and comfort to men, and this is usually in the shape of attachment figures, routine and structured activity. Yet, the biggest appeal by far, is the relationship that the men have with one another. This is reflected in the quasi-religious dedication that men show to the gym. It is through this mechanism of change, that the gym is able to demonstrate its potential not only to incapacitate, but also to further work alongside young men in developing a more positive manner. With the dedication shown by those who attend, and the incapacitating element of the gym itself, boxing is able to captivate an audience that otherwise might be disengaged from mainstream activities.[3] This was evidenced by the dedication and admiration shown by the younger amateurs in the gym towards Marcus and Eric, the trainers:

> 'Marcus is my role model, he came from the streets like me and he turned it around, I'm gonna do that too, my picture will be up there one day I'm tellin you.' (Carl, 16 years old, amateur)

The crux of these arguments, and ultimately the success of this activity, sits with the skills and perspectives of those in charge – the trainers. It is *their* outlooks and ideologies that underpin the overall ethos of the gym, and subsequently the attitudes of those who attend. The trainers in the gym did indeed act as surrogate parents for most of the young professionals, and it was not uncommon for them to be referred to as a 'second dad'. The relationship between trainer and trainee was the most significant in the gym and the most interesting in terms of this research, as it provided a significant other who often seemed to be lacking from other areas of the young men's lives.

Both Butt (1987) and Coakley (1990) consider the importance of interpersonal relationships in sport settings, and discuss the impact of the coach–athlete relationship in both positive and negative ways. They claim that sporting institutions and clubs offer young people a sense of belonging, attachment and purpose. I could not agree more, and when analysing this from a social bonding perspective, it is the quality, strength and consistency of these social bonds that play a crucial role. Furthermore, Mutz and Baur (2009:309) claim 'that most sports clubs provide bonds that encourage pro-social behaviour patterns', and therefore assume that such involvement tightens adolescents' bonds to moral codes and limits their propensity to commit acts of violence.

On the surface, I saw this happening on many occasions in the gym. Eric, in particular, would attempt to lecture the young men about refraining from violence outside the ring; however, this did not always seem sincere and the young professionals often smiled and made empty promises whenever he broached the subject. Engagement in violence outside the gym walls could result in a revoking of their professional boxing licence, and most were aware of this. Yet, it seemed to be a chance that some would take, if faced with threats to their personal identity – especially when out drinking after a contest.

Hirschi's (1969) social bonding theory focuses on these mechanisms for change, and posits that unless an individual is effectively bound to moral standards and socialised into conventional social structures, then deviance is likely. From this perspective, participation in a boxing club would therefore be regarded as a conventional activity that is socially appreciated, as there is an assumption that being a member of a club inadvertently 'bonds' members to strong and stable relationships (coaches, peers, teammates) with whom individuals feel attached. But as previously discussed, the moral codes that these men inculcate via coaches and trainers are somewhat flawed, even though delivered with the best intentions.

Moreover, the violent relationships that most participants had with their fathers/peers prior to joining the gym contributed to many of them seeking further male attachment figures in the boxing coach and gym. This was evidenced on more than one occasion in my data. Sal, in particular, discussed how his boxing coach replaced a father figure he so desperately craved in his home and family life, whereas Marcus, the hard-faced boxing trainer, confessed to thinking about his deceased boxing coach every day.[4]

Eric liked to discuss how he instilled morals in his professionals and amateurs, and he felt that he was a "good example":

> 'I did some voluntary youth work for a while, you know playing football with the kids and taking them on trips. They liked me because I was a boxer; I wanted to put something back, you know, be a good example.' (Eric, 51 years old, boxing trainer)

However, the good example that Eric liked to portray of himself was riddled with hypocrisy and ambivalence, as I witnessed Eric reinforcing negative attitudes and propensity for violence in his athletes on numerous occasions. He expressed violent attitudes in his own life, and disclosed how as a young athlete he would become involved in illicit fighting when challenged. He disclosed that when he was once referred to as "pathetic" by a competitor outside the ring, he wanted to "smash his face in" for being "disrespectful". Outside of Eric's awareness were the implicit messages he bestowed on his gym members, as he often talked of just "walking away" when faced with violent challenges, but more often than not, he was complicit with a discourse that saw boxing as a weapon that could be used if necessary. Eric therefore sanctioned retaliation, often stating "always stand your ground" and "don't let no-one take the piss".

The athletes listened to Eric and Marcus religiously. Usually, after the weekends, tales of retaliation from the boxers themselves could be heard around the gym:

> 'I know I shouldn't of, but when little dickheads in the take-away act all hard and that, I have [to] tell 'em they're dickheads.' (Carl, 16 years old, amateur)
>
> 'Funny when they reckon they can have me an all, I just "one bomb" [one punch] 'em innit. Shut the fuck up then don't they.' (Baz, 38 years old, amateur)

Similar to the paradox of the gym environment, the relationship between coaches, boxers and peers was also riddled with ambivalence. Despite the young boxers' tales of weekend violence, Eric was instrumental in developing habitual behaviours among his athletes. He promoted constant attendance and participation in gym life, and from this perspective he contributed to a form of incapacitation by virtue of them simply attending. Nonetheless, the messages inherent in this hyper-masculine world were complicit with those that reinforced competition, retaliation, strength, virility and instrumental aggression. Besides, the athletes invested in an environment that sanctioned violence, while further developing a significant relationship with one that legitimised it. Arguably over time, the identities of these men will inevitably become imbued with hyper-masculine ideals, supported and sanctioned by significant others who are complicit in the rehearsal of such behaviours. This is because both athlete and trainer function collectively, in creating a social world that views violence as an acceptable solution to a problem.

Respect: the gym, opportunities and the street

Lind and Tyler (1988) suggest that people care deeply about whether they are treated fairly by others, because fair treatment indicates something important about our social status and identity as judged by others. Likewise, the notion of 'respect' involves treating another as though they are worthy of consideration, and this is viewed as crucial for the development of a secure sense of self (Kant 1964; Tyler and

Lind 1992; Tyler and Bladder 2000). In contrast, disrespect entails a disregard for the individual, and when others behave in ways that are perceived as disrespectful it conveys a message that they are not worthy (Miller 2001). Perceived insults or disrespect are often reported as catalysts for aggression and violence among men (Scheff and Retzinger 1991; Toch 1992), and in the world of boxing, disrespect is seen as the ultimate insult.[5]

Insults of a disrespectful nature seemed to penetrate the men deeply, and they were cited as the cause of aggressive behavior outside the gym on more than one occasion. However, in the gym itself, incidences of disrespect tended to be of a playful nature, and were not usually taken that seriously. These could range from taunts in relation to body weight or dietary requirements, and more often than not, they were received as a jest and no further action was taken:

> 'I hate dieting, eating salad isn't my thing, but if you wanna make the weight, seriously, you have to cut out the burgers and stuff.' (Leroy, 32 years old, professional)
>
> 'He's worse than a woman that one, he'll be asking if his arse looks big in them jeans next.' (Marcus, 42 years old, professional trainer)

It seemed from this account, and others witnessed, that in the confines of the gym, the concept of banter was accepted – men were taunted on the premise that it was part of the game, part of the sport, and not an attack on status or identity. Yet, on the street it was a very different scenario, and men would retaliate against the slightest remark and often cited them as "disrespectful". This led me to believe that the confines of the gym acted as a safety net, and therefore the comments uttered in the gym were not taken seriously.

The gym itself possessed a certain cohesion that provided a temporary space for men to feel safe and welcome, regardless of their social standing in the wider community. As Wacquant (2004:53) stated: 'The gym culture is ostensibly egalitarian in the sense that all participants are treated alike'. Indeed, the ethos of the gym was simply 'train hard', and most men invested in this discourse with relish. Training hard encapsulated endurance, stamina and bodywork, sculpting and honing the body to resemble their perceptions of the masculine ideal. In turn, this reflected a sense of achievement for most men, and praise was always dispensed to those who had successfully crafted the perfect torso, so much so that advice was usually sought from the most 'ripped' (toned), and diet plans were openly exchanged among followers.

Outside the gym it was a different story altogether, as the younger boxers would often become embroiled in disputes in the local community:

> 'The boys were out running and heading back to the gym when two lads asked them "who do you think you are?" Jonny and Ricky didn't take kindly to that and marched over to the lads sat on the wall. I had to go over and prise them apart as they would of fuckin' killed 'em.' (Eric, 51 years old, boxing trainer)

The men arguably felt more vulnerable to attacks and were less likely to engage in friendly banter and exchangeable advice. They generally retaliated in defence of their perceived identity and status as a boxer, with some reporting that attacks were inevitable by virtue of simply being a boxer. It seemed that other men would try to pit themselves against the pugilists as a way of dominating one another, and this is not uncommon. Winlow (2001) has attested that men's violent encounters, or potential violent encounters, are viewed much in the same way as a bookmaker may decide the favourite in a forthcoming sporting event. The odds are calculated in a similar fashion, as men gamble on who will beat who, based on mental calculations and prior victories. Notwithstanding, to be dominated, or to let an affront go, was and is a process that can strip many working-class males of their image of themselves and ultimately change their image in the eyes of others (Winlow 2001). It is this concept – and the subsequent fear of losing respect – that unnerves the boxers when outside the gym. This is because 'losing face' or not living up to the expectations of other males' mental calculations of victories, can plunge men into a pool of shame and humiliation (Winlow and Hall 2009).

Blok (1974:62) stated that what earns men respect is their 'capacity to coerce with physical violence and invoke fear in others'. In this research, boxing played such an important part in men's self-concepts and identities that it proved very difficult for some of them to back down from a violent reproach. They viewed retaliation, or lack of, as a life or death situation. Michael, a 40-year-old boxer and ex-convict, described this as such:

> 'Nah, you can't never back down, because that's seen as weak. If I back down then people are gonna think that I'm an easy target. Don't matter whether it's inside, or on the

> streets, you got to act like you won't put up with anyone coming at you.' (Michael, 40 years old, boxer)

Michael's testimony demonstrates perfectly Blok's earlier point. By demonstrating the capacity to coerce with violence, Michael was able to invoke fear in others and signify that he was not vulnerable to attack, nor present as an "easy target". When faced with violent encounters – particularly those perceived as 'disrespectful' – Michael was able to rebuke any concept of desistance, as he arguably felt culturally obliged to respond. This is because the cultural importance of violence, reputation and violent reputation are exceptionally strong among criminals and 'hard' men alike (Winlow 2001). Moreover, for men like Michael and those who have also spent significant periods in prison, the cultural importance of violence becomes a form of 'survival', with violence further serving as a defence mechanism in the sublimation of feelings of inadequacy and shame (Gilligan 1996; Butler and Maruna 2009).

Violence and violent potential are viewed as a 'cultural expectation' (Winlow 2001), especially for working-class men. It is seen as a way to sublimate shame and overcome humiliating experiences, both past and present. (Wolfgang 1959; Toch 1992; Scheff 2000; Winlow and Hall 2009; Ellis et al 2017). The majority of men in this sample identified as working class, or stated that they came from a working-class background, and out of the ten boxers interviewed in this study, nine reported growing up in difficult circumstances. These circumstances ranged from absent and abusive fathers to neglectful mothers, and lack of educational qualifications, with longs spells of truancy from school.

Previous ethnographic research in this area has suggested that when an individual's access to social capital and/or social status is limited, being treated in a respectful manner becomes vastly important for one's sense of self-worth (Gilligan 1996; Bourgois 1996; Sennett 2003). Anderson (1999:66) also writes that: 'In the inner-city environment, respect on the street may be viewed as a form of social capital that is very valuable, especially when other forms of capital have been denied or are unavailable'. It was not uncommon in the boxing gym to hear men discuss the lack of employment in the surrounding area, and most complained of the difficulties they faced when looking for work. These difficulties were mainly as a result of criminal records, but most reported that they could not imagine doing a "regular 9-5 job".

Bouncing, or door work, was one example of an accepted profession, as many of the boxers in this research moonlighted as bouncers to supplement their income and reputation. Boxing therefore acted as a pastime during the day for some men who "didn't wanna sit at home watching telly" before their nightshift started; for others, it provided the physical capital needed to ensure continued employment in their chosen profession. Moreover, the men chided anyone with a successful career outside boxing, bouncing or security work, and the head coach often stated that "the posh 'uns have come to the wrong end of town to mix with the real boys", when the white-collar boxers entered the gym.[6] This led me to believe that some of the boxers saw those members who were in full-time, white-collar employment as something to be scorned. They felt that full-time work that did not involve the physical body was somehow effeminate, and it was not uncommon to hear remarks in relation to this:

> 'Can't imagine sat at a desk all day me. I'd get bored just sat there. I need to be up and doing stuff otherwise I'd get bored and then just end up saying something to someone.' (Lewis, 19 years old, trainee plumber and amateur boxer)
>
> 'I'd rather not have a job than have to be told what to do all day.' (Sam, 23 years old, unemployed amateur boxer)
>
> 'Boxing is a proper job, don't even feel like a job, just show up and train, get good and then become top of your game and earn money, none of this 9-5 shit.' (Jonny, 19 years old, professional boxer)

These seemed interesting statements, as they reflected an aversion to anything classified as subordinate in these men's eyes – being told what do, or having to be somewhere at a particular time. The likes of these men, particularly Jonny, saw full-time employment as something to be avoided, especially if it involved structured practices or adherence to a set of rules stipulated by an organisation. Yet, interestingly, Jonny complied with the structured practices of the gym and the rules set by this accompanying culture. I would argue that the ethos and status associated with gym culture fitted more closely with Jonny's idea of himself as independent, tough and physical, and therefore reminiscent of Willis's (1977) 'lads' when he discusses how working-class ideals are part of a strategy to demonstrate one's masculinity and differentiate themselves from authority (Willis 1977).

Male activities in the world of boxing are not entirely divorced from wider working-class culture, as Tolson (1977:43) has observed: 'Aggression is the basis of "style", of feeling physical, of showing feelings and protecting oneself', and in this context, masculine performativity meant exhibiting a measure of the general lower-class masculine role. Cloward and Ohlin (1960) termed this the 'conflict orientated sub-culture' and suggested that in particular group settings, access to opportunities – illicit or otherwise – may be lacking. Working to this premise, the conditions in the boxing gym created opportunities for the emergence of a conflict, or a fighting-orientated subculture, as men would demonstrate their potential for violence as a means to further themselves when other opportunities were not forthcoming.

Matza (1964:28) claimed that the 'delinquent transiently exists in a limbo between convention and crime', whereby young men postpone commitment and evade decisions in their everyday life. This idea of 'drift' (Matza 1964), and the concept of a 'conflict orientated' delinquency, allowed for many of the boxers' behaviours to be 'neutralised', as they were able to view their behaviour as being normative for the environment in which they lived (Sykes and Matza 1957, 1961). Indeed, comments in relation to criminal activity usually focused on the normative elements of their surrounding culture, and men would justify their behaviours as being "just what happens around here". This could be anything from selling pirate DVDs in the gym, to retaliatory behaviour for issues concerning respect. Moreover, the financial rewards and opportunities that certain elements of criminal activity could provide became a source of income for some gym members, as those without legal professions sought to "make ends meet" with illicit activity:

> 'Between me and you, I do a bit of other boxing on the side, just a bit to make a few quid, coz I don't have a professional licence. A few of the lads organise other fights in a gym across town where there's usually a wager and a cash prize, that's why I normally look mashed after the weekends!' (Derek, 32 years old, amateur)

> 'I do a few hours personal training at a gym near where I live, it's cash in hand so I can scratch [claim benefits] at the same time, frees me up to try and turn pro and keeps my fitness up at the same time.' (Jason, 27 years old, amateur)

> 'If a couple of the Asian lads ever need back up then they ring me, I can round a few of the boys up and give them a hand, I scratch their back and they scratch mine.' (Marcus, 40 years old, professional trainer)

In summary, being respected, creating opportunities and earning money was an important element in the culture of the boxing gym.

Men young and old, amateur and professional, sought to become infallible, respectable and employable through sheer physical force and intimidation. These ideas were sanctioned and perpetuated by those in charge as well as by those participating, and were reflective of the subcultural norms inherent in the surrounding community where most of these men came from. Opportunities and employment mainly focused on masculine validating professions, and the men would pick and choose the areas they wished to forge a career in, particularly those that reinforced their physicality. Moreover, these professions accompanied the boxers' identities and spoke volumes in terms of the way they negotiated certain behaviours and attitudes, thus reinforcing their self-concepts and structural positioning as 'hardmen'.

Identity and desistance from violence: the inside/ outside gym paradigm and the use of techniques of neutralisation

Brookman et al (2011:398) posit that: 'The study of self and identity provides valuable insights into the links between structural conditions, cultural influences and individual behavior'. They argue that selves are situated identities, and that these identities form part of a concept that people create for themselves and express to others – how a person 'likes to think of himself as being and acting' (McCall and Simmons 1966:65). As such, an individual's construction of self plays a part in how he evaluates situations, chooses lines of actions, makes sense of behaviours and presents himself to the world. Therefore, aspects of the self not only represent how one likes to be viewed in the world, but further demonstrate consensus with wider cultural and subcultural understandings. Stoke and Hewitt (1976) argue that aligning one's actions with the beliefs and expectations of a larger group, makes it possible to explain both action and construction of personal identities. People construct identities in various ways – personal appearance, physical appearance, choice of leisure pursuits and choice of partners.

For the majority of the boxers in this study, identity work and self-concepts were key to understanding the way in which they viewed themselves and others. They especially liked to think of themselves as masters of their own fates and decision-making processes, and in some respects, this is complementary to the desistance process. Indeed, Eric, Marcus and Frank all at one time or another discussed how they could no longer imagine doing anything but boxing or bouncing. Frank, in particular, talked of attempting college, when he realised that his dream of 'world champion' was not forthcoming:

> 'I attempted college, thought about going into my own business, but it got too much with the boxing and wanting to go out and stuff, that I sacked it and just focused on the gym. It got me a job bouncing so it didn't really matter that much anyway.' (Frank)

Eric originally trained to be an electrician, but became disillusioned with the trade and devoted his time to fashioning his career in professional boxing. Marcus disclosed never having a "proper job", as he knew early on that he wanted a career in sport. He therefore set about his career straight after school, believing he had limited prospects in any other profession:

> 'I knew when I left school that there was fuck all else going for me, I went to a sports school and I was pretty good at basketball. When I left school, I was just hanging out on the streets as there was not much going on when I was growing up. It was only when I found boxing that I knew I had a way out.' (Marcus)

A 'way out' was a common theme in the men's narratives, as they framed their identities around the limited opportunities they believed had beset them, or around working-class discourses that they hoped to transcend. Jonny, the youngest professional in the gym at the age of 19, stated that boxing "forms a massive part of who I am". Having lost his mother the year before, at the age of 18, Jonny confessed to relying on the gym as a form of social support, and as a result he spent vast amounts of time there, even when not training. Jonny's father was a bouncer and worked most nights, so when Jonny was not "at his girlfriend's house", he would most definitely be in the gym. Jonny identified as a boxer so much so that he only "hang[s] around" with boxers. He "[wasn't] interested" in much else and defined himself as a professional boxer "above anything else". Jonny felt that boxing was "in his blood", as his dad had "tried his hand" in the past. Accordingly, Jonny felt that boxing as a sport reflected his heritage and personality and his subsequent class positioning:

> 'It takes a certain kind of person to wanna get hit for fun, you know what I'm saying? I don't think you'd get many kids from posh areas taking it up. Boxing is for lads who can take a punch, none of this "glass jaw" stuff. Growing up where I did you had to be able to look after yourself,

> and that set me up for boxing, you know what I mean?'
> (Jonny, 19 years old, professional boxer)

Most of the men in this study were raised in highly disadvantaged circumstances – places where you "had to be able to look after yourself" or "be on your toes". Most of those that I interviewed had experienced familial abuse and fear throughout their childhoods, and therefore were familiar with the implicit codes of violent milieus. The majority of the men who did experience violent upbringings became finely attuned to incidences of disrespect, and viewed any attack as an attack on their identity and self-concept. Boxing therefore became embedded in a sense of self, as Jonny attested, and formed a huge part of the way they wished to be perceived – to such an extent that any attack – potential or actual – was met with force and an almost life or death commitment. This was justified as a way of maintaining honour and respect, and retaliatory or instigated violent action was passed off as necessary.

When challenged outside the gym, many of the boxers *felt* that they must react, although this did differ slightly between the professionals and the amateurs. The messages inherent in their environments, both in and outside the gym, supported this response. The professionals had more to lose in terms of their boxing licence than the amateurs did, and in some respects, they were slightly more cautious; in other words, they chose their battles more wisely. Yet, to not respond at all, even just verbally, would not only result in emasculation and leave the men potentially vulnerable to further attack, but would also threaten their self-concept and identity.

In the boxing world, the culture of masculinity that pervades the gym is all-inclusive, and therefore reinforces hierarchies based on physical dominance. This can lead to confrontations, as some boxers attempt to replace feelings of psychological anxiety with feelings of pride obtained through an aggressive display of 'masculine' behaviour (Gaylin 1984; Gilligan 1996; Miller 2001). This experience of personal indignation is what raises the risk that boxers will engage in violent behaviour, as feelings of disrespect do not so much trigger retaliatory violence as make it possible.

For men in this study, the fact that they were boxers dictated – in their eyes at least – a suitably violent response to confrontations that reinforced their self-concepts and their place in the subculture of the boxing gym. For Ricky and the others to have gone against the expected moral code and predictable violent response, would not only have endangered their identities as boxers, but also made their positions in the social world of boxing untenable. Moreover, it would have rendered their identities (and locations in the group) fragile.

According to Gilligan (1996), such individuals rehearse violent behaviour to deflect threats to their identity, as they attempt to replace feelings of shame with feelings of respect; therefore, they demonstrate aggressive behaviour with pride and masculine prowess. Likewise, Katz (1988:24) argues that when individuals feels wronged in some way, they may experience themselves as the object of another, and thereby seek to regain their 'lost control of identity' through aggressive and violent behaviour. In addition to feeling 'righteous' (Katz 1988:24), some men justify their violence and aggression as a way of 'reasserting one's dignity and identity' (Young 2002:408).

In this study, concepts of dignity and identity were so important to the men that they would do almost anything for it to remain intact. Marcus, the retired boxing champion turned trainer, encapsulates this, when he discusses how he was involved in an altercation with the police. He disclosed that when challenged for parking illegally, he responded with a violent act, to the point of confronting the police officer and requesting that they "go round the corner and sort it out". When I asked Marcus why it felt so important for him to challenge the officer, he responded:

> 'I would go to jail man, in my book you're either right or you're wrong and I was 100% right there. And I wouldn't regret it either. I'm serious I wouldn't. I'd go jail to be right. I'd die doing it. Simple as. 100% die for being right. So, jail is minor you know what I mean?' (Marcus)

It transpired that Marcus felt disrespected by the police officer, and felt him to be racist, as he believed that the police perceived him as: "Another black man, another drug dealer in a BMW". However, there was a sense that Marcus just did not like to be challenged, particularly by those in authority, as he felt that "no-one has the right to tell another person what to do". He viewed most disagreements and challenges as "disrespectful" and generally responded to them in the same manner. Marcus, having previously spent a period of time in prison for a crime he "didn't commit",[7] often portrayed a hyper-vigilant attitude to any form of challenge, particularly ones from the police, and was very quick to respond to any small sign that inferred he was somehow inferior or wrong.

This retaliatory tale was one of many from the men in the gym, and it was not uncommon to hear tales of fighting outside the ring among the amateurs and professionals, particularly in response to challenges from other men and authority figures. Traffic wardens were obvious targets, and on more than one occasion a pugilist could be seen running out of the ring and down the gym's stairs to "stop some fucking cunt" putting a ticket on their car with threats of violence. The professionals seemed less likely to pursue violent altercations, as they raised concerns over their boxing licences and worried over injuries to hands. Indeed, Jonny, a young professional climbing the ranks, voiced this concern:

> 'Why bother with the dickhead "weekend warriors", you know those guys who wanna drink 10 pints and start a fight. I could take them but I'm not arsed, don't wanna break my hand doing it you see, coz it would put me out of the game for a few months and I can't afford that.' (Jonny)

Jonny's vignette here is interesting, as it demonstrates boxing's ability to promote a 'primary' form of desistance from violence (Maruna 2001), and Giordano et al (2002:1040) discuss how: 'The ability to imagine a negative sequence of hypothetical consequences that might flow from one's deviant behaviour can have a deterrent effect'. Nonetheless, Jonny's story is purely instrumental and offers no evidence by way of 'wilful cognitive distortion' (Maruna 2001), as his outlook and understanding of violence do not form part of a new self-identity (Maruna 2001). Jonny refrained from "taking them out" due to fear of breaking his hand. While it is arguable that this is desistance promoting, it does not offer evidence of any cognitive transformation, as Jonny still felt the need to enact violence. Had he not been in fear of injury, or worried about losing income as a result, it is more than likely that he would have engaged in violent behaviour, as he felt that boxing "forms a massive part of who I am, and when I'm not training, I get a bit 'snappy'". Indeed, this instrumental desistance-promoting element did not always take effect, as Jonny relayed stories of fighting when out running with Eric and Ricky. Hence, the desisting element of potentially breaking one's hand becomes temporary and situational – and not part of a redemption narrative or 'new self' (Maruna 2001).

Worryingly, some of the younger amateurs were not in fear of losing any income or sustaining injuries, and were therefore more than happy to engage in violent behaviour outside the gym. Carl, a 16-year-old refugee, felt that boxing gave him "street cred", and his friends looked to him to "sort out any problems":

> 'Yeah, coz, a 25-year-old gang member wanted to fight with my 12-year-old friend, and he ran away, so the 25-year-old tried to punch me didn't he, but I beat him and earned respect by standing my ground.' (Carl)

For most of these men, their attitudes and involvement in urban environments such as boxing gyms enabled them to call upon street codes and boxing cues as a convenient and acceptable way to make sense of their violence. By providing storylines and excuses that reflected codes relevant to the social audience, participants were able to depict their experiences more generally, and portray themselves specifically as bastions of an accepted moral code and related behaviours (Anderson 1999). Anderson claims that there is a 'set of informal rules governing interpersonal public behaviour, particularly violence' (Anderson 1999:33), and that the rules prescribe both proper comportment and the proper way to respond if challenged. They regulate the use of violence and supply a rationale, allowing those inclined to aggression to precipitate violent encounters in an approved way.

Evidence procured in the gym demonstrated that any lack of response from these men would have conveyed a message that they tolerated victimisation. This was unthinkable for the majority of men in this study. With most heralding from violent and abusive upbringings, the fear of repeat victimisation became acute, and under no circumstance would this be tolerated. The men were therefore hyper-vigilant to any affronts. Being classified as a victim was so damaging to their sense of identity in this masculine domain, that men like Eric, Leroy and Marcus would do everything in their power to abdicate the subject position. Quite often they would call upon the code of the street to justify their violence, and neutralise their retaliatory behaviour as an acceptable response.

Seen in this light, codes become yet another linguistic device for maintaining a positive self-concept, much like techniques of neutralisation (Sykes and Matza 1957). When the men were questioned about their wrongdoings, the way they justified their actions became central to maintaining a particular sense of self. Moreover, these explanations demonstrated an endorsement of a code – a cultural expectation and narrative identity that signified these men's self-images with the potential to react violently.

Working to this premise, Gilligan (1996), Bourgois (1996) and Sennet (2003) all suggest that when an individual's access to social capital becomes scarce, being treated respectfully becomes hugely important for one's sense of self-worth. An individual may lack the skills and confidence to assert themselves sufficiently to get basic respect needs met from others, and this lack of capability may lead to increased subjective emotional experiences of frustration and humiliation. This is usually relieved or comforted through aggressive release (Ward and Maruna 2007). To avoid the consequences of such outbursts, individuals may then seek to 'neutralise' their behaviours to remain bound to the dominant social order, and therefore defend their actions with justifications and rationalisations.

Sykes and Matza (1957:666) argue that neutralisation is 'delinquency based on what is essentially an unrecognised extension of defences to crimes in the form of justifications for deviance'. They identified five techniques of neutralisation available to the offender that not only allowed for denial of responsibility, but also denial of injury, denial of the victim, condemnation of the condemners, and lastly, appeal to higher loyalties (Sykes and Matza 1957: 666). Sykes and Matza argue that it is through these techniques that juveniles become delinquent, as they allow for moral disengagement and lack of self-sanction. According to this theory, young offenders are fully aware of the wrongfulness of their actions, yet, if they are to maintain commitment to the dominant social order, then they must find ways to assuage guilt and shame. This guilt, and its potential for producing a negative self-image, helps the average person to refrain from committing an immoral act most of the time. In order to participate in deviant behaviour under such conditions, individuals must find methods to rationalise the actions or neutralise the guilt associated with it. These five techniques form part of this procedure, and provide 'defences to crimes in the forms of justifications' (Sykes and Matza 1957:666). If these neutralisations are to carry any psychological weight, then they must be at least partially believed by the person enacting them (Maruna and Copes 2005).

In this research, techniques of neutralisation were used to justify violent behaviour. Excuses usually focused around narratives of disrespect and loyalty to the code of the street, as men felt justified in their defence of what they perceived as "honour". The men felt that their narrative identity or self-concept was somehow being compromised by a lack of retaliation, as they defined their actions as a form of rightful retaliation or punishment. In the case of Eric, he justified the beating of his children as a punishment for "lying", whereas Marcus felt justified in violating a parking restriction to the point where he was unable to take responsibility and became aggressive. Marcus was also quick to condemn the police, justifying his retaliatory behaviour as "standing up for me and my community". He felt that asking an officer to accompany him around the corner to settle the altercation in a violent way was somehow permissible.

In Frank's case, an appeal to higher loyalties was evident, as he would informally talk of his job "on the doors", and how sometimes he "manhandled" punters to present an impression of not being "someone to fuck with". Unfortunately, this once involved punching a deaf man, as Frank was unaware of the man's disability when reprimanding him in a noisy bar. Thinking him to be "arrogant", Frank punched him and threw him outside, only then realising that the man was deaf and unable to comprehend his instructions at the time. This was a saddening tale, and in some respects, I could see that Frank felt guilty. However, this was largely laughed off as being part of the job, and a "mistake anyone could have made". This story added a new dimension to Frank, and at it was at this point that the bravado he had successfully managed to convey became fractured and tenuous.

The projected images of Frank and the others started to seem untenable as the stories of retaliation and violence outside the gym began to reek of fragility. Eric was terrified of replicating his father's violence, but also ruled his own family home with the belt. He was able to defend against this behaviour, by rationalising it to himself: "Good for instilling discipline" in his children, he said.

Marcus, on the other hand, condemned the condemners, believing that the police were responsible for his false imprisonment, and thus felt it important to stand up for the community. Appealing to higher loyalties, Marcus felt that he was a community activist, and stated that "if it could happen to me it could happen to anyone". He therefore took it upon himself to wage arguments with the police for "the people's sake".

Frank also demonstrated his vulnerability on numerous occasions and had developed a sense of hyper-vigilance to matters of disrespect. I often wondered how he managed to sustain his job.

Leroy, a championship boxer, often thought people were laughing at his inability to competently read and write, and felt that if he did not have boxing, he would "have nothing going for him". Ricky, who once revealed that he was "bottled" in a restaurant, felt that the beating he administered afterwards was justified, due to the injuries *he* had sustained. Leroy also rationalised his deviant behaviour as a teenager, stating that the theft of designer clothes from his affluent peers was "only right as they could afford it", insisting that affluent individuals are not entitled to be victims.[8]

It became evident throughout my research that victimhood was denied to most parties; interestingly, this included the men themselves.

The participants would refer to victims as "pussies", therefore viewing this subject position as feminine, and as far removed from their own self-concept as humanely possible. The idea of being a victim, or even creating one, was immediately dismissed, as most men would see victims as ineffectual or weak – the irony being, that most of them had been one at some point in their lives.

Boxers employed neutralisation techniques designed to assuage guilt or deny their own vulnerability. In keeping with the cultural mores of the gym, there was always an excuse to evade responsibility or place the blame elsewhere. Brookman et al (2011) argue how violent inmates employ 'formula stories' to maintain 'street codes', and thereby secure valued identities and positionings in cultural worlds that adhere to these practices.

The nature of the violence in these men's lives was an interesting topic and one that began to unravel throughout my time in the gym. The logic of gym-based violence coincided with street violence; they reinforced each other. As a result, cognitions stayed intact. These allowed men to justify both their own autobiographical violence and their potential theoretical violence, using core moral neutralisation techniques. These techniques therefore maintained and supported the idea that violence was an acceptable solution to most problems. This violence was consistently reinforced by the attendant culture of the boxing gym and the wider community that most of these men inhabited. As a result, these men's psyches became imbued with violence both in and outside the gym walls, and thus formed part of the fabric of their lives.

Summary

Desistance from violence proved to be difficult for the majority of these men. They had too much of their own identity resting upon their construction of muscle, their performance of masculinity, and their own subjective denial of vulnerability. To resist retaliation would not only victimise them, but also deny the very existence that they had fashioned for themselves via the masculine domain of boxing. By using neutralisation techniques, boxers were able to align their actions with social expectations (Stoke and Hewitt 1976; Brookman et al 2011), which further allowed them to maintain desired identities. When participants discussed violence, the way they explained their actions became a central way of maintaining a particular sense of self. The narrators elevated their stories as evidence that they were acting accordingly, as "real blokes" should. Their violence became an easily understandable and expected reaction to unfolding events (Brookman et al 2011), and demonstrated the salience of retaliation in the social worlds they inhabited.

Giordano et al (2002) highlight the degree to which cognitive and linguistic processes themselves play an important role in behavioural change. According to Giordano et al, for there to be a change in behaviour, there must be an 'openness to change', described as an agentic desire and receptivity to a 'hook for change'. Posited as catalysts for lasting behaviour, these 'hooks' supposedly energise fundamental shifts in identity, and therefore support changes in the meaning and desirability for deviant and criminal behaviour. More importantly, these hooks enable a participant to craft a satisfying 'replacement self', one that is seen as incompatible with continued criminal behaviour (Giordano et al 2002).

Yet the men interviewed in this study had not adapted their behaviour. Their identities were still bound up in masculine discourses and 'codes of the street' (Anderson 1999). Whilst boxing arguably acted as a hook – much in the same way as religion or prison might – evidence was primarily supportive and supplementary to self-concepts that denied vulnerability. Men were attuned to perceived incidences of humiliation and disrespect, and neutralised their violent outbursts as evidence of cultural and psychic defences. It would seem that the only 'replacement self' was the one from 'victim' to 'boxer', and this would be defended against at any cost. In the words of Marcus: "I would go to jail to be right; I would die doing it".

Identity formation, especially when combined with the prevention of repeat victimisation, took precedence over anything else. The maintenance of desired identities, coupled with a desperate need to deny a sense of vulnerability, was paramount in this study. In environments that do not tolerate weakness, men invest in discourses that enable them to view violence as a part of everyday life (Gilligan 1996), and the boxing gym is no different. Desistance was only achieved through incapacitation in the gym itself, as it prevented men from physically engaging in illegitimate violence when present. While the implicit code of the gym was generally respectful and legal, the culture of the space and the significant others present often reinforced discourses that spoke of competition, masculinity, violence and retaliation. Therefore, the boxers embraced this social world wholeheartedly, and fashioned identities and cognitions in line with expected behaviours. They did not demonstrate attitudes or subsequent actions that were cognisant with desistance from violence.

Evidence did, however, show an openness to change, as some men on re-entry from prison or those "sick of being in trouble" saw it as a positive way to occupy their time. Hence, boxing has the potential to act as a 'hook for change', as it incapacitates men at a time when they may otherwise be engaged in crime. However, hooks vary in their transformative potential and, as Giordano et al (2002) argue, for a cognitive transformation to take place, an identity transformation (or what Maruna (2001) refers to as a 'redemption script') must be evident. Men in this sample did not provide any evidence of redemption scripts nor 'willful cognitive distortion' (Maruna (2001). They did not take ownership of their violence or recast themselves in new lights. In fact, the participants saw no wrongdoing in violent retaliation, and therefore neutralised any violent interaction as part of a code by which they lived.

For desistance to occur, Giordano et al emphasise that hooks have to offer a broad outline of a replacement self – a new identity that is open to change and susceptible to redemption. Boxing does not offer this. It may offer an element of incapacitation or employment, or as a connection to some 'positively valued themes' (Giordano et al 2002), but the masculine discourse of the sport, coupled with the discursive meanings of violence, only serves to reinforce self-concepts that define violence as acceptable and necessary in certain situations. Ward and Maruna (2007:151) write that 'in order to construct viable identities people draw on the discursive [sources of meaning] resources in their social and cultural environment'. Thus, in the social environment of boxing, discursive resources are complicit with dominant masculinities, and arguably reinforce violence as an expected outcome. As Presser (2005) also argued, self-identity is not constructed in a social vacuum, and each one of us draws on available cultural narratives in constructing our own worldviews.

Indeed, the attitudes fostered in the gym led me to believe that not only had the men not changed their attitudes towards violence, but that boxing and the gym environment could potentially reinforce them. It is therefore a legitimate argument that, in some cases, boxing can elaborate on the rehearsal of violence. All too often, boxers could be heard talking about altercations they had been involved in, both historically and potentially. It was disappointing, yet it was this particular element that assisted in the surmising of my theory. The discursive meanings that were entrenched in the social world of boxing saw men finely attuned to violence, and the trajectories of these men had already demonstrated a significant relationship towards it. As Jonny stated: "It takes a certain kind of person to want to get hit for fun".

The habitus of the gym, with its emphasis on competition, muscle and violent potential, proved to be not only reflected in the bodies of these men (Bourdieu 1977), but also ingrained in their consciousness as a system to live by. Boxers are committed to violence. Violence sustains their identity as men who demand total respect and are unable to compromise, as this would remove the essence of their identity – their self-concept. The gym is a reinforcing mechanism that prescribes these very discourses. Indeed, every semblance of a boxer's body is 'packed into a framework of confrontational options which are then manifested as violent potential' (Hobbs 1995:122), and these men defined themselves in terms of a cultural inheritance that gives primacy to violence, both inside and outside the gym. As a result, it cultivates a willingness to engage in violence wholeheartedly, which makes boxers unique from the rest of the general population, who generally shy away from violent reproach. Boxers can command fear and obedience through their potential for physical damage; their bodily armour, honed daily in the confines of the gym, adds to this image.

The ability to command such fear and obedience results in the propensity to also command respect. As Frank stated: "I respect someone I fear". Boxing therefore acts as a gateway to respect, in the same way that a high-powered job or financial success might. Indeed, the men often compared Roger the boxing promoter to Alan Sugar, the businessman-turned-television star, who became famous for being rich and mean. In their eyes, this was respect. Money signified an ability to behave in ways that were not usually considered polite and law-abiding, and it provided these men with a blueprint for success.

The majority of men in the gym knew that professional success happened to the mere few. Those who were left behind were viewed as being restricted to the area in which they grew up. To achieve success and status meant sheer dedication, and in some cases, sheer brutality. Daly and Wilson (1988) claim that men's violence towards other men involves an element of competition and bravado, and that violence can be seen as a common means by which men can rise above the throng of working-class youth who also inhabited their locality. With this in mind, the men used violence as a crucial signifier of self-image; maintaining a credible threat through a well established and adhered to pecking order (Winlow 2001).

Because of this, men did not consider "walking away". This would only demonstrate fear and a reduction in their credible threat. Therefore, men invested in violent retaliation to avoid shame and humiliation, and to stay engaged in a hyper-masculine domain that places onus on retaliation as a way to maintain respect. As a result, men's self-narratives and self-concepts were increasingly imbued with violence, their cognitions were wired with it, and ultimately, this prevented them from rewriting a narrative of change – or what Maruna (2001) refers to as a 'redemption script'.

Boxing does not offer anything by way of cognitive transformation (Giordano et al 2002), when it comes to desistance from violence. The logic of gym violence reinforces the sagacity of street violence, and this became evident through men's narratives of illicit fighting when outside the gym. The rewarded behaviours of courage, competitiveness and respect become counter-productive and thus criminogenic, when applied to the street. This is demonstrated by the pre-emptive aggression, particularly the idea of "getting in there first". Hence, the gym has the potential to encourage repertoires of violence, and also to reinforce toxic masculine identities.

In conclusion, the rationales by which the majority of participants lived their lives remained intact through core moral neutralisation techniques and justifications for further action. The men in this study always had an excuse for their behaviour. In an environment where the majority of men spent their time, these rationales and excuses became supported and sanctioned by significant others, thus allowing boxers to craft identities that spoke to violent recidivism. Unfortunately, more so than pro-social development theories seemingly think.

Notes

1 The professionals also trained during the day at least three out of every five days and reported that they went running when not in the boxing gym.

2 From a Darwinian perspective, staring at another animal with a fixed gaze serves the purpose not of looking but of communicating a message of intimidation. This can be heightened in front of potential copulatory mates.

3 This is evidential, particularly with the rise of alternative education programmes such as The Boxing Academy in London, and Fight for Peace in both the UK and Brazil.

4 Reminiscent of Nouwen's (1979) concept of the 'wounded healer', whereby a healer's own wounds carry curative powers for the mentee or client.

5 Originally starting with Muhammad Ali, 'pre-fight banter' has become as essential to professional boxing as the throwing of punches in the ring. David Haye, speaking of his opponent Wladimir [Klitschko] in 2011, said: "This is going to be the most brutal execution you have seen of a boxer in many years". Klitchko responded by saying that Haye's words were: "Disgraceful and disrespectful" (*The Guardian* (2011) 'Boxing Trash Talk That Stings Like a Bee', Tuesday 28 June).

6 White-collar boxing is a form of boxing in which men and women who work in white-collar professions train to fight at special events. Most have had no prior boxing experience.

7 Marcus was accused of nine attempted murders, but managed to clear his name. This was only after having spent six months in jail.

8 In the case of Simon, note that he denies the theft of the teacher's purse, then later admits to it, when the dictaphone has stopped recording. Perhaps this demonstrates the salience of Sykes and Matza's (1957) theory, as Simon felt it important to remain 'bound to the social order' – at least while on tape.

8

Discussion

To conclude, I will discuss the overarching themes that emerged from the findings and also from the case studies of Frank, Eric and Leroy. I will briefly discuss the commonalities of each case and also the differences, and summarise my overall conclusions in relation to both the appeal and desistance potential of boxing.

I argue that the gym – and 'gym life' – incapacitates to the extent that it consumes men's time, but offers little in the way of positive behavioural change or cognitive transformation (Giordano et al 2002). The discourses inherent in the gym and the broader habitus of these men reinforce a self-concept that views violence as a solution to self-perceived problems of masculinity. Boxing traps men in a culture of 'respect' and constructs habits of proactive and reactive violence that are not always conducive to criminal desistance. I finish with a discussion of the implications for the sport, and for future youth policy and practice, and thus close with a brief discussion of ways forward for the sport and its relationship to desistance from crime.

The enduring appeal of boxing

The enduring *public* appeal of the boxing gym resides in an ill-conceived notion that it can offer a 'way out'. In this study, men often perceived the sport as capable of helping them overcome some form of economic, social or academic barrier. In their words, boxing was about "money, status and fame", and "getting out from round 'ere". It was personal for most of these men, and many saw the gym as being more than just a place to "let off steam". However, beyond the veneer of these status accomplishments and 'routes out of poverty' statements, boxing also offered a way for these men to deny fragility and previous victimisation, and invest in specific discourses that contributed to them achieving what they deemed to be "respect". The masculine discourses inherent in this social world reinforced this ideal, as men built their physical capital not only to gain a sense of respect, but also to increase their sense of status among peers both inside and outside the gym setting.

Men viewed the concept of 'respect' as being coterminous with 'fear'. The very idea of being disrespected or perceived as weak was so abhorrent, that they would do anything in their power to avoid it. This was demonstrated not only in the ring, whereby men would fight through pain to achieve a sense of valour, but also on the street, as men would call upon the 'Code of the Street' (Anderson 1999) to negate a sense of responsibility for their violent retaliations. This negation was achieved via neutralising techniques (Sykes and Matza 1957) that allowed men to maintain masculine 'fronts', and place the responsibility for their actions elsewhere.

As demonstrated in the case studies, most of the men had suffered, or had been subject to, violent abuse in their formative years, either within the community, in the family, or both. As a result, the boxing gym represented 'an island of stability and order' (Wacquant 2004) and a place where men such as Frank could experience a sense of control in an otherwise hostile, unpredictable world. For Eric and Leroy, it provided a form of self-defence against environments where you had to be "on your toes", and therefore helped to create both ontological security and self-efficacy. The victimhood and violence that these men had once been subject to was displaced by investing in boxing, as it provided a physical, social and psychological space for them to invest in. This space was conterminous with masculine discourses that confronted and defended against the certainty of future victimhood, and thus allowed men such as Frank and the others to disavow the emasculating victim status they so despised.

By investing in 'physical capital' and the creation of muscle, the men were able to present as individuals who would not tolerate victimisation, nor be made 'subject to the will of others' (Connell 1990). Furthermore, the masculine accomplishments of competitive wins – strength, courage and virility – all contributed towards the rejection of female elements (being a "pussy"). By disowning these feminine attributes, Eric, Frank, Leroy and others were able to perform their masculinity in line with hegemonic sporting discourses. By risking the body in performance (Feldman 1991), and demonstrating bodily capital, these men were able to present as the epitome of 'hardness' – the opposite of feminine 'softness' – and that which is fearful.

Woodward (2004:7) has argued that 'men's boxing evokes hegemonic masculinity', a view that this data strongly supports, as boxing is most certainly an investment in a gendered habitus that creates distance from a subjective interpretation of the feminine 'other'. To be classified as feminine is to be classified as subordinate in these men's eyes, and this leads to a fear of being disrespected and subject to the will of other males. Accordingly, the concept of being 'respected' becomes aligned with their sense of masculinity, as Eric attested – when his trainer referred to him as "having no balls" – "it was an insult to me as a man". As Gilligan (1996:231) wrote: 'Men are honoured for activity (ultimately, violent activity); and they are dishonoured for passivity, which renders them vulnerable to the charge of being a non-man'.

This construction of the feminine other as fragile, vulnerable and subordinate is the main reason why the majority of men in this sample disliked the idea of women's boxing; it threatened their sense of masculine accomplishment, and blurred the lines between masculine and feminine subject positions. Boxers develop self-concepts that are consistent with ideas of respect, honour and winning, further combined with an external locus of evaluation that places emphasis on robust and dominant masculinities. Hence, the environment, the significant others (peers, trainers, parents) and the conditions of worth inherent in the gym all contribute to the way in which individuals view and understand violence and desistance.

Moreover, the occupational culture that forms the habitus of a boxer can become so deeply ingrained in ideas and the presentation of self, that violence and retaliation as a means to 'maintain face' (Goffman 1959; Katz 1988; Anderson 1999; Winlow 2001) override most forms of desistance. This is because the identity of a boxer, and the occupational culture of boxing, places violence as central to the concepts of the male self, as Maruna (2001:17) observes: 'Sustained desistance most likely requires a fundamental and intentional shift in a person's sense of self'. From this vantage point, desistance proved too difficult for men who identify as boxers, especially when combined with the respect they could lose if domination, winning and violence were not adopted as potential strategies. Losing is not considered an option in a boxer's self-project, nor is it seen as a viable subject position in a habitus where violence and respect are given primacy.

Partly through self-defence and partly through fear of being perceived as a loser (economically, socially and academically), Frank, Eric and Leroy, among others, all invested in boxing for reasons that allowed them to reshape a sense of their own masculinity. Frank felt pressured by the gang violence that enfolded him, and therefore saw boxing as a way to escape it without compromising his masculinity. With an abusive father who tried to murder both him and his brother, Eric invested in boxing to overcome his fear of repeat victimisation, and also as a way to stand up to his father when the time came. For Leroy, the competitive element of the gym provided opportunities for him to feel like a "winner", particularly in an environment that perceived young working-class lads like him as "losers".

For these men, and I suspect many more, boxing offers a site (both physically and psychologically) to deny a sense of inadequacy and vulnerability. By investing in becoming boxers, Frank, Eric and Leroy, were able to reconfigure a self-concept that took winning and success as a central theme. It helped to distort any incoming messages that spoke to prior victimhood, and assisted in their personal quest to achieve what they perceived as appropriate masculine, physical and economic status. The 'hook for change' was not necessarily about pro-social development and desistance, but was about masking their fear of bullying and repeat victimisation. Their ideas of respect, what Emmanuel Kant (1964)refers to as 'being worthy of consideration', became so important to them, that the very idea of losing it was non-negotiable.

The fear of being disrespected, coupled with the emasculating properties of this, allowed men to justify their violent behaviour in moralistic ways. The maintenance of respect becomes young men's *raison d'être*, when the fear of repeat victimisation and bullying looks imminent. This is worrying in the current climate, as recent reports show a 77 per cent increase in homicides committed by knives by males under 18 (Home Office 2018). Some might say it is a tenuous link, to attribute the fear of losing respect to the rise in knife crime, but I believe it is a valid conversation to start. Indeed, this very conversation has prompted local boxing clubs such as Collyhurst and Moston Boxing Gym in Greater Manchester to run campaigns such as #putdownth eknivesandputonthegloves and boxing initiatives in London such as Gloves not Guns. The Home Office #knifefree campaign (2019) has also made the link, by challenging common tropes that knives will offer power and protection, and thus promotes boxing as a disciplining tool.

The desistance-promoting potential of boxing

The gym was an important site for the men in this study. As previously discussed, it offered a space that many men interpreted as being safe and secure. The gym was always busy and the men in attendance devoted a huge amount of time to their weekly (and sometimes daily) workouts, underlining the ascetic nature of the sport. Boxing for them was habit-forming and an incapacitating function in their lives, and this is boxing's biggest selling point. Yet, most of the men in attendance had at some point been involved in crime. In the gym they openly discussed their trajectory of offences; petty crimes, like selling unlicensed DVDs in the gym, to the more serious issues of being accused of attempted murder and police assault.

Having said that, a large majority saw the gym as an activity that "kept them off the streets", conveying an impression that boxing alone was somehow responsible for their current lack of involvement in crime. I see this view clearly, and for some this was probably the case. I err on the side of caution, however, as this incapacitating function did not prevent them from possessing attitudes that were favourable to the 'code of the streets' (Anderson 1999).

This code made violence permissible when it was employed as a resource for enforcing and upholding ideas around interpersonal violence. These ideas take respect as the key goal and regulate the use of violence as a defensive structure, condoning individuals to precipitate violence in socially approved ways. Evidence demonstrated that this code was embedded in men's outlooks, and was often called upon when they felt that they were somehow being threatened or disrespected. This was adhered to across the sample, from the trainers through to the amateurs, as men often discussed how they retaliated to reinforce an identity that would not tolerate abuse or becoming subject to attack.

As much as the trainers encouraged the young men to refrain from illegitimate violence by discouraging acts of revenge, issues concerning disrespect and emasculation were defended against. Men legitimised their violence as part of maintaining their male identity, as any threats to their self-concepts and social status were too painful to bear, particularly if victimhood was already evident in their personal history. As a result, they neutralised and negated their violence as part of the code, as imperative in the accomplishment of their masculinity in a domain that takes respect very seriously.

As Ward and Maruna (2007) have suggested, submissive individuals may lack the skills to assert themselves sufficiently to get basic respect needs met from others. This lack of capability can lead to increased subjective emotional experiences of frustration and humiliation that may be relieved or comforted through aggressive release. As Winlow and Hall (2009) and Ellis et al (2017) also attest, humiliated or victimised men sometimes invoke social situations, in which they may face dark memories of passive victimhood. This, in turn, allows men to employ new-found techniques of violence and domination to gloss over previous images of humiliation and victimisation. Boxing contributes to this idea, as the men involved in this research had mostly suffered humiliating abuse and lacked the capabilities to assert themselves prior to signing up. Boxing therefore acted not only as a cathartic mechanism, by providing a comfort release for their latent aggression, but also allowed the participants to gain respect through aggressive means. 'Responding to threats in ways idealised by the embodied habitus thus enables the individual to shuffle a little closer to the sense of self that signifies the ceaseless desire of the disturbed (victimised) psyche to find tranquillity' (Winlow and Hall 2009:30).

Members in authoritative positions constantly maintained this idea, as trainers were also complicit in the discourses and habitus of the gym culture. Attachment figures in the shape of trainers and other sporting role models therefore played a significant role in the formation of attitudes of those that they supervised. While illegitimate violence was generally discouraged, it was also condoned, particularly when maintaining valued masculine identities. Seen in this light, the trainers and role models in the gym culture contributed to the formation of attitudes that were not necessarily conducive to desistance from violence.

Structurally, boxing acts as a social arrangement or activity that can enable or limit action as part of the desistance process. As Sampson and Laub (2003) have argued, commitment to work, mutual ties and employers all increase informal social control, and for some of the professional boxers this was most certainly the case. In the main, the involvement in the gym setting detained the men and provided an habitual activity that was both rewarding and demanding, as the culture and habitus of this social world allowed men to share similar assumptions, beliefs and patterns of behaviour that were passed on from one generation to the next. Having said that, trainers such as Eric and Marcus saw no problem with violence when defending "honour", and this inevitably formed part of the gym's culture and, therefore, of the men they taught.

Giordano (1986) argues that the more individuals value membership in a group, the more likely they are to accede to group influences in order to maintain or enhance their social standing (for further discussion, see Warr 2002). If this is the case, it is arguable that the likes of Ricky, Jonny and other young professionals will be susceptible to the influences of their trainers and peers as part of maintaining their position in the gym. Bottoms et al (2004:377) further argue that 'desistance cannot be considered outside the social context in which it occurs'. Therefore deviance is also likely to be shaped by social context, with opportunities, cultural views, self-identity, friends and the activities of social control agents all likely to play their part (see Cloward and Ohlin 1960; Cressey 1964; Bandura 1977). This was evidenced by demonstrations of violence outside the ring by Marcus, Frank, Eric, Ricky and Jonny, and also towards those amateurs they deemed as subordinate in the ring.

In the same way that social context affects the professions to which young people aspire (Willis 1977), the language they speak, their faith, the ways in which they are victimised and other aspects of daily life, the men in this study mostly originated from socially disadvantaged areas and most had left school with few or no qualifications. Furthermore, the social links outside family life and the gym were scarce. The men would often state that boxing was the "only friend" they had, reinforcing the impression that the gym acted as some form of stability for these men, however fragile that may be. I sensed that boxing as an "only friend" was interpreted by these men as a form of stability and reassurance; when boxing, the men had a sense of control and ownership in a climate where they felt otherwise powerless.

Some of the men had part-time jobs outside the gym, based in security work or 'grey' economies involving cash-in-hand labouring or building work, but these were usually casual and transient. Accordingly, the 'attachment communities' (Bottoms et al 2004) of work, marriage, friends and education were limited. Men often spent substantial amounts of time in the gym as a result. As Putnam (2000) has argued, aspects of community spaces have the power to create change from within, as they have the capacity to 'bridge social capital'. The gym community did create social cohesion, and I often wondered what would replace it if it ever closed, especially having witnessed the sense of community and structure it brought to many.

Without the sport, men like Frank, and particularly Marcus, professed that they could have seen themselves either in prison or dead, and it would seem that boxing does provide some opportunities for men with limited options. However, the desire to offend, or the motivation to react violently in certain situations, still exists for the men in this study, as they view the concept of retaliation as part of their identities and self-concepts. Working from this premise, the parameters of social control that the gym possesses are limited. For desistance to commence, there is a need for an integral cognitive shift as part of the process (Giordano 2002). As discussed in Chapter 2, it is these cognitive elements that provide lasting change in the meaning and desirability of deviant/criminal behaviour, and although boxing provides a 'hook for change', it does not provide a site for positively valued themes, nor does it provide an outline for a replacement self (Giordano 2002).

What boxing does provide is a culture based on hegemonic masculine sporting discourses and attachment figures that are complicit within in it. The informal control mechanisms that boxing provides are only one side of the coin, as the habitual patterns and time spent in the gym environment contribute to the formation of attitudes that are complicit with masculine and working-class codes. Thus, boxing merely incapacitates and diverts young men away from crime by virtue of detainment, and offers little by way of cognitive transformation. This is evidenced from this study by the data suggesting that the masculine discourses of this social world override theories of incapacitation and pro-social development, as the men presented in this study would barely think twice about engaging in retaliatory or defensive behaviours outside the gym setting.

Implications for policy and practice

Throughout this study, I have tried to establish whether the sport of boxing can be employed as a strategy for criminal desistance, particularly the reduction of violent behaviour and attitudes among young males. It is often thought that boxing has the potential to reduce criminal activity, and that young people can personally benefit from participating (Sampson 2009; Meek 2018), and this is true to some extent. Boxing has the ability to engage, inspire and provide opportunities for young men (and women) when other avenues seem blocked or unattainable. Additionally, sport and physical activity have great meaning for those who box, and the gym provides a cohesive site that brings together varying communities that otherwise may not get the chance to meet. It is helpful in reducing barriers to engagement and in building relationships among segregated communities, and I commend boxing in the way it creates a family structure for people who may not have that in their lives. Furthermore, participants experience rewards from strenuous exercise, and many of those interviewed discussed how exercise contributed to their feelings of increased self-esteem. The sport also gave participants a sense of belonging, loyalty and support, and members often discussed how peers and trainers in the gym acted as second parents or brothers and sisters.

As discussed in previous chapters, the last decade has seen several research reviews being commissioned to examine the evidence for sport's claimed benefits (Audit Commission 2009; McMahon and Belur 2013; Centre for Social Justice 2011; Meek 2018; Walpole et al 2018). The general consensus of these reviews is that there is a lack of robust, research-based evidence on the outcomes of sports participation, and more evidence is needed to make an affirmative link. As Coalter (2007:79) has suggested, 'policymakers lack the evidence required to make informed policy decisions and to connect sport issues to other policy priorities', which, he goes on to say, is as a result of methodological problems, due to a lack of control groups and longitudinal research. The research that does exist divides itself into two main categories: research on programmes seeking to use sport with 'at risk' populations to prevent crime, commonly referred to as 'diversionary activities'; and also, research on programmes that use sport to rehabilitate offenders, commonly referred to as 'secondary' or 'tertiary' forms (Cryer 2005).

Evaluations of both of these approaches suggest that the salience and popular appeal of sport can be effective in attracting young people to programmes, and I do not disagree. However, evidence has demonstrated that sport itself is part of a process, and not an end in its own right; therefore, its benefits need to be managed sensitively and with the right workforce for the task (Nichols 2007). This will require an awareness of the process and an ability to match the needs of the participants with the experience and benefits that sport can offer.

Furthermore, considerations of the perceptions of sport are also imperative to its success in reducing criminogenic attitudes, and success requires an awareness of boxing's association with masculine discourses and physical risk. Hence, it is important to unpick the underlying cultural messages transmitted in hyper-masculine arenas and to provide young men with positive role models who they can identify with; albeit, by providing positive alternatives to the dominant hegemonic prototype commonly seen in gyms (Jump 2017).

With recent work by the Ministry of Justice and Rosie Meek (Meek, 2018), there has been a general sway towards developing the recommendations she suggests in her independent review of sport in youth and adult prisons. This is a welcome report, and I converge with Meek in her suggestion to pilot and evaluate boxing-related programmes as part of a targeted intervention. However, I believe that this intervention must sit alongside more therapeutic and pro-social identity change mechanisms than it currently does, and help to facilitate a change in identity that provides hope for the future, as well as addressing a young person's readiness to change (Stephenson et al 2010; Fitzpatrick et al 2015). There has been a move towards this with recent work by Deuchar et al (2016) and Søgaard et al (2016), and their work around 'boxing transformation narratives'. These narratives are defined as the 'utilisation of masculinised narratives to assist in the reimagining of young men's cognitions to motivate them to become active and responsible partakers in their own reformation process' (Søgaard et al 2016:102). Put simply, more responsibility is placed at the feet of young men in the gym, and with the help of experienced counsellors and boxing coaches, young men are encouraged to view their masculinity in a more inclusive manner. For example, hyper-masculine discourses in the gym are challenged and reframed in a more inclusive situational context, whereby the gladiatorial imagery and retaliatory tropes are channelled into the desistance process as opposed to the code of the street (for further discussion, see Jump and Smithson forthcoming).

The Department for Culture, Media and Sport and Strategy Unit (2002) argue that sport can have a positive impact on behaviour, and can therefore lead to reduced offending when employed as part of a wider developmental programme of education and support. Indeed, it is hoped that by achieving improvements in personal and social skills, a process of change will be stimulated that will impact favourably on the participant's offending behaviour. As stated previously, there is little to suggest that participation in sport alone will reduce offending, as there is a real difference between using sport as part of a programme to deliver positive social outcomes and assuming that sport will automatically deliver these on its own.

The beneficial impact of participation in boxing is hard to measure, as it may eventually appear as one of a number of linked positive changes in an individual. Hence, it becomes increasingly difficult to identify the effect of one particular activity in isolation from other factors, such as change in family circumstances, change in peer networks or relationship patterns, or the commencement of employment. One area where there is a clear consensus, however, is that of the coaches and their impact on sporting environments and outcomes for participants (Jump and Smithson forthcoming). Previous research by Coalter (2012) found that young people expressed a stronger preference for coaches who provided social support and encouragement, and who adopted a more empathic, democratic approach to coaching compared to their parents.

Fitzpatrick et al (2015) further suggest that a crucial function in any relationship is that of providing identity support, as individuals see themselves in a variety of roles, whereby it becomes important that others provide them with enough support to maintain visions of roles that they rank highly. In the gym environment, the roles promoted by the coaches were ones of a competitive nature, which sometimes came at the expense of an individual's welfare (Sandford et al 2006). This is because competition is often seen as an imperative part of sporting activity, and that taking part in lessons about winning and losing will somehow enhance an individual's understanding of 'fair play'. This idea presumably becomes transposable to wider arenas, and the lessons learnt in sport can be translated and applied when the gloves are off.

Undoubtedly, the culture of the ring did enforce a version of fair play. When confined to the rules of the sport, men did adhere to these versions, and responded well to the setting of boundaries. These versions are not necessarily transposable to the outside world, as the men in this research – while respectful and obedient to the rules in the gym – often viewed the sport as a form of domination or as a resource in maintaining valued identities. The version of 'fair play' and training rules regulating sportsmen's behaviour outside the gym is a common misconception when applied to boxing and other hyper-masculine combat sports. This is because sporting activity in a boxing gym involves an element of aggressive competitiveness and domination. It is these elements, I would argue, that make it so appealing to young, disenfranchised men, in particular. The young men in the gym saw boxing as a way to further accomplish their masculinity, and eradicate any notions of disrespect. Moreover, the environment of the gym that I studied was equipped to support this idea.

Kidd (1990:37) has argued that 'the current debate about boxing is still about competing masculinities', and that there is little scope for the full expression of differing masculinities in boxing gyms. Anderson's (2010) work into 'inclusive masculinities' may disagree. I would welcome a sea-change moment, whereby hegemonic masculine discourses are re-theorised and enacted in combat sports such as boxing. Notwithstanding, the residual prevalence of these hyper-masculine discourses in combat sports ultimately leaves this research with one outstanding question: *how do we combat hyper-masculine violent discourses in boxing?*

This is a difficult question to answer, and even more difficult to embed in practice, but answering it is ultimately imperative to the success and future direction of combat sports in the youth-focused sphere of welfare-based approaches. In other words, sports targeted towards youth provision – either primary or secondary forms of diversion and reform – need to consider the implicit messages transmitted through aggressive competitive sports, if they are to be successful in reducing criminogenic attitudes and behaviours.

There are no magic solutions to the situation described, as it is deeply rooted in long-established patterns of socialisation and human interaction. As Matthews (2014:16) suggests in his work around male identity in a boxing gym: 'it was clear that the power of biology to justify their understanding of male physicality was used in a relatively socially acceptable manner'. Moreover, these ideas are perpetuated and maintained by both powerful and political interests. We cannot dismiss boxing, nor would we want to; yet, if boxing is to be taken seriously as a diversionary activity that can assist in the personal and social development of young people, then more work needs to be done.

Considering that the Department for Culture, Media and Sport (2013:12) confirmed a £40 million increase in funding to extend the 2012 Olympic sport legacy to 2017, with an aim to 'increase school sport and regular participation in competitive sport', issues concerning sport's short- and long-term effects on young people's attitudes need to be addressed. Indeed, boxing alone received £1,171,195 of funding from Sport England's Olympic Legacy programme in 2012, therefore funding numerous amateur boxing clubs across the UK. In April 2019, the Home Office announced a drive to fund more sporting schemes over the next ten years, with an injection of £200 million into the Youth Endowment Fund, specifically aimed at tackling knife crime and serious youth violence.

If money is to be invested in sports such as boxing, then I believe a conversation needs to start about how we make boxing gyms more inclusive and less hyper-masculine. I believe it is possible to challenge the hegemonic masculine discourses evidenced and perpetuated in combat sports, however this needs to be a top-down approach. By this I refer to the coaches and trainers, as they need to be the starting point. They could start by actively questioning the pervasive masculine bias in the boxing world, as the language and discourses of these combat sports reinforce the male dominant gender order. Challenging sexism and homophobia as Anderson (2010), Burstyn (1999) and Channon and Matthews (2015) have attested would be imperative to making a change, as would 'undoing gender' (Channon 2014) and promoting more positive feminist role models in the boxing world (Van Ingen 2003).

Combat sports are often seen as masculine battles, and competition forms part of a discourse that views opponents as enemies, as opposed to co-contributors. It is no wonder that many discourses on combat sports call upon military speech and gladiatorial imagery as a way to evoke competition. A sports culture that did not place so much emphasis on winning – and therefore emphasised an exploration of skill, creative interaction and appreciation of one another – would be much less repressive. As one of the policy makers in this research attested, "non-contact boxing would be less aggressive but arguably also less attractive".

Both male and female coaches (and members of the LGBTQI community) delivering boxing training, could go some way to start readdressing the gender imbalance in this field. This may help to challenge those individuals who commonly view violence as a male self-expectation and a viable solution to a problem when their masculinity is assumedly brought into question. If women and non-binary individuals can also be seen to be successful at boxing, then it can potentially be looked upon as a sport that is accessible to all. This will go some way towards challenging the common misconception that boxing is a 'male only preserve' (Dunning 1986). There is no doubt that the gym is an important site for young men, and increasingly young women, and the attachments formed in it can contribute to feelings of safety, security, involvement and commitment. However, what is important is the culture that is fostered. As the boxing coach generally dictates this, it would make sense for this cultural change to begin with them.

Yet as it stands, the relationship between coach and participant in the gyms I observed and participated in, were non-conducive to the development of these attributes, as the trainers themselves were immersed in the culture of sporting masculine domination and the search for respect. Thus, the masculine discourses inherent in combat sports became cyclical and ever-present as the men consistently reinforced and accomplished their masculinity in space-occupying, dominant ways.

Research by Joliffe and Farrington (2007) on the impact of mentoring on reoffending suggests that even long-term mentor/mentee relationships are not statistically significant in terms of reducing offending. While these scholars recognised that mentoring is often viewed as influential in increasing life success for those 'at risk' of offending, criticisms are also apparent (Buck 2018). Nonetheless, I align with Coalter (2012) and Joliffe and Farrington (2007), when they suggest that mentoring can be successful in reducing offending, particularly when combined with a successful 'hook' such as boxing. This can only be achieved when it forms part of a number of interventions, whereby behaviour modification, supplementary education and employment programmes are established, and when the mentor themselves are in a position to actively challenge aggressive dominant behaviours as part of a process of lasting change. For all their good intentions, the coaches presented in this study would perhaps not be ideal candidates for this role, as their understanding of desistance and violence is clouded by their own scarred histories. This is not uncommon, and also not dissimilar to recent work by Greenfield (2001) into the church and ministry, as he describes how the concept of the wounded healer is not always best placed to heal from and prevent further attacks.

Accordingly, the task of providing a better sporting experience across the spectrum, especially for young people and particularly for those who are coming to the gym from disadvantaged or vulnerable backgrounds, requires a more rounded approach to sport coaching. The key to this is through the coaches themselves, and their personal understanding and experiences of violence, and how this is disseminated and transmitted in the gym environment for the young people to absorb. Buck (2018) suggests that for mentoring to be successful, Rogerian theory (Rogers, 1995) must be applied – thus, the core conditions of 'caring', 'listening' and 'encouraging small steps' must form part of the mentoring relationship. To apply this to boxing, would require coaches and mentors to be congruent with their own process of desistance and views of masculinity, and this is not always an easy feat. Having said that, it is not impossible. I believe this is a step in the right direction, and one that could build upon Søgaard's concept of 'boxing transformation narratives' (Søgaard et al 2016).

It is a misguided assumption that taking part in boxing will automatically result in individuals developing a sense of discipline and control, or learning lessons in dealing with success and failure. Instead, what matters more than participating in an activity is the way in which it is presented. If we value participation in sport and boxing for its alleged ability to develop outcomes for young people, it makes sense to ensure that coaches and trainers are able to present activities in a way that increases the likelihood that legitimate violence in the pursuit of winning is correctly understood, and not embedded in men's identities as a way to achieve respect and status.

Sport alone will not be sufficient to counter criminal activity, as the social bonds formed with attachment figures such as coaches are often viewed as an essential element for the internalisation of values and norms, and are therefore related to the conception of internal personal control (Hirschi 1969). Developing this coach-athlete dyad in more positive and forward-thinking ways, and emphasising the relationship as a vehicle to develop internal personal control, could be a contributory factor in the quest to promote desistance from violence among young males. By developing Hirschi's concept of commitment and involvement – which boxing clearly has the potential to do – coaches have the power to foster environments that challenge misconceptions around competitiveness, homophobia and misogyny.

Indeed, given that an important condition for the development of individuals through sport is regular attendance at a programme or club, it is important that the sporting environment is one to which young people are keen to return. Yet, this has to be a constructive approach, if the environment is to have any impact on positive outcomes for young people. Based on research in the field of youth development,

Roth and Brooks-Gunn (2003) outlined key principles as being imperative to the success of sporting programmes and mentorship. These are: positive view of one's actions and capability; internal sense of self-worth and being good at things; positive bonds with people and institutions; respect for rules; correct behaviour and integrity; and a sense of sympathy and empathy for others, regardless of gender, sexuality, race or class.

If these elements could be achieved, and these documents disseminated and embedded in sporting clubs of this kind, then I believe there is hope – and a future for boxing as an engagement tool and as a potential vehicle for change.

Limitations of this research

All research has limitations. I appreciate that the 'knowledge' of the social world that I have accrued is only a small part of understanding what this world actually means to individuals who dwell in it. More importantly, I acknowledge that as a female researcher in a social world that is mainly dominated by men, my gender subject position may not be the best equipped to understand the meaning and habitus of these men, as they negotiate their understanding and positioning in this competitive hierarchical world (see Jump 2016 for a further discussion). Accordingly, the accounts and narratives of these men are always situated within the particular power relations of this research.

As Lois Presser (2005) has stated, the interview and subsequent narrative constructions are consequential to men's narratives of self, including Presser's response to their power plays. In other words, the ongoing understanding of gender relations, particularly in the social sciences, must go beyond simply writing the researcher into the research, and must pay closer attention to the exchanges of dialogue within them. How did the men wish to be seen by a female academic researching their understanding of violence? Were their responses and actions part of a further construction and accomplishment of their masculinity in the interview process? Missing from this data is a systematic investigation into how gender power relations between interviewer and participant become part of interview data. As one of many female researchers in this subject area (in particular Presser 2005; Woodward 2008; Trimbur 2009), further research ought to consider these 'research effects'.

Feminist critiques, although rarely applied to boxing, have a great deal to offer for resolving some of the methodological problems that have emerged, particularly those concerning validity that underpin subjective/objective dualism, and it is these that I attempted to call upon in my research. Despite my 'insider' status, it became clear that regardless of my level of expertise, or the knowledge that I had managed to accrue, I could not adopt a gender-neutral stance. Indeed, women can only go so far in 'doing masculinity'. This may be because the masculinity that is enacted in the boxing gym is predicated upon a history of risk-taking, danger, adventure, the practice of physical force and exclusivity, all of which constitute the making of traditional masculinities. These masculinities are juxtaposed with bodies with which they are associated; that is, men's bodies as perceived by those who box (Woodward 2008). Moreover, researchers, whether situated as women or men, inhabit lived bodies that are also constituted through the practices of gender. Therefore, reflections on the gender identity and positioning of the researcher helps to illuminate the representations of masculinities that emerged in the research process.

To conclude, men who box, despite common disadvantages, take various approaches in their interpretations of how they can act as individuals in relation to the obstacles that structure – and are structured into – their daily lives. In short, identity formation, and the development of both desisting and recidivist identities are a function of the individual's interpretation of his place in the social structure. These differences in interpretation and consequent action suggest that desistance, while of obvious importance, tells us little on its own about the range of ways in which pugilistic men interpret and negotiate their place in the world. In this research, I tried to remain open to the possibilities of interpretation, and to focus more on the understanding of violence that men possess, as opposed to just measuring levels of violence prior to or after joining the gym.

In some respects, this limited my ability to speak clearly, and I acknowledge this, when ascertaining whether or not boxing contributes to a process of desistance. However, the knowledge gained, and recommendations made, are valid when considering the future relationship between sport and crime. Indeed, policy makers and politicians are still wringing their hands when trying to solve the complex problem that is desistance from violence, especially among young disenfranchised men. While boxing may present as an attractive option, it is not always the best avenue for these young men, as the findings in this particular study demonstrate.

It is because of my love for boxing and my experience in youth justice that I researched this area. It was always my intention, when writing this book, to improve the lives of those who box, and to help those who champion it as a desistance-promoting tool. I believe that the messages inherent in this monograph can work towards doing this.

Boxing has a lot to offer, if it can only deconstruct – or at least, reflect on – its inherent masculine properties and discourses. In late modern social worlds, the traditional patriarchal gender order is being increasingly challenged, and boxing is part of that challenge. With the #metoo movement, and notions of gender being no longer classified as strictly binary, boxing has a long way to go to address its thinking in these terms. I hope that the 'sweet science' of boxing can comprehend this, and that boxing can 'punch above its weight' in its quest to engage young people and the communities it serves.

References

Abrahams, R.D. (1970) *Positively Black,* Englewood Cliffs, NJ: Prentice-Hall.

Akers, R.L. (1998) *Social Learning Theory and Social Structure: A General Theory of Crime and Deviance,* Boston, MA: Northeastern University Press.

American Medical Association (1983) 'Brain injury in boxing', *Journal of the American Medical Association,* 249(2): 255.

Anderson, E. (1999) *Code of the Street: Decency, Violence, and the Moral Life of the Inner City,* New York: Norton.

Anderson, E. (2002) 'Openly gay athletes: Contesting hegemonic masculinity in a homophobic environment', *Gender and Society,* 16: 860–77.

Anderson, E. (2005) *In the Game: Gay Athletes and the Cult of Masculinity,* New York: State University of New York Press.

Anderson, E. (2008) 'I used to think women were weak': Orthodox masculinity, gender-segregation and sport', *Sociological Forum,* 23: 257–80.

Anderson, E. (2009) *Inclusive Masculinity: The Changing Nature of Masculinity,* New York: Routledge.

Anderson, E. (2010) *In the Game: Gay Athletes and the Cult of Masculinity,* New York: State University of New York Press.

Atkinson, M. (2011) *Deconstructing Men and Masculinities,* Ontario, Canada: Oxford University Press.

Audit Commission (2009) *Tired of Hanging Around: Using Sport and Leisure Activities to Prevent Anti-Social Behaviour by Young People,* London: Audit Commission.

Baglivio, M.T., Wolff, K.T., Piquero, A.R. and Epps, N. (2015) 'The relationship between adverse childhood experiences (ACE) and juvenile offending trajectories in a juvenile offender sample', *Journal of Criminal Justice,* 43(3): 229–41.

Bandura, A. (1977) *Social Learning Theory,* Englewood Cliffs, NJ: Prentice Hall.

Barry, M. (2010) 'Youth transitions: From offending to desistance', *Journal of Youth Studies*, 13(1): 121–36.

Bartky, S. (1988) 'Foucault, Femininity and the Modernization of Patriarchal Power', in I. Diamon and L. Quinby (eds) *Feminism and Foucault: Reflections on Resistance*, Boston: Northeastern University Press, 61–86.

Bathrick, D. (1990) 'Max Schmeling on the Canvas: Boxing as an Icon of Weimar Culture', *New German Critique*, 51, 113–36 cited in Jefferson, T. (1998) 'Muscle, "Hard Men" and "Iron" Mike Tyson: Reflections on Desire, Anxiety and the Embodiment of Masculinity', *Body and Society*, 4(1), 77–98.

Begg, D. J., Langley, J. D., Moffitt, T., & Marshall, S.W. (1996). Sport and delinquency: an examination of the deterrence hypothesis in a longitudinal study. *British Journal of Sports Medicine, 30*(4), 335-341.

Bertaux, D. (1981) *Biography and History: The Life History Approach in Social Sciences*, Beverly Hills, CA: Sage.

Blok, A. (1974) *The Mafia of a Sicilian Village 1860–1960: A Study of Violent Peasant Entrepreneurs,* Oxford: Blackwell.

Blok, A. (1981) 'Rams and Billy Goats: A Key to the Mediterranean Code of Honour, *Royal Anthropological Institute of Great Britain and Ireland,* 16 (3) 427-440.

Bordo, S. (1989) 'The body and the reproduction of femininity: A feminist appropriation of Foucault', in A. Jagger and S. Bordo (eds) *Gender/body/knowledge: Feminist reconstructions of being and knowing*, New Brunswick, NJ: Rutgers University Press, 13–33.

Bottoms, A., Shapland J., Costello, A., Holmes, D. and Muir, G. (2004) 'Towards desistance: Theoretical underpinnings for an empirical study', *The Howard Journal*, 43(4): 368–89.

Bourdieu, P. (1977) *Outline of a Theory of Practice*, Cambridge, UK: Cambridge University Press.

Bourdieu, P. (1986) 'The Forms of Capital', in John. G Richardson (ed), *Handbook of Theory and Research for the Sociology of Education*, New York: Greenwood Press, 241–58.

Bourgois, P. (1996) *In Search of Respect: Selling Crack in El Barrio*, Cambridge, UK: Cambridge University Press.

Brookman, F., Copes, H. and Hochstetler, A. (2011) 'Street codes as formula stories: How inmates recount violence', *Journal of Contemporary Ethnography*, 40: 397.

Buck, G. (2018) 'The core conditions of peer mentoring', *Criminology and Criminal Justice*, 18(2): 190–206.

Burtsyn, V. (1999) *The Rites of Men: Manhood, Politics, and the Culture of Sports,* Toronto, Canada: University of Toronto Press.

Butler, J. (1999) *Gender Trouble.* New York: Routledge.

Butler, M. and Maruna, S. (2009) 'The impact of disrespect on prisoner's aggression: Outcomes of experimentally inducing violence-supportive cognitions', *Psychology, Crime and Law*, 15(2–3): 235–50.

Butt, D.S. (1987) *The Psychology of Sport, the Behaviour, Motivation, Personality and Performance of Athletes*, New York: Van Nostrand Reinhold.

Centre for Social Justice (2011) *More Than a Game: Harnessing the Power of Sport to Transform the Lives of Disadvantaged Young People.* Available at: www.centreforsocialjustice.org.uk/library/game-harnessing-power-sport-transform-lives-disadvantaged-young-people [Accessed 1 April 2019].

Channon, A.G. (2014) 'Enter the discourse: Exploring the discursive roots of inclusivity in mixed-sex martial arts': *Sport in Society*, 13: 935–51.

Channon, A. and Matthews, C.R. (2015) '"It is what it is": Masculinity, homosexuality, and inclusive discourse in mixed martial arts', *Journal of Homosexuality*, 62(7): 936–56.

Chodorow, N. (1978) *Reproduction of Mothering; Psychoanalysis and the Sociology of Gender*, Berkeley: University of California Press.

Cloward, A. and Ohlin, L.E. (1960) *Delinquency and Opportunity: A Theory of Delinquent Gangs*, New York: The Free Press.

Coakley, J. (1990) *Sport in Society: Issues and Controversies*, 4th edn, St Louis, MO: Times Mirror/Mosby.

Coakley, J. (2001) *Sport in Society: Issues and Controversies*, 7th edn, Boston, MA: McGraw Hill.

Coalter, F. (1988) *Sport and Antisocial Behaviour: A Literature Review*, Research Report, Scottish Sports Council, Edinburgh.

Coalter, F. (2007) *A Wider Social Role for Sport: Who's Keeping the Score?*, Oxford: Routledge.

Coalter, F. (2012) 'What is the development in sport-for-development', *Sports Governance, Development and Corporate Responsibility*, 88–106.

Coalter, F., Alison, M. and Taylor, J. (2000) *The Role of Sport in Regenerating Deprived Urban Areas*, Edinburgh: Scottish Executive.

Cohen, A.K. (1955) *Delinquent Boys: The Culture of the Gang*, New York: The Free Press of Glencoe.

Cohen, P. (1976) 'Working Class Youth Cultures in East London', in S. Hall and T. Jefferson (eds) *Resistance through Rituals*, London: Hutchinson.

Coleman, J. (1961) *The Adolescent Society: The Social Life of the Teenager and its Impact on Education*, New York: The Free Press of Glencoe.

Colinson, M. (1996) 'In search of the high life', *British Journal of Criminology*, 36(3): 428–44.

Collins, M. and Kay, T. (2003) *Sport and Social Inclusion*, London: Routledge.

Connell, R.W. (1983) *Which Way is Up? Essays on Sex, Class and Culture*, Sydney: Allen and Unwin.

Connell, R.W. (1985) 'Theorising gender', *Sociology*, 19(2), 260–72.

Connell, R.W. (1987) *Gender and Power*, Cambridge, UK: Polity Press.

Connell, R.W. (1990) 'An Iron Man: The Body and Some Contradictions of Hegemonic Masculinity', in M. Messner and D. Sabo (eds) *Sport, Men and the Gender Order*, IL: Human Kinetics.

Connell, R.W. (1995) *Masculinities*, Cambridge, UK: Polity Press.

Connell, R.W. (2005) *Masculinities*, Cambridge, UK: Polity Press, 2nd edn.

Cooley, C.H. (1922) *Human Nature and the Social Order* (rev. edn), New York: Scribner, 352.

Costello, E.J., Erklani, A., Fairbank, J. and Angold, A. (2003) 'The prevalence of potentially traumatic events in childhood and adolescence', *Journal of Traumatic Stress*, 15, 99–112.

Coward, R. (1984) *Female Desire: Women's Sexuality Today*, London: Paladin.

Cox, S. (2012) *Game of Life,* Sport and Recreation Alliance. Available at: www.sportandrecreation.org.uk/policy/research-publications/game-of-life [Accessed 1 April 2019].

Crabbe, T. (2006) 'Reaching the "hard to reach": engagement, relationship building and social control in sport based social inclusion work', *International Journal of Sport Management and Marketing*, 2(1–2): 27–40.

Cressey, D.R. (1964) *Delinquency, Crime and Differential Association*, The Hague, The Netherlands: Martinus Nijhoff.

Crossett, T.W. (1999) 'Male athletes' violence against women: A critical assessment of the Athletic Affiliation, Violence Against Women Debate' *Quest* 51:244–57.

Crosnoe, R. (2001) 'The social world of male and female athletes in High School', *Sociological Studies of Children and Youth*, 8: 87–108.

Cryer J. (2005) *Ruff Guide to Sport and Youth Crime*, Sports Development. Available at: www.sportdevelopment.org.uk/index.php/rgsd/53-rgcrime [Accessed 1 April 2019].

Curry, T.J. (1991) 'Fraternal bonding in the locker room: A pro-feminist analysis of talk about competition and women', *Sociology of Sport Journal*, 8(2): 119–35.

Curry, T.J. (1998) 'Beyond the locker room: Campus bars and college athletes', *Sociology of Sport Journal*, 15(3): 205–15.

Daly, M. and Wilson, M. (1988) *Homicide*, New York: De Gruyter.
Davies, N. (1992) *Maxwell: The Inside Story*, London: Pan.
de Garis, L. (2002) '"Be a Buddy to Your Buddy", Male Identity, Aggression, and Intimacy in a Boxing Gym', in J. McKay, M. Messner and D. Sabo (eds) *Masculinities, Gender Relations and Sport*, London: Sage, 87–107.
Denzin, N.K. (1988) *Interpretive Biography,* New York: Sage.
Department for Culture, Media and Sport (DCMS) and Strategy Unit (2002) *Game Plan: A Strategy for Delivering Government's Sport and Physical Activity Objectives.* London: Cabinet Office.
Department for Culture, Media and Sport (DCMS) (2013) *Mid Year Report to Parliament April-September 2013.*
Department of the Environment (1975) Parliamentary White Paper on Sport and Recreation. National Archives.
Deuchar, R., Søgaard, T.F., Kolind, T., Thylstrup, B. and Wells, L. (2016) '"When you're boxing you don't think so much": pugilism, transitional masculinities and criminal desistance among young Danish gang members', *Journal of Youth Studies*, 19(6): 725–42.
Dubbert, J.L. (1979) *A Man's Place: Masculinity in Transition.* Englewood Cliffs, NJ: Prentice Hall.
Dunning, E.G. (1986) 'Sport as a Male Preserve: Notes on the Social Sources of Masculine Identity and its Transformations', in N. Elias and E. Dunning (eds) *Quest for Excitement: Sport and Leisure in the Civilizing Process*, New York: Basil Blackwell.
Dunning, E.G. and Sheard, K. (1979) *Barbarians, Gentlemen and Players, A Sociological Review of the Development of Rugby and Football,* Oxford: Martin Robertson.
Dunning, E.G., Murphy, P. and Williams, J (1988) *The Roots of Football Hooliganism,* London: Routledge.
Durkheim, E. (1973) *Emile Durkheim on Morality and Society*, Chicago: University of Chicago Press.
Dutton, K.R. (1995) *The Perfectible Body: The Western Ideal of Physical Development*, London: Cassell.
Eder, D. and Kinney, D.A. (1995) 'The effect of middle-school extracurricular activities on adolescents popularity and peer status', *Youth ad Society*, 26: 298–324.
Eder, D., Evans, C. and Parker, S. (1997) *School Talk: Gender and Adolescent Culture*, New Brunswick, NJ: Rutgers University Press.
Edreson, I.M. and Olweus, D. (2005) 'Participation in power sports and antisocial involvement in preadolescent and adolescent boys', *Journal of Child Psychology and Psychiatry* 46(5): 468–78.

Elias, N. and Dunning, E. (1986) *The Quest for Excitement,* Oxford: Basil Blackwell.

Ellis, A., Winlow, S. and Hall, S. (2017) '"Throughout my life I've had people walk all over me": Trauma in the lives of violent men', *The Sociological Review*, 65(4): 699–713.

Epstein, S. (1991). Cognitive-experiential self theory: Implications for developmental psychology. In M. R. Gunnar & L. A. Sroufe (eds), *The Minnesota symposia on child psychology, Vol. 23. Self processes and development* (pp. 79–123), Hillsdale, NJ, US: Lawrence Erlbaum Associates, Inc.

Evans, J. (2003) 'Vigilance and vigilantes: Thinking psychoanalytically about anti-paedophile action', *Theoretical Criminology*, 7(2): 163–89.

Evans-Chase, M. (2014) 'Addressing trauma and psychosocial development in juvenile justice-involved youth: A synthesis of the developmental neuroscience, juvenile justice and trauma literature', *Laws*, 3, 744–58.

Faludi, S. (2000) *Stiffed: The Betrayal of the American Man*, New York: William Morrow and Company.

Farrell, W. (1974) *The Liberated Man*, New York: Random House.

Farrington, D.P. (1992) 'Criminal career research in the United Kingdom', *British Journal of Criminology*, 32, 521.

Farrington, D.P. and West, D.J. (1995) 'Effects of marriage, separation, and children on offending by adult males', *Current Perspectives on Aging and the Life Cycle*, 4: 249–81.

Featherstone, M. (1992) 'The heroic life and everyday life', *Theory, Culture & Society*, 9(1): 159–82.

Feldman, A. (1991) *Formations of Violence*, London: University of Chicago Press.

Felitti, V.J., Anda, R.F., Nordenberg, D., Williamson, D.F., Spitz, A.M., Edwards, V. and Marks, J.S. (1998) 'Relationship of childhood abuse and household dysfunction to many of the leading causes of death in adults: The Adverse Childhood Experiences (ACE) Study', *American Journal of Preventive Medicine*, 14, 245–58.

Felitti, V. J., Anda, R. F., Nordenberg, D., Williamson, D. F., Spitz, A. M., Edwards, V., and Marks, J.S. (2019). 'Relationship of childhood abuse and household dysfunction to many of the leading causes of death in adults: The Adverse Childhood Experiences (ACE) Study', *American Journal of Preventive Medicine*, *56*(6), 774–786.

Fine, G.A. (1987) *With the Boys: Little League Baseball and Preadolescent Culture*, Chicago IL: University of Chicago Press.

Fitzpatrick, E., McGuire, J. and Dickson, J.M. (2015) 'Personal goals of adolescents in a youth offending service in the United Kingdom', *Youth Justice*, 15(2): 166–81.

Fletcher, M. (1992) 'An Investigation into Participation in Amateur Boxing, Unpublished dissertation in part-requirement for MSc in Sport and Recreation Management Sheffield University', in G. Nichols (2006) 'A Consideration of why Active Participation in Sport and Leisure Might Reduce Criminal Behaviour', *Sport, Education and Society*, 2(2): 181–90.

Freud, S. (1975). *Beyond the Pleasure Principle*, New York: Norton.

Frosh, S. (1997) 'Screaming under the Bridge: Masculinity, Rationality and Psychotherapy', in J. Ussher (ed) *Body Talk*, London: Routledge.

Fussell. S. (1991) *Muscle: Confessions of an Unlikely Bodybuilder*, New York: Poseidon.

Gadd, D. (2000) 'Masculinities, violence and defended psychosocial subjects', *Theoretical Criminology*, (4): 429–46.

Gadd, D. (2002) 'Masculinities and violence against female partners', *Social & Legal Studies*, 11(1): 61–80.

Gadd, D. (2004) 'Making sense of interviewee–interviewer dynamics in narratives about violence in intimate relationships', *International Journal of Social Research Methodology*, 7(5): 383–401.

Gadd, D. and Farrall, S. (2004) 'Criminal careers, desistance and subjectivity: Interpreting men's narratives of change', *Theoretical Criminology*, 8(2): 123–56.

Gadd, D. and Jefferson, T. (2007) *Psychosocial Criminology*. London: Sage.

Gadd, D., Corr, M.L., Fox, C.L. and Butler, I. (2014) 'This is Abuse … Or is it? Domestic abuse perpetrators' responses to anti-domestic violence publicity', *Crime, Media, Culture*, 10(1): 3–22.

Gaylin, W. (1984) *The Rage Within: Anger in Modern Life*, New York: Simon and Schuster.

Gilligan, J. (1996) *Violence: Our Deadly Epidemic and its Causes*, New York: GP Putnam.

Giordano, P.C., Cernkovich, S.A. and Pugh, M.D. (1986) 'Friendship and delinquency', *American Journal of Sociology,* Vol 91 (5) pp 1170-1202.

Giordano, P.C., Cernkovich, S.A. and Rudolph, J.L. (2002) 'Gender, crime, and desistance: Toward a theory of cognitive transformation', *American Journal of Sociology*, 107(4): 990–1064.

Glassner, B. (1989) 'Men and Muscles' in M. Kimmell and M. Messner (eds) *Men's Lives*, New York: Macmillan.

Glueck, S. and Glueck, E. (1943) *Criminal Careers in Retrospect*, New York: The Common.

Goffman, E. (1959) *The Presentation of Self in Everyday Life*, Garden City, NY: Doubleday.

Goffman, E. (1967) *Interaction Ritual*, New York: Anchor.

Gorn, E.J. (1986) *The Manly Art: Bare-Knuckle Prize Fighting in America*, New York: Cornell University Press.

Gottfredson, M.R. and Hirschi, T. (1990) *A General Theory of Crime*. Stanford: Stanford University Press.

Graham, J. and Bowling, B. (1995) *Young People and Crime*. Home Office Research Study 145, London: Home Office.

Greenfield, G. (2001) *The Wounded Minister: Healing from and Preventing Personal Attacks*. Michigan: Baker Books.

Groombridge, N. (2016) *Sports Criminology: A Critical Criminology of Sport and Games*. Bristol: Policy Press.

Guardian, The (2012) 'Women's boxing comes of age at 2012 Olympics' Thursday 9 August 2012.

Gunaratnam, Y. (2004) 'Bucking and Kicking': Race, Gender and Embodied Resistance in Healthcare', in P. Chamberlayne, J. Bornat and U. Apitzsch (eds) *Biographical Methods and Professional Practice*, Bristol: Policy Press.

Hall, L. (1991) *Hidden Anxieties: Male Sexuality, 1900–1950*, Cambridge, UK: Polity Press.

Hall, S. (1997) 'Visceral cultures and criminal practices', *Theoretical Criminology*, 1(4): 453–78.

Halpern, D. (1988) 'Distance and Embrace', in J.C. Oates and D. Halpern (eds) *Reading the Fights*, New York: Prentice-Hall, 275–85.

Hannerz, U. (1996) *Transnational Connections: Culture, People, Places*, New York: Taylor & Francis US.

Hargreaves, J. (1986) '"Where's the virtue?" Where's the grace? A discussion of the social production of gender relations in and through sport', *Theory, Culture and Society*, 3(1).

Hargreaves, J. (1997) 'Introducing Images and Meanings', *Body and Society*, 3(4): 33–49.

Hartmann, D. (2001) 'Notes on midnight basketball and the cultural politics or recreation, race, and at-risk urban youth', *Journal of Sport and Social Issues*, 25: 339–71.

Healy, D. (2010) 'Betwixt and between: The role of psychosocial factors in the early stages of desistance', *Journal of Research in Crime and Delinquency*, 47(4): 419–38.

Hendry, L.B., Shucksmith, J., Love, J.G. and Glendinning, A. (1993) *Young People's Leisure and Lifestyles*, London: Routledge.

Hirschi, T. (1969) *Causes of Delinquency*, Berkeley, CA: University of California Press.

Hobbes, T. (1968) *Leviathan*, Harmondsworth: PenguHobbs, D. (1994) 'Mannish Boys', in T. Newburn and E. Stanko (eds) *Just Boys Doing Business,* London: Routledge.

Hobbs, D. (1995) *Bad Business*, New York: Oxford University Press.

Hobbs, D., Hadfield, P., Lister, S. and Winlow, S. (2003) *Bouncers: Violence and Governance in the Night-Time Economy*, New York: Oxford University Press.

Hoch, P. (1979) *White Hero, Black Beast: Racism, Sexism, and the Mask of Masculinity,* London: Pluto Press.

Hodge, K. and Danish, S. (2001) 'Promoting life skills for adolescent males through sport', *Handbook of Counseling Boys and Adolescent Males: A Practitioner's Guide*, 55–71.

Holdaway, S. (1988) 'Blue Joke: Humour in police work', *Humour in Society: Resistance and Control*, 106–22.

Hollway, W. and Jefferson, T. (1998) 'A kiss is just a kiss': date rape, gender and subjectivity', *Sexualities*, 1(4): 405–23.

Hollway, W. and Jefferson, T. (2000) *Doing Qualitative Research Differently: Free Association, Narrative and the Interview Method*, London: Sage.

Holt, R. (1989) *Sport and the British*, Oxford: Oxford University Press.

Home Office (2018) *Serious Violence Strategy*. Available at: www.gov.uk/government/publications/serious-violence-strategy [Accessed 1 April 2019].

Horne, A. & Kiselica, M. (1999). *Handbook of Counseling Boys and Adolescent Males: A Practitioner's Guide,* Thousand Oaks, CA: SAGE Publications.

Hughes, R. and Coakley, J. (1991) 'Positive Deviance Amongst Athletes: The Implications of Over-conformity to the Sport Ethic', *Sociology of Sport Journal*, 8: 307–25.

Jefferson, T. (1998) '"Muscle, "hard men" and "Iron" Mike Tyson: Reflections on desire, anxiety and the embodiment of masculinity', *Body and Society*, 4(1): 77–98.

Jefferson, T. (2002) 'Subordinating hegemonic masculinity', *Theoretical Criminology*, 6(1), 63–88.

Jefferson, T. and Walker, M.A. (1992) 'Ethnic minorities in the criminal justice system', *Criminal Law Review*, February (8): 3–9.

Joliffe, D. and Farrington, D. (2007) 'A Rapid Evidence Assessment of the Impact of Mentoring on Re-offending', *Home Office Research Development and Statistics Directorate*. Available at: www.youthmentoring.org.nz/content/docs/Home_Office_Impact_of_mentoring.pdf [Accessed 21 March 2014].

Jump, D.L. (2015) 'Fighting for change: Narrative accounts on the appeal and desistance potential of boxing', *ECAN Bulletin,* May 2015.

Jump, D.L. (2016) 'They didn't know whether to 'fuck me or fight me': An ethnographic account of North Town boxing gym' in *Mischief, Morality and Mobs, Essays in Honour of Geoffrey Pearson.* Edited by Dick Hobbs, New York: Routledge, 37–54.

Jump, D.L. (2017) 'Why we should think some more. A response to "When you're boxing you don't think so much": pugilism, transitional masculinities and criminal desistance among young Danish gang members', *Journal of Youth Studies*, 20(8): 1093–107.

Jump, D.L. and Smithson, H. (2020) 'Dropping Your Guard: The Use of Boxing as a Means of Forming Desistance Narratives Amongst Young People in the Criminal Justice System', *International Journal of Sport and Society.*

Kant, I. (1964) *Groundwork of the Metaphysics of Morals* (trans H.J Paton), London: Harper and Row.

Katz, J. (1988) *Seductions of Crime: The Moral and Sensual Seductions of Doing Evil*, New York: Basic Books.

Kelly, L. (2011) '"Social inclusion" through sports-based interventions?', *Critical Social Policy*, 31(1): 126–50.

Kidd, B. (1990) 'The Men's Cultural Centre: Sports and the Dynamic of Women's Oppression/Men's Repression' in M.A. Messner and D. Sabo (eds) *Sport, Men and the Gender Order*, Illinois: Human Kinetics.

Kimmel, M. (1990) 'Baseball and the reconstitution of American masculinity', *Sport, Men, and the Gender Order: Critical Feminist Perspectives*, 55–56.

Kinney, D.A. (1993) 'From nerds to normal: Adolescent identity recovery within a changing school system', *Sociology of Education*, 66: 21–40.

Klein, A.M. (1986) 'Pumping iron: Crisis and contradiction in bodybuilding', *Sociology of Sport*, 3(2): 112–33.

Klein, A.M. (1990) 'Little Big Man' in M. Messner and D. Sabo (eds) *Sport, Men and the Gender Order*, Illinois: Human Kinetics.

Kreager, D.A. (2007) 'Unnecessary roughness? School sports, peer networks, and male adolescent violence, *American Sociological Review*, 72: 705–24.

Landers, D.M. and Landers, D.M. (1978) 'Socialization via interscholastic athletics: Its effects on delinquency', *Sociology of Education*, 51(4): 299–303.

Langbein, L. and Bess, R. (2002) 'Sports in school: Source of amity or antipathy?', *Social Science Quarterly*, 83: 436–54.

Larson, R. (1994) 'Youth Organisations, Hobbies, and Sports as Developmental Contexts', in R.K Silberiesen and E. Todt (eds) *Adolescence in Context*, New York: Springer-Verlag, 46–65.

Laureus Report (2011) *Sport for Good Foundation*. Available at: www.Laureus.com [Accessed 19 July 2011].

Laureaus and Ecorys (2012) *Sport Scores: the costs and benefits of sport for crime reduction, Laureaus Sport for Good Foundation and Ecorys*. Available at: www.sportanddev.org/sites/default/files/downloads/laureus_sports_scores_report_1.pdf [Accessed 1 April 2019].

Leder, D. (1990) *The Absent Body*, Chicago: The University of Chicago Press.

Lensky, H. (1986) *Out of Bounds: Women, Sport and Sexuality*, Toronto, Canada: Women's Press.

Lind, E.A. and Tyler, T.R. (1988) *The Social Psychology of Procedural Justice*, New York: Plenum.

Lorber, J. (1993) 'Believing is seeing: Biology as ideology', *Gender & Society*, 7(4): 568–81.

Luckenbill, D.F. (1977) 'Criminal homicide as a situated transaction', *Social Problems*, 25: 176–86.

Lyng, S. (1998) 'Dangerous Methods: Risk-Taking and the Research Process', in J. Ferrell and M.S. Hamm (eds) *Ethnography at the Edge*, Boston: Northeastern University Press, 221–51.

Mahoney, J.L. (2000) 'School extracurricular activity participation as a moderator in the development of antisocial patterns', *Child Development*, 71: 502–16.

Mahoney, J.L., Cairns, B.D. and Farmer, T.W. (2003) 'Promoting interpersonal competence and educational success through extracurricular activity participation', *Journal of Educational Psychology*, 95(2): 409.

Malekoff, A. (1997) 'Planning in group work: Where we begin', *Group Work with Adolescents: Principles and Practice*, 53–80.

Martinson, R. (1974) 'What works? Questions and answers about prison reform', *The Public Interest*, 35, 22.

Maruna, S. (1997) 'Going straight', *The Narrative Study of Lives*, 5, 59–93.

Maruna, S. (2001) *Making Good: How Ex-Convicts Reform and Rebuild Their Lives*, Washington, DC: American Psychological Association.

Maruna, S. and Copes, H. (2005) 'What have we learned from five decades of neutralization research?', *Crime and Justice*, 221–320.

Maruna, S. and Matravers, A. (2007) 'N=1: Criminology and the person', *Theoretical Criminology*, 11(4): 427–42.

Matthews, C. (2014) 'Biology ideology and pastiche hegemony', *Men and Masculinities*, 17(2): 99–119.
Matza, D. (1964) *Delinquency and Drift*, New York: Wiley.
McAdams, D.P. (1993). *The Stories We Live by: Personal Myths and the Making of the Self*, New York: The Guilford Press.
McAdams, D.P. (1996) 'Personality, modernity, and the storied self: A contemporary framework for studying persons', *Psychological Inquiry*, 7(4), 295–321.
McAdams, D.P. (1999) 'Personal narratives and the life story', in L. Pervin and O. John (eds) *Handbook of personality: Theory and research*, 2nd edn, New York: The Guilford Press, 478–500.
McBee, T.P. (2018) *Amateur: A True Story About What Makes a Man*, Edinburgh: Canongate.
McCall, G.J. and Simmons, J.L. (1966) *Identities and Interactions*, New York: Free Press.
McDowell, L. (2003) *Redundant Masculinities? Employment Change and White Working Class Youth*, Oxford, England: Blackwell.
McGhee, F. (1988) *England's Boxing Heroes*, London: Bloomsbury.
McGuire, W.J. and McGuire, C.V. (1996) 'Enhancing self-esteem by directed-thinking tasks: Cognitive and affective positivity asymmetries', *Journal of Personality and Social Psychology*, 70(6): 1117.
McGuire, J. and Priestley, P. (1995) 'Reviewing What Works: Past, Present and Future', in J. McGuire (ed) *What Works: Reducing Offending*, Chichester: Wiley.
McMahon, S. and Belur, J. (2013) *Sports-based programmes and reducing youth violence and crime,* https://project-oracle.com/uploads/files/Project_Oracle_Synthesis_Study_02-2013_Sport_interventions.pdf [Accessed 13 December 2019].
McNeal, R.B. (1995) 'Extracurricular activities and High School dropouts', *Sociology of Education*, 68: 62–81.
McNeill, F. and Whyte, B. (2013) *Reducing Reoffending*, Willan: Devon.
Meek, R. (2018) *A Sporting Chance: An Independent Review of Sport in Youth and Adult Prisons*, Ministry of Justice, August.
Meisenhelder, T. (1977) 'An exploratory study of exiting from criminal careers', *Criminology*, 15(3): 319–34.
Merleau-Ponty, M. (1962) *Phenomenology of Perception* (trans, C. Smith), London: Routledge.
Merton, R.K. (1938) 'Social structure and anomie', *American Sociological Review*, 3(5): 672–82.
Merton, R.K. (1968) *Social Theory and Social Structure*, Glencoe: The Free Press.

Messerschmidt, J.W. (1993) *Masculinities and Crime: Critique and Reconceptualization of Theory*, Maryland: Rowman and Littlefield.

Messner, M.A. (1990) 'When Bodies Are Weapons: Masculinity and Violence in Sport', *International Review for the Sociology of Sport*, 25(3): 203–20.

Messner, M.A. (1992) *Power at Play: Sports and the Problems of Masculinity*, Boston, MA: Beacon Press.

Messner, M.A. (2005) 'Still a Man's World? Studying Masculinities and Sport', in M. Kimmel, J. Hearn and R.W. Connell (eds) *Handbook of Studies on Men and Masculinities*, California: Sage.

Messner, M.A. and Sabo, D. (eds) (1990) *Sport, Men and the Gender Order*, IL: Human Kinetics.

Miller, D.T. (2001) 'Disrespect and the experience of injustice', *Annual Review of Psychology*, 52, 527–53.

Miller, K.E., Melnick, M.J., Farrell, M.P., Sabo, D.F. and Barnes, G.M. (2006) 'Jocks, gender, binge drinking, and adolescent violence', *Journal of Interpersonal Violence*, 21(1): 105–20.

Moffitt, T.E. (1993) 'Life-course-persistent and adolescence-limited antisocial behavior: A developmental taxonomy', *Psychological Review*, 100(4): 674–701.

Mullender, A., Hague, G., Imam, U.F., Kelly, L., Malos, E. and Regan, L. (2002) *Children's Perspectives on Domestic Violence*, London: Sage.

Mulvey, E.P. and LaRosa Jr, J.F. (1986) 'Delinquency cessation and adolescent development: Preliminary data', *American Journal of Orthopsychiatry*, 56(2): 212–24.

Mutz, M. and Baur, J. (2009) 'The Role of Sports for Violence Prevention: Sports Club Participation and Violent Behaviour Amongst Adolescents', *International Journal of Sports Policy*, 1(3): 305–21.

Neff, J.A., Prichoda, T.J. and Hoppe, S.K. (1991) 'Machismo, Self-Esteem, Educational and High Maximum Drinking Among Anglo, Black and Mexican American Male Drinkers', *Journal of Studies on Alcohol*, 52: 458–63.

Nichols, G. (2006) 'A Consideration of Why Active Participation in Sport and Leisure Might Reduce Criminal Behaviour', *Sport, Education and Society*, 2(2): 181–90.

Nichols, G. (2007) *Sport and Crime Reduction: The Role of Sports in Tackling Youth Crime*, Oxon: Routledge.

Nichols, G. and Crow, I. (2004) 'Measuring the Impact of Crime Reduction Interventions Involving Sport Activities for Young People', *The Howard Journal*, 43(3): 267–83.

Nouwen, H.J. (1979). *The Wounded Healer: Ministry in Contemporary Society*, New York: Image.

Oates, J.C. (1987) *On Boxing*, London: Bloomsbury.

Pawson, N. (2006) *Evidence-based Policy: A Realist Perspective*, London: Sage.

Pleck, J.H. (1982) *The Myth of Masculinity*, Cambridge, MA: MIT Press.

Plummer, K. (1983) *Documents of Life: An Introduction to the Problems and Literature of a Humanistic Method*, London: Allen and Unwin.

Plummer, K. (1995) *Telling Sexual Stories*, London: Routledge.

Presser, L. (2005) 'Negotiating power and narrative in research: Implications for feminist methodology', *Signs, New Feminist Approaches to Social Science*, 3(4).

Purdy, D.A. and Richard, S.F. (1983) 'Sport and juvenile delinquency: An examination and assessment of four major theories', *Journal of Sport Behaviour*, 6(4): 179–93.

Putnam, R.D. (2000) *Bowling Alone: The Collapse and Revival of American Community*, New York: Simon and Schuster.

Ricoeur, P. (1991) 'Narrative identity' (trans D. Wood) in D. Wood (ed) *On Paul Ricoeur: Narrative and Interpretation*, London: Routledge.

Riemann, G. and Schutze, F. (1987) 'Trajectory as a Basic Theoretical Concept for Analyzing Suffering and Disorderly Social Processes', in D. Maines (ed), *Social Organization and Social Process: Essays in Honor of Anselm Strauss*, New York: Aldine de Gruyter, 333–57.

Rogers, C.R. (1995 [1980]) *A Way of Being* [Reprint], New York: Houghton Mifflin Harcourt.

Roth, J.L. and Brooks-Gunn, J. (2003) 'What exactly is a youth development program? Answers from research and practice', *Applied Developmental Science*, 7(2): 94–111.

Rubin, L.B. (1982) *Intimate Strangers: Men and Women Together*, New York: Harper and Row.

Rubinstein, W. (1973) *City Police*, New York: Ballantine.

Sabo, D. F., & Runfola, R. (1980). *Jock: Sports & Male Identity,* pp. 365 Englewood Cliffs, NJ: Prentice-Hall.

Sabo, D. (1985) 'Sport, patriarchy, and male identity: New questions about men and sport', *Arena Review*, November, 9(2).

Sabo, D. (1986) 'Pigskin, Patriarchy and Pain' in M. Messner and D. Sabo (eds) *Sex, Violence and Power in Sports: Rethinking Masculinity*, Freedom, CA: Crossing Press, 82–8.

Sampson, A. (2009) *Fight for Peace Academy UK: An Independent Assessment*, University of East London.

Sampson, A. (2015). *An Evaluation of the Longer Term Outcomes of the Pathways Programme at Fight for Peace*, University of East London.

Sampson, A. and Vilella, M.R. (2013) *Fight for Peace Academies in Rio and London -assessing their progress and impact,* University of East London, Centre for Social Justice and Change.

Sampson, R.J. and Laub, J.H. (1993) *Crime in the Making: Pathways and Turning Points Through Life*, Cambridge, MA: Harvard University Press.

Sampson, R. J., & Laub, J. H. (2003). Life-course desisters? Trajectories of crime among delinquent boys followed to age 70. *Criminology*, *41*(3), 555–592.

Sanders, C. (1989) *Customizing the Body: The Art and Culture of Tattooing*, Philadelphia: Temple University Press.

Sandford, R.A., Armour, K.M. and Warmington, P.C. (2006) 'Re-engaging disaffected youth through physical activity programmes', *British Educational Research Journal*, 32(2): 251–71.

Schafer, W.S. (1975) 'Sport and male sex role socialisation', *Sport Sociology Bulletin*, 4: 47–54.

Scheff, T.J. (1994) *Bloody Revenge*, Boulder, CO: Westview Press.

Scheff, T.J. (2000) 'Shame and the social bond', *Sociological Theory*, 18(1): 84–99.

Scheff, T.J. and Retzinger, S.M. (1991) *Emotions and Violence: Shame and Rage in Destructive Conflicts*, Lexington, MA: Lexington Books.

Schulian, J. (1983) *Writers' Fighters and Other Sweet Scientists*, Kansas City: Andrew and MacMeel.

Scraton, S. and Flintoff, A. (2002) *Gender and Sport: A Reader*, London: Routledge.

Sennett, R. (2003) *Respect: The Formation of Character in an Age of Inequality*, London: Penguin Books.

Sennett, R. and Cobb, J. (1973) *The Hidden Injuries of Class*, New York: Vintage.

Shipley, S. (1989) *Boxing. Sport in Britain: A Social History*. Edited by Mason, T. Cambridge, UK: Cambridge University Press, 78–115.

Sky News (2012) 'Olympics: Boxing Wins Funding Boost for Rio', 6:23pm (UK), Tuesday 18 December.

Sky News (2019) 'Mark Prince tells Sky Sports about how he uses boxing to spread a strong anti-knife crime message', 6:08pm (UK), Saturday 19 January.

Smith, A. and Waddington, I. (2004) 'Using "sport in the community schemes" to tackle crime and drug use among young people: some policy issues and problems,' *European Physical Education Review*, 10(3): 279–98.

Smith, M.D. (1974) 'Significant other influence on the assaultive behavior of young hockey players', *International Review of Sport Sociology*, 9(3): 45–58.

Søgaard, T.F., Kolind, T., Thylstrup, B. and Deuchar, R. (2016) 'Desistance and the micro-narrative construction of reformed masculinities in a Danish rehabilitation Centre', *Criminology and Criminal Justice*, 16(1): 99–118.

Sport England (2016) *Active People Survey*. Available at: www.sportengland.org/research/about-our-research/active-people-survey/ [Accessed 1 April 2019].

Stearns, P. (1987) 'Men, Boys and Anger in American Society, 1860–1940', in J.A. Mangan and J. Walvin (eds) *Manliness and Morality: Middle-Class Masculinity in Britain and America, 1800–1940*, New York: St Martin's Press, 75–91.

Stebbins, R. (1997) 'Serious Leisure and Wellbeing' in J. Haworth (ed) *Work, Leisure and Wellbeing*, London: Routledge.

Stephenson, M., Giller, H. and Brown, S. (2010) *Effective Practice in Youth Justice*, London: Routledge.

Stoke, R. and Hewitt, J.P. (1976) 'Aligning Actions', *American Sociological Review*, 41: 838–49.

Sugden, J. (1996) *Boxing and Society: An International Analysis*, Manchester and New York: Manchester University Press.

Sullivan, H.S. (1938). 'The interpersonal theory of psychiatry', New York, 1953. *The Interpersonal Theory of Psychiatry 1953*, 6.

Sullivan, H.S. (1950) 'The illusion of personal individuality', *Psychiatry: Journal for the Study of Interpersonal Processes, 13*(3), 317-332.

Sutherland, E.H. (1947) *Principles of Criminology*, 4th edn, Philadelphia, PA: JB Lippincott.

Swaddling, J. (1999) *The Ancient Olympic Games*, 2nd edn, Austin: University of Texas Press.

Sykes, G.M. and Matza, D. (1957) 'Techniques of neutralization', *American Sociological Review*, 22, 664–70.

Sykes, G.M. and Matza, D. (1961) 'Juvenile delinquency and subterranean values', *American Sociological Review*, 26 (5), 712–719.

Taylor, P., Crow, I., Irvine, D., and Nichols, G. (1999) *Demanding Physical Activity Programmes for Young Offenders under Probation Supervision*, London: Home Office.

Taylor, P. and Godfrey, A. (2003) 'Performance measurement in English local authority sports facilities', *Public Performance & Management Review*, 26(3): 251–62.

Tedeschi, J.T. and Felson, R.B. (1994) *Violence, Aggression, and Coercive Actions*. Washington, DC: American Psychological Association.

Telegraph, The (2016) 'From Drug Offences to Heavyweight Superstardom: The Making of Anthony Joshua' 5:17pm (UK) Wednesday 6 April.

Theberge, N. (1991) 'Reflections on the body in the sociology of sport', *Quest*, 43.

Toch, H. (1992) *Violent Men: An Inquiry into the Psychology of Violence* (revised edn). Washington, DC: American Psychological Association.

Tolson, A. (1977) *The Limits of Masculinity*, London: Tavistock Publications.

Trimbur, L. (2009) '"Me and the Law is Not Friends": How Former Prisoners Make Sense of Re-entry', *Qualitative Sociology*, 32: 259–77 (online 18 June).

Trimbur, L. (2013). *Come Out Swinging: The Changing World of Boxing in Gleason's Gym*. Princeton: Princeton University Press.

Turner, B. (1984) *The Body and Society.* Oxford: Basil Blackwell.

Tyler, T.R. and Bladder, S.L. (2000) 'Cooperation in Groups: Procedural Justice, Social Identity and Behavioural Engagement', *Essays in Social Psychology*, Philadelphia, PA: Psychology Press.

Tyler, T.R. and Lind, E.A. (1992) 'A Relational Model of Authority in Groups', in L. Berkowitz (ed) *Advances in Experimental Social Psychology*, Orlando, FL: Academic Press, 115–92.

Utting, D. (1996) *Reducing Criminality Among Young People: A Sample of Relevant Programmes in the United Kingdom* (Home Office Research Study No. 161) London: Home Office.

Van Ingen, C. (2003) 'Geographies of gender, sexuality and race: Reframing the focus on space in sport sociology', *International Review for the Sociology of Sport*, 38(2): 201–16.

Van Ingen, C. (2011) 'Spatialities of anger: Emotional geographies in a boxing program for survivors of violence', *Sociology of Sport Journal*, 28(2), 171–88.

Vaz, E.W. (1980) 'The Culture of Young Hockey Players: Some Initial Observations', in *Jock, Sports and Male Identity*. Sabo and Runfola (eds) New Jersey: Prentice-Hall.

Vazsonyi, A.T. and Jiskrova, G.K. (2018) 'On the development of self-control and deviance from preschool to middle adolescence', *Journal of Criminal Justice*, 56, 60–9.

Wacquant, L. (1989) 'Corps et Ame: Notes Ethnographique d'un Apprenti-Boxeur', *Actes de La Recherche en Science Sociales*, 80 (November): 33–67.

Wacquant, L. (1995a) 'Pugs at Work: Bodily Capital and Bodily Labour Among Professional Boxers', in C.L. Cole, J. Loy and M.A. Messner (eds) *Exercising Power: The Making and Remaking of the Body*, Albany: State University of New York Press.

Wacquant, L. (1995b) 'The pugilistic point of view: How boxers think and feel about their trade', *Theory and Society*, 24(4): 489–535.

Wacquant, L. (2004) *Body and Soul: Notebooks of an Apprentice Boxer*, New York: Oxford University Press.

Walpole, C., Mason, C., Case, S. and Downward, P. (2018) *Safer Together: Creating Partnerships for Positive Change*, StreetGames and Loughborough University.

Ward, T. and Maruna, S. (2007) *Rehabilitation*, London: Routledge.

Warr, M. (2002) *Companions in Crime: The Social Aspects of Criminal Conduct*, Cambridge, UK: Cambridge University Press.

Weeks, J. (1981) *Sex, Politics and Society*, London: Longman.

Wengraf, T. (2001) *Qualitative Research Interviewing: Biographic Narratives and Semi-Structured Methods*, London: Sage.

White, J.C. and Sweet, W.H. (1955) *Pain: Its Mechanisms and Neurosurgical Control*, Springfield, IL: Charles C. Thomas.

Widom, C.S. (1989) 'The Cycle of Violence', *Science*, 244(4901): 160–66.

Wiley, R. (1989) *Serenity: A Boxing Memoir*, New York: Henri Holt and Company.

Willis, P. (1977) *Learning to Labour: How Working Class Kids Get working Class Jobs*, Aldershot: Gower.

Wilson, E.O. (1978) *On Human Nature*, Cambridge, MA: Harvard University Press.

Winlow, S. (2001) *Badfellas: Crime, Tradition and New Masculinities*, Oxford: Berg.

Winlow, S. and Hall, S. (2009) 'Retaliate first: Memory, humiliation and male violence', *Crime, Media, Culture*, (5): 285–304.

Winlow, S., Hobbs, D., Hadfield, P. and Lister, S. (2001) 'Get ready to duck: Bouncers and the realities of ethnographic on violent groups', *British Journal of Criminology, Special Issue: Methodological Dilemmas of Research*, 41(3): 536–48.

Witt, P.A. and Crompton, J.L. (1997) 'The protective factors framework: A key to programming for benefits and evaluating for results', *Journal of Park and Recreation Administration*, 15(3): 1–18.

Wolff, K.T., Baglivio, M.T. and Piquero, A.R. (2017) 'The relationship between adverse childhood experiences and recidivism in a sample of juvenile offenders in community-based treatment', *International Journal of Offender Therapy and Comparative Criminology*, 61(11): 1210–42.

Wolfgang, M.E. (1959) *Patterns in Criminal Homicide*, New York: John Wiley and Sons.

Wolfgang, M., Figlio, R. and Sellin, T. (1972) *Delinquency in a Birth Cohort 1972,* Chicago: University of Chicago Press.

Woodward, K. (2004) 'Rumbles in the jungle: Boxing, racialization and the performance of masculinity', *Journal of Leisure Studies*, 23(1): 5–17.

Woodward, K. (2007) *Boxing, Masculinity and Identity: The "I" of the Tiger*, London: Routledge.

Woodward, K. (2008) 'Hanging out and hanging about: Insider/outsider research in the sport of boxing', *Ethnography*, 9: 536–60.

Wright, W. (2006) 'Keep it in the ring: Using boxing in social group work with high-risk and offender youth to reduce violence', *Social Work with Groups*, 29(2–3): 149–74.

Young, J. (2002) 'Merton with energy, Katz with structure: The sociology of vindictiveness and the criminology of transgression', *Theoretical Criminology*, 7: 389–414.

Zimmerman, D. (1998) 'Discourse identities and Social Identities', in C. Antaki and S. Widdicombe (eds) *Identities in Talk*, London: Sage.

Index